Writing the Caribbean in Magazine Time

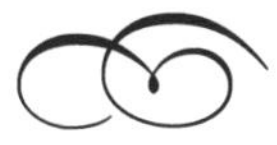

CRITICAL CARIBBEAN STUDIES

Series Editors: Yolanda Martínez-San Miguel, Carter Mathes, and Kathleen López

Focused particularly in the twentieth and twenty-first centuries, although attentive to the context of earlier eras, this series encourages interdisciplinary approaches and methods and is open to scholarship in a variety of areas, including anthropology, cultural studies, diaspora and transnational studies, environmental studies, gender and sexuality studies, history, and sociology. The series pays particular attention to the four main research clusters of Critical Caribbean Studies at Rutgers University, where the coeditors serve as members of the executive board: Caribbean Critical Studies Theory and the Disciplines; Archipelagic Studies and Creolization; Caribbean Aesthetics, Poetics, and Politics; and Caribbean Colonialities.

For a list of all the titles in the series, please see the last page of the book.

Writing the Caribbean in Magazine Time

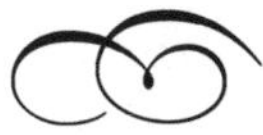

Katerina Gonzalez Seligmann

RUTGERS UNIVERSITY PRESS
NEW BRUNSWICK, CAMDEN, AND NEWARK,
NEW JERSEY, AND LONDON

Names: Seligmann, Katerina Gonzalez, author.

Title: Writing the Caribbean in magazine time / Katerina Gonzalez Seligmann.
Description: New Brunswick, New Jersey : Rutgers University Press, [2021] |
Series: Critical caribbean studies | Includes bibliographical references and index.
Identifiers: LCCN 2020042816 | ISBN 9781978822429 (paperback) | ISBN 9781978822436 (hardcover) | ISBN 9781978822443 (epub) | ISBN 9781978822450 (mobi) | ISBN 9781978822467 (pdf)
Subjects: LCSH: Caribbean literature—Periodicals—History—20th century. | Caribbean periodicals—History—20th century. | Discourse analysis, Literary—Caribbean Area. | National characteristics, Caribbean, in literature. | Caribbean Area—Intellectual life—20th century.
Classification: LCC PN849.C3 .S35 2021 | DDC 809.89729—dc23
LC record available at https://lccn.loc.gov/2020042816

A British Cataloging-in-Publication record for this book is available from the British Library.

Maps by Kyle Engstrom, Illustrator and Art Director

www.rutgersuniversitypress.org

Manufactured in the United States of America

For Esther, Julieta, Kurt, and Raúl, my grandparents

Contents

Maps

Writing the Caribbean in Magazine Time

CHAPTER 1

Location Writing in Magazine Time

The year World War II ended—1945—has been hailed as a turning point of empire. In some genealogies, 1945 marks the transition from dominion to independence for the colonized world. However, the initiation of the International Monetary Fund (IMF) may be the most transformative event of that year for the global political economy. The IMF established the U.S. dollar as a normative global currency—overtaking the dominance of the British pound—and paved the way for a new style of imperialism. That year ushered in the framework of development that continues to normalize the distribution of economic power facilitated by the history and predominance of imperial relations.[1] I maintain that the transformative force of 1945 dramatically reconfigured the Caribbean archipelago as I trace the decade of the 1940s when the dominant paradigm of development had not yet become normative and multiple forms of anti-imperial critique were incubated in and around Caribbean literary magazines. The decade ushered in numerous changes for the region. Plans to implement the West Indies Federation as a transitional governing body for the British colonies in the Caribbean were put into motion during the second half of the 1940s. In 1946 the remaining French colonies in the Caribbean would transition to states, or departments, of France. The Cuban Revolution's 1959 triumph that would become an iconic symbol of the region would be incubated during the 1940s after the Cuban Revolution of 1933 and the subsequent legalization of the Cuban Communist Party in 1938. As these political developments were under way, Caribbean peoples experienced a sharpening of archipelagic vision that was as important for geopolitics as it was for literature.

World War II was a key catalyst for these transformations. The Caribbean region was a strategic location during the war and a site of naval blockades. Through the 1940 wartime arrangement facilitated by the destroyers-for-bases deal between the United States and the United Kingdom, the United States would occupy British naval bases and greatly expand its already growing military and economic presence in the region. By this time the United States already occupied a naval base at Guantánamo Bay in Cuba, held territorial dominion over Puerto Rico and the U.S. Virgin Islands, controlled the Panama Canal, and had occupied Haiti (1915–1934) and the Dominican Republic (1916–1924). The 1940 agreement would extend the U.S. presence in the Caribbean to British military bases in Jamaica, Trinidad, Guyana (then British Guiana), St. Lucia, Antigua, the Bahamas, and Bermuda. The expansion of the U.S. military presence alongside active Caribbean participation in the world war would incite the rise of Pan-Caribbean discourse as a vessel for an expanded awareness of and desire to understand the Caribbean region's presence in the world as a space affiliated through shared geography and imbricated histories.

Literature produced during the 1940s would both register and contribute to the rising Pan-Caribbean tide. Leading Cuban poet Nicolás Guillén's Pan-Caribbean poetry collection from 1934, *West Indies Ltd.*, anticipated this movement. Acclaimed Martinican poet Aimé Césaire's epic poem first published in France in 1939 and next published in Cuba in 1943, *Cahier d'un retour au pays natal* (Notebook of a Return to the Native Land) would follow suit.[2] Influential Cuban poet Virgilio Piñera would then offer the archipelagically configured poem *La isla en peso* (The Weight of the Island) in 1943. Transformative Martinican cultural theorist Suzanne Césaire's Caribbeanist essay "Le grande camouflage" (The Great Camouflage) would emerge in 1945. In 1948 Nobel Laureate Derek Walcott would publish archipelagic poetry in his less well-known first book, *25 poems*, and the same year lauded Barbadian writer George Lamming would engage West Indian identity in his first work of short fiction, "Birds of a Feather." The next year, Cuban writer of great fame Alejo Carpentier would publish his trans-Caribbean novel about the Haitian Revolution, *El reino de este mundo* (*The Kingdom of This World*). Most of these works would appear in literary magazines during the 1940s.

During World War II literature produced abroad would circulate even less than usual in the Caribbean, and perhaps due to the resulting demand for reading material, literary magazines featuring many of the writers who would go on to become spotlights of Caribbean literature proliferated. Amid paper shortages brought on by the war and the disparaging of homegrown literature over foreign imports prevailing among middle-class reading audiences throughout the region, literary magazines contributed to uplifting locally and regionally produced literature, fomenting cultural capital for Caribbean literature and bolstering political transformations. As I argue throughout this book, literary magazines produced during the 1940s assembled and advanced the debates that structure many of the Caribbean's political, social, and aesthetic trajectories until the present. This book thus highlights the centrality of the magazine form to the history of literature and politics in the region and examines the aesthetic and political strategies authors, editors, critics, and publishers used to imaginatively construct and circulate the Caribbean as a literary and geopolitical location.

The potential for Pan-Caribbean community that circulated in and around literary magazines during this decade gave form to the possibility of a decolonizing transformation. A perfect example of Pan-Caribbean vision as a decolonial horizon appears in a letter that leading Martinican poet, playwright, and politician Aimé Césaire wrote in April 1945 upon his return to Martinique from Haiti, the same year that he concluded *Tropiques*, the literary magazine he had coedited since 1941, and launched his political career. As he described his great admiration for working-class Haitians to his friend and comrade Henri Seyrig, who then served as the cultural attaché for the Free French, Césaire remarked that he had consolidated his Antillean vision: "Je crois qu'il y a un génie antillais, un style antillais. Pour fixer mes idées à ce sujet, il me tarde de connaître une Antille de langue espagnole—Cuba—une Antille de langue anglaise: la Jamaïque" (I believe that there is an Antillean genius, an Antillean style. To clarify my ideas on this subject, I need to learn about a Spanish-speaking Antille—Cuba—and an English-speaking Antille: Jamaica)" (Seyrig).[3] Although Césaire lays claim to a Pan-Caribbean "genius" and "style" in this passage, his curiosity to test this vision by visiting Spanish-speaking Cuba and English-speaking Jamaica also reveals that his regional vision was under construction at this time.

Césaire contributes to that construction even in this moment moreover, as the vision he proffers hinges on a linguistic bridge between French and Spanish: "*une Antille*," the singular form of "Antilles" he employs in reference to Cuba and Jamaica. As Kora Véron has indicated, the lexeme "*antille*" is itself a neologism in French expressed here through what Césaire would later go on to call "*géographie cordiale*," or geography of the heart (Personal conversation).[4] The singular "*Antille*" also recalls the trace of Caribbean construction that predates Colón's famed 1492 voyage of imperial conquest: an island called "Antillia" is recorded on a portolan map as early as 1424, and since classical antiquity, there are records and myths surrounding islands in the Atlantic, the most famous of which is the myth of Atlantis. These myths resonate in the inscription of "Antilles" that would be used to name the Caribbean after 1492 and the exoticist imaginaries projected onto the region from imperial worldviews (Babcock 109–124; Fritzinger 25–33).

Césaire's division of the islands into singular bodies alongside his suggestion of a collective Antillean way of being and thinking evokes the ambivalence of archipelagic vision potentialized by literary magazines during the 1940s. Even as Césaire neologizes the singular form of *antille* instead of employing "*isle* / island" or "*Caraïbe* / Caribbean," his letter demonstrates that he was at once curious to translate Cuba and Jamaica into his conception of the francophone islands *and unable* to access them. The 1945 articulation of his regional imagination was structured precisely by the part of the region he knew best from language, travel, and literature: the French-colonized islands. Fueled by his sojourn in Haiti, Césaire's vision of the region was also imbued with the unfulfilled desire to see beyond the Francophone Antilles.

The limits of Césaire's prophetic regional vision are less remarkable than his desire and efforts to overcome them, for the Caribbean region had been constructed primarily in fragments that correspond to its multiple imperial histories. As Franklin Knight has reflected about the competing European empires that colonized the region, each empire tended to refer to the Caribbean as if "their" sector represented it as a whole (ix). I have found that this tendency persists in the anti-imperial tradition, shaping intellectual discourse defining the Caribbean region until the present day. As such, I understand Pan-Caribbean discourse as synecdoche, or as a mode of signification that enunciates a whole by referring to part of the region.

Césaire's own Pan-Caribbean vision, like the region-making of the 1940s literary periodicals central to this book, was *on the edge* of the imperial view of the archipelago. His archipelagic imagination was located in the French-colonized parts of the Caribbean, but in order to express a way to see beyond his particular location, he expanded the French lexicon. Césaire thereby prophesized a regional community beyond the imperial borders that nonetheless delimited his vision and the region's articulation.[5]

Writing the Caribbean in Magazine Time tells the story of the Caribbean archipelago as a particular kind of choice for literary and political representation. In particular, this book excavates what choosing to write the Caribbean archipelago—or not—meant to the literary, social, and political transformations incubated by literary magazines during the 1940s. I examine the potent power of representing Caribbean locations in and around magazines, highlighting location strategies that increased the archipelago's visibility and fomented regional unity in geopolitical and literary world systems. I interrogate how magazine editors, creative writers, and literary critics have deployed (and resisted) the Caribbean as a locus of enunciation for their work in Spanish, French, English, and creolized linguistic forms. In the literary, political, and cartographic archives probed by this book, the Caribbean—named as such or as las Antillas, les Antilles, or the West Indies—tends to evoke the archipelago as a decolonial horizon. The Caribbean as a region repeats itself as a creatively constructed location with purpose: to articulate a colonial record in common of racial and gendered violence that persists into the present, to imagine an anti-imperial (and in some cases anticapitalist) regional and planetary solidarity, and / or to offer political, social, and aesthetic alternatives to the hierarchies buttressed by imperial infrastructures.[6]

Representations of Pan-Caribbean discourse are multifaceted, however, and it would be too easy—and inaccurate—to position them as wholly resistant to imperial structures. What we might call "methodological resistance" in postcolonial literary studies, or the overstatement of literary and cultural forms as resistance, too often overshadows the complex, incomplete, and often paradoxical ways that resistance to empire is necessarily embedded in imperial designs, sometimes captured, sometimes intervening, often both captured and intervening at the same time.[7] It is precisely because I am committed to understanding how resistance to empire has been elaborated, however, that I seek to avoid overstating its presence in the historical record. Instead, I examine *the extent to which* the archives in and around literary magazines offer decolonial imaginaries. I understand a decolonial imaginary, in its most realized form, as a "structure of desire" oriented toward undoing the social, economic, and intellectual work of empire. Writing such a structure of desire consists of elucidating and inscribing alternatives: to the state of war imposed by colonial rule; to the racialized class and gender hierarchies grown out of empire, genocide, slavery, and indenture; and to contemporary forms of imperial violence, dispossession, and representation that naturalize the geopolitical hierarchies wrought by empire.[8]

Even when Pan-Caribbean discourse activates a decolonial imaginary, it is nonetheless highly limited in its reach. It is difficult—impossible even—to state the totality of an archipelago, and I seek neither to express such a totality nor to suggest that it has ever actually been expressed. In this book I highlight instead how Caribbean-located discourse makes meaning. In this sense, I trace through literary magazines what Yolanda Martínez-San Miguel has identified as "the meaning of the archipelago in the *symbolic* articulation" of the Caribbean ("Colonial and Mexican Archipelagoes" 156). I interrogate each symbolic turn of Pan-Caribbean articulation to decipher a limited yet meaningful intervention in imperial and nationalist frameworks of understanding. Archipelagic representations of the Caribbean are propositional and asynchronous, I argue, differing from the dogmatic certainties of national affiliation. They appear, rather, as interrogations of being-in-relation to a broader present and future community, a practice of creatively instilling wonder about the resilience and transformations of peoples oriented against the grain of imperial violence.[9]

I use "Caribbean" tentatively to name the archipelago because it has become a normative term in English. Following Edward Said's designation of the "Orient" to bring imperial histories of producing such a location into question, I name the "Caribbean" even as I investigate anti-imperial projects of making such a location visible. In *Orientalism*, Said focuses on the work of the French and British empires to launch an "Orient" into existence. In *Writing the Caribbean in Magazine Time* I am less concerned with the imperial processes of launching a "Caribbean" into circulation than I am with how literary magazines offer literary and cartographic strategies to represent ways of thinking, feeling, and desiring out of the imperial capture of the Caribbean.

The literary and cartographic ways of writing the Caribbean that I examine in this book evolved in literary magazines produced in Cuba, Martinique, and

Barbados during the 1940s. I propose that the magazine, also known as *revista* and *revue* (both meaning "review") in Spanish and French, respectively, emerges as a source for literary, social, and political articulations of the Caribbean and as a principal *articulator* of the Caribbean archipelago. Although furnishing publishing infrastructure can hardly be included among the imperial achievements of European and U.S. rule and occupations of the Caribbean, the dearth of literary infrastructure available to writers in the region is rarely accounted for in debates about the form and value of the ideas and creations they have circulated. One of the fundamental queries of this book pertains to how to recover and interpret literary and intellectual interventions in imperial ways of thinking and feeling when multiple forms of censorship, including the lack of (and imperially dominated) infrastructure, have been preconditions to circulation. I also interrogate the relationship between the medium of the literary magazine and the construction of literary and geopolitical visibility in global routes of circulation. Alejandra Bronfman has argued for the role of Caribbean sound technologies "in the production of knowledge about shifting relationships to the wider world" and in the articulation of "changing geographies of power" (6). I similarly position the medium of the literary magazine as an agent in the transformation of geopolitical and aesthetic routes of circulation.

The literary magazines generated during the 1940s that I focus on for this book would catapult the disparate literatures woven by decades of magazine work into greater international circulation and contribute significantly to social, political, and aesthetic frameworks for decolonization, including Pan-Caribbean discourse.[10] In Martinique, *Tropiques* was born in 1941 and had a five-year run. It was coedited by Aimé Césaire with the writer and cultural theorist he was married to, Suzanne Césaire, and their comrade and collaborator, the philosopher René Ménil. In Cuba, two magazines in conflict with each other—*Gaceta del Caribe* and *Orígenes*—emerged at about the same time in the spring of 1944. *Gaceta del Caribe* was a brief publication that only ran through December of the same year. It was coedited by leading poet, chronicler of Cuban society, and political activist Nicolás Guillén with his comrades in literature and politics, the poets and literary critics Mirta Aguirre, José Antonio Portuondo, and Angel Augier. *Orígenes* was the culminating manifestation of several literary magazines edited or coedited by leading poet and literary critic José Lezama Lima and his assemblage of high modernist aesthetes, known posteriorly as the *Orígenes* group. *Orígenes* would run until 1956 under the helm of Lezama Lima with the literary translator and critic José Rodríguez Feo. In 1942 Barbados, the poet, fiction writer, and actor Frank Collymore would begin to edit the literary magazine *Bim*, which he continued to edit with various coeditors until 1973. *Bim* would begin as an outlet for local literature in Bridgetown and expand gradually to become a broadly West Indian publication. Although I have investigated numerous Caribbean magazines for this book, I have by no means been exhaustive.

Rather, I offer theoretical and methodological possibilities for expanding our understanding of Caribbean literary magazines based on extant interdisciplinary paradigms of Caribbean studies.

I elect the term "literary magazine" as opposed to "cultural journal" or "little magazine" to name the sources of this archive for several reasons. In Spanish-language history, the literary and cultural "*revista*" includes magazines that are explicitly literary alongside those that are more interdisciplinary and commercial, and the framework of the "little magazine" and "*petit revue*" utilized for the study of literary modernisms in English and French are more explicitly literary conceptions of magazines or journals. Furthermore, I am interested in conceptualizing literary magazines that emerge out of and in many cases against empire, and their timelines across the South Atlantic (Latin America, the Caribbean, and Africa) from the nineteenth century to the present, both include and exceed the timeline of the "little magazine." I seek to use language that may address publications large and small, depoliticized as well as political periodicals, and the hybrid formation of the literature *and* politics magazine that recurs throughout the Caribbean in the twentieth century. Finally, however, I am interested in enunciating both the relative literariness of a broad range of periodicals and the bellicose etymology of the "magazine." As Jill Lepore indicates, "The metaphor is to weapons. A magazine is, literally, an arsenal; a piece is a firearm. A magazine is an arsenal of knowledge. It is also a library, dissected: bits of this book and bits of that. A magazine is a library—knowledge—cut into bits, so that more people can use it" (128). Lepore's etymological portrait of the magazine as somewhere between an arsenal and a library translates well to the work of Caribbean literary magazines writing against the grain of empire. *Tropiques* deployed poetry in Martinique as an intellectual weapon against the Vichy regime while functioning as an itinerant library to replace the insufficiently stocked colonial one. *Gaceta del Caribe* and *Orígenes* were engaged in a highly politicized literary battle for the terms that would shape the Cuban literary canon, both of which combated Cuba's imperial subjection in differing and even conflicting ways. *Bim* in turn critically confronted colonial ideology in the West Indies by compiling a library of local-regional short fiction. In all four of these cases, the collection of pieces served as a moving library as well as a weapon of literary representation and circulation. Up against the imperial Goliath of the global book industry, these Caribbean literary magazines waged a guerrilla pursuit of geopolitical and literary dimensions for the terms of Caribbean representation.[11]

Locating the Archipelago

The earliest maps from the sixteenth century do not name the Caribbean Sea as such. They name it "Golfo de Tierra Firme" and "Mer des Entilles" (Gaztambide-Géigel, "The Invention" 131). By the seventeenth century as the French and English empires increasingly competed with the Spanish Empire's domination of the region, new terminologies such as "West Indies," "Entilles," and later "Antilles" became regularly employed on maps in reference to the chain of islands in the archipelago (132). French and English maps from the seventeenth and eighteenth century also call the Caribbean Sea the "Mexican Sea" and the region the "Mexican archipelago" (Martínez-San Miguel, "Colonial and Mexican Archipelagoes" 158–159). By the eighteenth century as English maps proliferated, "Caribbee" and Caribby" would become regularly employed on maps, including the famous one by Thomas Jefferys, *A Map of the Caribbee Islands* (1756) (Gaztambide-Géigel, "The Invention" 131–132). As Antonio Gaztambide-Géigel puts it, "And thus, English-speaking administrators, colonizers, and seafarers began the slow process of transferring the name given to the former masters of the islands to the sea waters the latter delimited" (132). If English colonizers projected ownership of the sea onto the Native peoples of the region by naming it "Caribbean," they would also primarily refer to the islands and coastal areas they colonized in and along this sea as the "West Indies."[12] By the nineteenth century the United States would enter the imperial contest for regional dominance and refer to the region using both "Caribbean" and "West Indies" and also absorb the area into a network of slaveholding planters called the "American Mediterranean" that extended between the U.S. South and South America (Guterl 19).

Each of the designations for the region elicits a different history of naming. Each one also refers to a different area, and the parameters of the area named are furthermore not always clear from a map, a policy document, a magazine, or a literary work. Each marks a location as much as it constructs one. As Michel-Rolph Trouillot indicates, "terminologies demarcate a field, politically and epistemologically. Names set up a field of power" (115). Naming practices would be added to the imperial infrastructure of the map to represent imperial fields of power that have both fueled and hidden the violence of empire. As J. B. Harley would indicate about the discursive power of maps, "To those who have strength in the world shall be added strength in the map" (7). Imperial maps and names of the Caribbean represent the region's capture by imperial terms of visibility at least as much as they approximate the spatial relations of a set of islands and coastal territories. The semisovereign literary strategies of naming and reclaiming the Caribbean would therefore contest the work of imperial maps to dominate the region's field of visibility.

As I chart designations of the Caribbean inside and outside of magazines, I work through a foundational premise of Decolonial studies rooted in Latin America, the Caribbean, and the borders of U.S. empire: that geographic and social *locations* are inherently embedded in the production of knowledge. This premise also proceeds from theoretical reflections by Aimé Césaire and George Lamming that I engage in this book. Césaire implies the centrality of location to knowledge production when he offers the practice of poetry as the producer of contextual knowledge left out of scientific empirism in his monumental essay, "Poésie et connaissance" (Poetry and Knowledge) (157–170) and George Lamming more explicitly suggests that the colonial structure of the Antilles locates vision (*The Pleasures* 35). Walter Mignolo would go on to offer a related idea in his suggestion that Homi Bhabha has posited postcolonial critique as a differential "locus of enunciation" ("La razón" 63), or the location from which knowledge production proceeds. After postcolonial critique, Mignolo explains, we may consider the location of knowledge production as a constitutive component of the knowledge produced. While I also presume the constitutive role of social and geographic locations in constructing knowledge, for this book I reflect especially on *how* the Caribbean has been produced as a locus of enunciation through the practice I call "location writing," which I understand as discursively producing and circulating a locus of enunciation. In my designation of "location writing," I am particularly concerned with the creative *construction* at stake in setting the terms of Caribbean aesthetic, social, and geopolitical representation. I seek to examine the partial process whereby Caribbean locations are written into being rather than assert location as an achieved or total *origin*.[13] I do recognize, however, the anterior role of social positions such as race, class, gender, geopolitics, geography, and other historical facets engaged by literary and rhetorical creativity. Therefore, I do not inscribe location as an exclusively creative *product*.[14] Examining the process of location writing draws attention, rather, to the transitive role of locations as imaginaries whose terms are consistently negotiated.

What I call "location writing" may appear to some as the kind of "local color" or auto-exoticist writing that appeals to foreign audiences by commodifying social and geographic locations. In my view, however, the location writing I examine in this book strategically maneuvers a world literary system unpoised to value Caribbean literature and still manages to avoid easy foreign consumption due to its sociopolitical density and / or aesthetic difficulty. The writers I examine in this book, whose literary works write locations into the circulating record, appear at least as concerned with the undervaluation of homegrown literature in the Caribbean as they are with how they might be read abroad. In other words, location writing is indeed mediated by foreign visibility but for different reasons, in my view, than is usually presumed: first because literary infrastructure has overwhelmingly lived abroad and second because positive appraisal abroad has been key to accruing cultural capital at home.

I understand the longstanding debate in Latin America and the Caribbean about the significance of grounding literary production at home through two related positions, one by the Argentine poet, fiction writer, and critic Jorge Luis Borges and the other by Brazilian critic Roberto Schwarz. In the essay "The Argentine Writer and Tradition," Borges draws attention to the constructedness of literature that self-consciously attempts to perform "local color" when he suggests a fundamental difference between "gaucheseque" literature and the folk tradition of gaucho poetry. Against the notion that literary artists serve the nation by developing the gauchesque literature he calls "localized," Borges suggests that it is a foreign imposition: "The Argentine cult of local color is a recent European cult which the nationalists ought to reject as foreign" (181). In other words, Borges deconstructs the notion of this literature's national "authenticity" by suggesting that it consists of imitating (rather than generating) popular folk forms and by indicating that it caters to foreign conceptions of literature. Schwarz in turn examines the way that Brazilian literature, at its best, serves to locate the gap between Western liberal ideologies and the actual histories of colonialism and slavery in his essay "Misplaced Ideas: Literature and Society in Nineteenth Century Brazil." As Schwarz explains, "Challenged at every turn by slavery, the liberal ideology—the ideology of the newly emancipated nations of America—was derailed" (21). Liberalism, he argues, would be limited by the particularity of the institution of slavery in shaping the social relations of the Americas. As he explains the literary artist's task before the problem of liberalism's mutation in Brazil, "In the process of reproducing its social order, Brazil unceasingly affirms and reaffirms European ideals, always improperly. In their quality of being improper, they will be material and a problem for literature" (29). The problem for literature would then be to articulate the "improper" gap between the European ideal and the material and social realities of the Americas, thus manifesting the ideological functioning of the social order. If Borges draws attention to the constructedness of writing "localized" literature and critiques commodifying ways of doing so for foreign gazes, Schwarz locates literature for the Americas in the gap between the material and social realities of empire and the plantation and the liberal ideals promulgated by Europe. In both cases, the past and present of imperial violence overdetermine the problem of locating writing.

The Caribbean location writing I examine in this book operates in a tension between Borges's and Schwarz's critiques. In *Tropiques* Suzanne Césaire would also criticize poetry that she called "literary tourism," which appeals to a foreign gaze by producing an exoticist version of the Caribbean in French ("Misère" 50). The debate over what it means to locate literature would also resonate in the context of the literary battle between *Gaceta del Caribe* and *Orígenes* and in the proliferation of West Indian literature to which *Bim* was central. My understanding of location writing is thus embedded in a self-conscious literary milieu in opposition to the tropes of empire and tourism that produce an exoticist and highly trafficked image of the Caribbean as a land of leisure to be enjoyed by foreigners. By "location writing" I do not refer to the playful inclusion of "localisms" or other forms of pandering to imperial or tourist tropes. On the contrary, I refer to work that intervenes in and disrupts those images. For example, the literary works of location writing I examine in this book utilize metaphors of combat, imprisonment, and the apocalypse; they articulate historical subjectivities shaped by the history of and the numerous revolts against slavery; and they use comedic irony to overwrite the tragedy of imperial domination. In most of the cases I examine, poetic, fictional, and critical location writing converge with editorial efforts in literary magazines to launch a Caribbean-located discourse into local, regional, and international circulation.

The incipient and propositional character of Pan-Caribbean discourse in the region's literary magazines of the 1940s suggests that the decolonizing tradition of reinventing the Caribbean had not yet become taken for granted and that the magazines participated in its fashioning in foundational ways. Lorgia García-Peña's archival deconstruction of the history of the Dominican Republic's "bordering" between Haiti and the United States also demonstrates how an alternative history of solidarity between the Dominican Republic and Haiti persists alongside what she calls the archives of "contradiction" submerged by the hegemonic construction and policing of borders that position Dominican nationhood in opposition to Haiti (5–6). Similarly, the anti-imperial legacy of reconstructing the Caribbean has been produced in contradiction with the imperial production of the region as a tourists' "paradise," grounding collective belonging by making the history of empire and the plantation visible through a tradition of revolt and rebellion. For example, the discourse that Édouard Glissant has called "*antillais*" (Antillean) produces, as he argues, a "detour" out of history produced by empire and the plantation (*Le discours* 28–36). Antonio Benítez-Rojo in turn has offered the idea of the "plantation machine" as the repeating engine of history across the region (9).[15] C.L.R. James would himself locate Caribbean history in revolt and revolution ("Appendix"). In a metacritical vein, Shona Jackson has suggested that the labor of slavery and indenture have been translated into Creole discourses of Caribbean sovereignty in ways that on the one hand omit Indigenous Caribbean labor and on the other hand put Indigenous Caribbean peoples to work for a "Creole social being" that nonetheless excludes them ("The Re / presentation" 529). Jackson's critique is an important indicator of the limits of Pan-Caribbean discourse imbued with decolonial desires.[16] What kind of work, then, does articulating a Pan-Caribbean locus of enunciation do? The one thing articulating a Pan-Caribbean locus of enunciation cannot *actually* do is encompass or resolve the diversity of experience and history of the region. Pan-Caribbean discourse necessarily asserts a "we" that is partial even as it addresses, or aims to signify, an inclusive totality.[17]

Against the genealogy of Pan-Caribbean discourse, there persists a long tradition of disavowing Caribbean location or pertinence, especially in the Spanish-speaking Caribbean. In "The Invention of the Caribbean in the 20th Century," Antonio Gaztambide-Géigel suggests that the widespread disavowal of Caribbean belonging in the Spanish-speaking countries and territories of the Caribbean archipelago stems from a reluctance in "accepting ourselves as Afro-American." As he elaborates, this reluctance can "be explained in part by the fact that we are indeed much more than that. We need to do it, nonetheless, because it is that part of us that distinguishes us from the rest of America and the world, and the part that in turn compels us to recognize ourselves as Caribbeans" (150). The call for Caribbean self-recognition in his formulation necessarily merges regional belonging with Afro-diasporic heritage.

In the Cuban context, as Alejandro de la Fuente has shown, "Antillean" has a longstanding history of usage to name migrant workers from other parts of the Caribbean (47). The idea of *los antillanos* as others presumes a Cuban exceptionality, as if Cubans were somehow not antillanos in their own right. Trinidadian poet and militant activist John La Rose would be disturbed to find Cuba's official disavowal of Caribbean pertinence at the 1968 Cultural Congress of Havana, where he traveled with C.L.R. James, Andrew Salkey, and Robert Hill. In the anti-imperial solidarity discourse of Tricontinentalism promulgated by the Cuban revolutionary state, Cuba would locate itself within Latin America instead (Seligmann, "Caliban" 63; Salkey 104).While the idea that Cuba is distinct from the Caribbean persists to the present, the 1959 Cuban Revolution simultaneously became central to the telling of Pan-Caribbean history.[18]

The Spanish-speaking context of the Caribbean also includes a strong tradition of Pan-Caribbean solidarity, however. In fact, the national independence movements from Spain in the Dominican Republic, Cuba, and Puerto Rico were tied to a Pan-Caribbean utopian project known as the Confederación Antillana (Antillean Confederation) in the nineteenth century.[19] As Jossianna Arroyo has demonstrated, the archive of this project is primarily secret as it circulated through Caribbean networks of freemasonry (*Writing Secrecy*). In Cuba, the twentieth-century tendency to dissociate the country from the Caribbean coexists with an undercurrent of strong Pan-Caribbean affiliation. John La Rose also noted, for example, that Nicolás Guillén and Juan Marinello were sympathetic to his concern that Cuba disavowed its Caribbean pertinence for the 1968 Cultural Congress of Havana (Seligmann, "Caliban" 63; La Rose "Notes").

Without relinquishing my argument that the discursive formation of Caribbean location writing, or Pan-Caribbean discourse, is necessarily partial and constructed, I would also like to suggest here that the countertendency to disavow Caribbean pertinence asserts a strategy of geopolitical passing. Throughout the archipelago in at least French, Spanish, and English, there are records of the same saying that belies both the prevalence of African heritage and its regular disavowal: "and your grandmother / *y tu abuela* / *et ta grand-mère*?" This question seeks to disclose the hypocrisy of anti-Black racism expressed by someone of unvisible or less visible African heritage who is racially passing, or assuming a racial identity of approximate whiteness. Dixa Ramírez argues that in response to the fear of Haiti that permeated the Euro-descendant ruling elites of the hemisphere and Europe after the Haitian Revolution, the Dominican Republic created a geopolitical strategy of racialized differentiation from Haiti in order to pass unnoticed as a territory of relative Black freedom (1–30). In my conception of geopolitical passing, I suggest that the kind of passing often condescendingly attributed to the Dominican Republic, which Ramírez reconsiders as camouflage, extends broadly throughout the Caribbean region and should be reappraised context by context. Even if white- or light-passing disavowers of Caribbean pertinence may not be covering up for unapprised forms of Black freedom in other contexts, "geopolitical passing" into Latin America and out of the Caribbean requires a closer examination.

Pan-Caribbean passing tendencies exemplify how easily the slave codes that encoded Africans and their descendants as dispossessed and always already subject to policing were transubstantiated into racial attitudes and values.[20] I understand racial values that persist throughout the Americas to emanate directly from the materiality of racism as a social structure built to favor colonialism and plantation slavery, structures that have been theorized to persist into the present through the frameworks of "coloniality" and "racial capitalism."[21] If European heritage or relative whiteness is capital under a system of coloniality and racial capitalism, then whiteness becomes coded as desirable: for survival, for comfort, for well-being.

In such a context, however, that "Caribbean" is almost coterminous with "Afro-Caribbean" should not be taken for granted. Locating the Caribbean in its Afro-American traditions as Gaztambide-Géigel suggests is a relatively recent intellectual project, one that a number of the magazines examined in this book contributed to, one that is unfinished. As a project, it is no decolonial panacea, however. The roots of racism are so deeply planted that it has proven all too easy for white-appearing subjects, myself included, to be overvalued while extolling Black legacies and for Black-appearing subjects to be disparaged in value and have their philosophical and aesthetic contributions dismissed, undermined, and rendered invisible. The region's Asian legacies that pass through the history of racial indenture have also been overwhelmingly underrepresented. Submerging the history of indenture produces an effect that Tao Leigh Goffe calls "racial sedimentation," which she explains as the process by which "different ethnic groups become ossified in the bedrock of the hemisphere" (29). In a contiguous record of violence, the region is named for Indigenous peoples at the same time that their presence is rendered invisible. And hegemonic discourses of Pan-Caribbean sovereignty have been persistently masculinist, as Sylvia Wynter has so well elucidated ("Afterword" 355–366). While attending to Pan-Caribbean discourse's composition and accounting for its incomplete and nonetheless potent decolonial orientation, I propose to interrupt thinking of the Caribbean as an obvious result of geopolitical, social, and / or literary developments.

Literary Infrastructure and Location Writing

Discursively producing and circulating Caribbean location writing would be shaped by the minimalism of publishing infrastructure across the region. Small private or state-owned presses were the primary means at the disposition of writers in the colonies, neo-colonies, and struggling states of the twentieth-century Caribbean, and these most often required self-financing or the purchasing of subscriptions. While there may have been cases of capital-backed publishing companies located in the insular Caribbean that financed book production for local writers during the early to mid-twentieth century, if they existed, they were rare.[22] For example, Derek Walcott's mother financed the publication of *25 Poems*, his first book of verse, and he sold it himself, along with his friends, for one dollar (King 56–59).[23] Although Walcott has become one of the most-read Caribbean authors and has won a Nobel Prize, his first and second self-published books are out of circulation today. These books served Walcott's career at home, but his contacts in London that would make his career possible were facilitated by his work being sent to Frank Collymore, the editor of the Barbados-based literary magazine *Bim*, where he also published early poems (Griffith 14–15; Nanton 95).[24] The magazine, however fragile and limited as infrastructure, offered writers a way to publish at home and circulate both at home and abroad. In cases such as Walcott's, magazines facilitated the possibility of book publishing abroad where robust infrastructure was backed by capital investments.

Throughout the Caribbean region during at least the first half of the twentieth century, writers most often sought literary infrastructure abroad to publish books—that is, if they could—as available infrastructures for bookmaking at home were highly limited. By literary infrastructure, I mean the book industry that includes publishers, editors, and mechanisms of national, regional, and international literary circulation. I also refer to smaller scale institutions that provide literary training, facilitate and promote the circulation of literary texts, and consecrate literary value, including commercial, noncommercial, and academic or state-supported cultural projects. Finally, my understanding of literary infrastructure also includes the smallest-scale variety: independent presses, literary magazines, literary associations, and specialized small-book production. Although fragile, these forms of literary infrastructure have sustained the development of Caribbean literatures, just as they have carried many marginal and avant-garde literary movements throughout the world. Given the importance of literature to various forms of social cohesion, it is not surprising that the European and U.S. empires that have dominated the geopolitical existence of the insular Caribbean have not readily invested in literary infrastructure throughout the archipelago.[25]

As Pamela Maria Smorkaloff has indicated, "All societies, past and present, lacking an infrastructure for literary culture, create alternative mechanisms to outwit the censors, overcome official hostilities and attempt to fill the void, although they never take its place" (31). The literary magazine was precisely such an alternative mechanism, as victorious as it was limited and unable fully to fill such a void.[26] Magazines also feature literary works by women of various racial backgrounds who never went on to circulate in book form, some of whom became perniciously unwritten from the records of literary and social history. The lack of infrastructure combined with race / gender hierarchies seems to have made it even more challenging for talented women writers to circulate and be remembered for the great influences they were in their time. If it had been easier to publish at home, perhaps the play Suzanne Césaire wrote might not have been lost (Wilks 108).[27] Likewise perhaps, the novel written by the still little-known writer Jan Williams who supported Collymore with the production of *Bim* would not remain lost (Low 105). The magazine, as the chapters that follow demonstrate, is a primary archive for the works of lesser-known women writers as well as a record of their influence on the works of canonized men.

But even canonized men were greatly impacted by the dearth of literary infrastructure. As George Lamming has averred of his own experience in both Barbados and Trinidad as a young writer, "You can't think of any cultural infrastructure that could have accommodated something called the novel" (Waters 196). Lamming would not, in fact, complete his first novel until he moved to London in 1950. Aimé Césaire would also publish his books abroad in France or in translation elsewhere with the exception of magazine and newspaper publishing. Nicolás Guillén, one of the few canonized Black writers in Cuba who participated in the Spanish-language Afro-centric literary movement known as *negrismo* or *afrocubanismo*, was able to finance the publication of his first book of poems in 1931 because he won the lottery (Smorkaloff 22; Augier, *Nicolás Guillén* 122). If getting a book contract that financed production had been readily accessible to talented writers, perhaps there would be more published *negrista* and *afrocubanista* books by Black writers.

Emilio Jorge Rodríguez, in his trailblazing study of Caribbean literary magazines, has argued that in much of the Caribbean literature has primarily been produced in the same way as other materials in an imperial economic system: "las obras cubren el mismo proceso de la materia prima procesada en la metrópoli que llega al consumidor nativo con la bendición de una prestigiosa casa editora" (the works undergo the same process as raw material processed in the metropolis that reaches the local consumer with the blessing of a prestigious publishing house) (29).[28] The dearth of local publishing ventures in colonized contexts have often assimilated the literary economy to the broader structure of the colonial economy, pace the prevailing ideology of the relative independence of literature from politics and economics. Although a short list of books was produced independently in the British Caribbean colonies by small presses during the first half of the twentieth century, the vast majority of what is known as West

Indian literature was printed in London. The same is true of the French Empire in the archipelago: Paris has largely governed its book production since the issue of what is considered the first Francophone novel, *Atipa: Roman guyanaise*, in 1885.[29] In independent Haiti too, although periodical publishing flourished upon independence and some books have been published by independent presses at home, many volumes of Haitian literature have been published in Paris.[30]

Furthermore, the dominant infrastructural framework for literary production in the Spanish-speaking Caribbean was closer to the other imperial contexts than has been widely acknowledged. Like other parts of the Caribbean at least until the 1960s, many works of Caribbean literature in Spanish were also published abroad. The primary difference is that Spain did not always monopolize local literary markets. Spanish-language writers from the Caribbean also found publishers for their works in the capitals of Mexico and Argentina, which in turn had been the seats of proxy colonial power under the Spanish viceroyalty system.[31] In Cuba, even though the volume of book and periodical publishing outpaced most other Caribbean contexts in the early to mid-twentieth century, the scale of production was quite similar to that of its Antillean neighbors. In a context in which periodicals were the principal means of circulating ideas and creativity at home, why is the primary focus in literary scholarship and teaching on Caribbean books?

Given the relative ephemerality of literary magazines in a context in which book production for Caribbean authors primarily occurred abroad, location writing became a particularly potent strategy of their guerrilla pursuit for the region's geopolitical and literary visibility. Pascale Casanova makes the compelling case that writers from "small literatures" unrecognized in the world literary system need to construct their literary locations in order to gain recognition and acquire literary value: "In order simply to achieve literary existence, to struggle against the invisibility that threatens them from the very beginning of their careers, writers have to create the conditions under which they can be seen. The creative liberty of writers from peripheral countries is not given to them straight away: they earn it as a result of struggles whose reality is denied in the name of literary universality and the equality of all writers" (177). Casanova's *World Republic of Letters* implies throughout what may be most closely seen in this passage: that literary prestige, or cultural capital, is accorded through the visibility of locations. She draws on numerous literatures throughout the world at their stage of symbolic emergence to demonstrate that negotiating located visibility is crucial to shaping literary careers and the value accorded to the literary communities in which writers' careers are located.

Casanova's insights about the relationship between a writer's creative depiction of her locus of enunciation have greatly shaped my thinking even though I develop my conceptual frameworks in a discordant tension with her work. For example, I understand her work to repress the role of literary infrastructure in the production of cultural capital, and in my estimation she rhetorically participates in reinvigorating the terms of literary domination that her book critiques.[32] The premise embedded in her book, that literary value is accorded through location, is nonetheless crucial to my work, as it is repeatedly corroborated by the arguments I develop throughout it.

Furthermore, although I find Casanova illuminating on the constitutive role of location in the distribution of literary value, I do not understand location, as she does, in national terms. For example, she indicates that "even the most international writers, at least in the formative stages of their career, are first of all defined, in spite of their wishes to the contrary, by their native national and literary space" (189). She limits her view of located literary capital to the nation even though she draws heavily from Latin American literature, which is itself a regional formation.[33] Although misapprehending regional formations strains Casanova's analysis, she is in good company, as the phenomenon of "methodological nationalism" is widespread in the humanities and the social sciences (Wimmer and Glick Schiller 576–610). Methodological nationalism limits the view of critics and scholars to national formations even when material does not pertain to a nationalist process or framework, thus repressing the presence of transnational or "un-national" processes. This tendency has indeed largely kept the transnational dimensions and networks of literary magazines from the view of scholars.

Literary magazines have also been fundamental in establishing canonical literary figures and accruing literary capital. As Bulson would explain, the centrality of the English-language modernist literary magazines known as "little magazines" to British and U.S. American modernism: "No little magazines, no modernism: it's as simple as that. No Gertrude Stein, No James Joyce, Ezra Pound, Marianne Moore, T. S. Eliot, Wyndham Lewis, Mina Loy, Hart Crane, Wallace Stevens, e. e. cummings, Williams Carlos Williams, or Ernest Hemingway" (*Little Magazine* 1). In the context of the Caribbean, the case is comprehensive: no literary magazine, no Caribbean literature. In a context in which magazines have been the principal local means of circulating ideas and creativity, their form and fields of power become crucial sites of inquiry.

Reading Community in Magazine Time

There is a tension at the center of this book between my impulse to locate the medium of the literary magazine in order to understand more deeply what is peculiarly at stake in literary magazines produced in the Caribbean and the way that universalizing debates about literary magazines alternately do and do not appear to translate in the Caribbean, a tension best elucidated through an investigation of the temporality of Caribbean literary magazines in relation to Pan-Caribbean discourse. I would like to draw attention to this tension without resolving it by outlining the relationship between the space-time, or chronotope, of Caribbean literary magazines and Caribbean-located discourse shaped—or evaded—by them. I would like to suggest that the stakes of this tension are heightened by two convictions that may appear to be at odds with each other: that Benedict Anderson's universalizing theory of the temporality of reading and community imaginaries does not entirely hold up in the case of Caribbean literary magazines and that as Nelson Maldonado-Torres warns: "*Trying to subvert imperial dynamics by reaffirming the particularity of the temporal mode of any particular region is bound to repeat that which is aimed to be vanquished*" ("Toward a Critique" 71). I heed this warning and resist succumbing to the imperial fantasy that the temporal mode of the Caribbean is intrinsically unique or inseperable from imperial infrastructures that shape space-time configurations. I am otherwise suggesting that the speed of periodical production and readership in the Caribbean emanates through the region's *infrastructural distance*—produced by empire—from the North Atlantic.

In Benedict Anderson's highly influential theory of the rise of nationalism throughout the world, he establishes a fundamental relationship among reading, time, and the projectability of the nation as an imaginary for community and belonging. As he explains, the forms of the novel and the newspaper "provided the technical means for 're-presenting' the *kind* of imagined community that is the nation" (25). More specifically, he argues that the representation of the nation was made possible by the new temporal form proliferated by the novel and the news daily: simultaneity. In other words, Anderson suggests that the possibility of reading simultaneously and the aesthetic rendering of simultaneity in the novel together allowed for the configuration of the nation, because they produced for readers the sense of existing at the same time as other readers who shared the same language and therefore a being-in-relation to those readers by way of the text, and by extension, the nation, as the spatial holder of this time-in-common.

In my understanding of this model, the novel and the newspaper become conceivable as proxy forms of the nation by way of the industrialization of print culture and the literary aesthetics tied to industrialization, which we may read together as the means of production for the ideology of national belonging. National belonging in this model is no seamless product of shared race or other ethnic homogeneity. Rather, it is a fiction fueled by imperial infrastructures for mass-producing books and newspapers, which codify vernacular languages, standardize mass education, and, finally, fund the literary arts—at home in metropolitan centers of empire. These infrastructures are in turn funded at least partially by the violent work of dispossession in the outposts of empire. I highlight the infrastructural dimensions of Anderson's theory in my description to draw attention to how partial it is to the seats of empire, even as it extends to the colonial and postcolonial outposts of empire. Although the applicability of this particular model of community formation on the colonized Caribbean is highly limited, I engage it critically to elaborate an analogical figure of reading, time, and community imaginary that would pertain to the relationship between Caribbean literary periodicals produced in disparate contexts during the 1940s and the community imaginaries they proliferated that exceed the form of the nation-state.

Isabel Hofmeyr, in her own dialogue with Anderson, has forwarded a model of "slow reading" that is germane to the form of a Caribbean literary periodical produced in the outposts of empire. Hofmeyr's concept of slow reading grows out of the smaller scale and slower tempo of *Indian Opinion*, the political periodical edited and printed by Mohandas Gandhi at the turn of the twentieth century in Durban, South Africa. As Hofmeyr notes about such smaller-scale periodicals, their "tempos are slower than the daily rhythms of the newspaper but, more importantly, are driven by the temporalities of circulation" (14). To describe what could very well be the reading habits around literary magazines, she also states that "reading such periodicals can never be a simultaneous experience with the daily newspaper; rather, their modes of consumption are punctuated and sequential" (14). Like the literary magazines in this book, *Indian Opinion* demanded a practice of reading in a "wider transnational frame" such that both the temporality and the figure of community would not align with Anderson's model of national reading (19). Hofmeyr's analysis makes room to imagine another kind of relationship between the periodical and community formation, one that bears precisely on the slowness and precarity of the infrastructure used to produce it, one at odds with or imperially marginalized by the fast pace of production fueled by industrial capitalism. This other kind of relationship between periodical and community bears on the formative role of literary magazines in the evolution of Pan-Caribbean thought.

The maps of authorship, influence, and circulation produced by the literary periodical protagonists of this book, like those of *Indian Opinion*'s readership, are dispersed and exceed the bounds of the particular nation or imperially interpolated colonial territory that produced it. Bakhtin indicates how time and space come together in literary work by describing that literary time "takes on flesh" and that literary space "becomes charged and responsive to the movements of time, plot and history" (84). Time takes up literary space, embodied in the flesh of works, of characters, of the reader of a work, and the space constructed by a literary work persists through the movements, or shifts, in time as they are plotted or referred to historically. In literary magazines, chronotope is multiplied: space is configured temporally within discrete literary pieces, each issue produces a located temporality, each magazine as a set of issues accrues a locus of enunciation over time, and the medium of the magazine itself when considered in light of its locus of production and the routes of circulation that expand its locales of reception demands being understood through the chronotope it projects.

The Caribbean literary magazine pertains to another chronotope than that of the simultaneously produced nation that Anderson theorizes. David Bennet has made a compelling case for the slowness of a literary magazine's reading temporality: "The reception of the magazine mimes its editorial production: reading, here, is an activity of selection and omission which produces the text as a (spatial) collage or (temporal) montage of fragments in provisional or indeterminate relations. The experience of periodical reading is an experience of discontinuity" (480). Even in industrial contexts, Bennet's reading of the literary magazine suggests an alternative to the commodity of the novel and the newspaper that Anderson mobilizes as the raw material of the nation. Bennet positions this definition in broad, universalizing terms without drawing attention to his parting of ways with critics of modernist periodicals who overwhelmingly position the magazine as a commodity of novelty and industrial speed.

My understanding of the temporality of Caribbean literary magazines is close to that of Bennet. In my analysis, the fragmentation of the literary magazine makes it a medium whose slower reading temporality creates a community imaginary more assimilable to the *asynchronous* fragmentation of the Caribbean archipelago segmented off into outposts of multiple empires. Mary Louise Pratt has noted that Anderson's theory of national imaginaries indicates that "the 'style of imagining' of modern nations is strongly utopian," suggesting that by "utopian" she means both idealization and that nations are "imagined as islands" (50). If a national imaginary functions like an island, a regional imaginary necessarily exceeds the form of the island and extends across a network of islands and territories. Gary Wilder indicates that "if there exists a determinate relationship between dwelling and thinking" we must consider relevant to this relationship the "imperial form and scale" to the form of thought (10). I would add to this conception that the infrastructural scale of empire has produced an asynchronous gap between empire and imperial outpost that pertains to both the circulation of ideas and the thinkability of community. Empires produce infrastructural distances within the archipelago that are greater than geographic distances by withholding or embargoing technology and other material resources and by producing shipping and travel routes created for the purpose of imperial extraction that often impede or complicate traversing imperial borders across short geographic distances. Therefore, blockages in synchronous communication across the region are regular, impinging on the very possibility of imagining a synchronous regional community. The circulation of Caribbean literary magazines, the slowness of their reading temporalities, and the forms of community imagining they may figure relate directly to the relationship among publishing, time, space, and infrastructure. The chronotopes of Caribbean literary magazines thus seem to approximate the asynchronous imaginary of the Caribbean archipelago itself.

Although discontinuity and asynchronicity may be generalizable for the reading temporality of literary magazines that in all contexts prioritize readers of high levels of literacy, the small-scale infrastructure of their production appears to particularly inflect the Caribbean literary periodical as a medium. In those contexts that mass-produce books in industrial time, the literary magazine can afford itself the task of becoming alternative, of opposing the literary market, of responding to the literary moment, of shaping nearby book production and ephemerally dissipating into the book-governed canon. In such a context, a literary periodical is also more likely to rely on ample funds and even a wide-ranging, highly literate readership. The Caribbean during the 1940s afforded no such luxuries to its periodical makers. What a number of them were able to do, however, was to become *themselves* the literary and critical canon, even if their canonicity is difficult to apprehend from the perspective of literary scholarship that still broadly assumes books are the primary object of study. The semipermanence of the magazine only becomes thinkable when the void of book production becomes properly considered.

Veritably, literary magazines became institutional placeholders in the Caribbean, and magazine producers understood themselves to be capable of exerting powerful influence. In fact, it is useful to consider the magazine medium itself *as* a field of power. I understand its operations of power in terms laid out by Leela Gandhi (who in turn glosses Foucault): "If power is at once the qualitative difference or gap between those who have it and those who must suffer it, it also designates an imaginative space that can be occupied, a cultural model that might be imitated or replicated" (*Postcolonial Theory* 14). I investigate the literary magazine's field of power as an "imaginative space that can be occupied" for launching aesthetic and political projects and for gradually tracing a decolonial horizon out of the war of empire. The urgency to critically recover these projects has heightened now given the danger that already fragile Caribbean archives are further threatened by the way climate change combined with the infrastructural precarity wrought by empire are poised to submerge the archipelago itself.

Methods: Slow Reading and Critique as Affiliation

Until recently, scholarship on the literary, social, and political work of periodicals has focused on assessing periodical "projects" by engaging primarily with their editorials and using these to synthesize their productive corpuses. Furthermore, works from magazines have at times been employed as sources without accounting sufficiently for the magazine contexts of their production. As Chelsea Stieber has indicated, the prevailing kind of work involves "sweeping accounts of the social and political significance of a literary magazine and its contributors that eschews close reading" (21). My view of Caribbean literary periodicals, predicated on the asynchronous temporality of their intervention, governs an approach to research that approximates the slow reading practices that I suggest they generate. While forms of distant reading popularized by Franco Moretti also enter this work—as I recognize the validity and practical use of taking stock of rates, trends, and networks that comprise the worlds of print culture—I predominantly practice and advocate for slow reading as a methodological approach to magazines.

Throughout the book I engage in an intertextual mode of critique sustained by historical archival research, which I understand methodologically as "affiliation" in dialogue with Said's theoretical elaboration of this concept. According to his work on how the "Orient" came to be produced as a Western imaginary, "each work on the Orient *affiliates* itself with other works, with institutions, with the Orient itself. The ensemble of relationships between works, audiences, and some particular aspects of the Orient therefore constitutes an analyzable formation" (*Orientalism* 20). Whereas Said is primarily concerned with affiliation as an already existing process to analyze, I investigate it as a method of inquiry into the status of the Caribbean (or el Caribe, les Antilles, and the West Indies) in the discursive practices generated by magazines. Affiliation as an interpretive strategy serves magazine studies well, as a magazine functions like an open textual system, evincing countless internal affiliations among the texts it publishes as well as external affiliations to the literary, philosophical, political, and historical record. In Said's later work *The World, the Text, and the Critic*, affiliation acquires another dimension that is also germane to my methodology: "What I am describing is the transition from a failed idea or possibility of filiation to a kind of compensatory order that, whether it is a party, an institution, a culture, a set of beliefs, or even a world-vision, provides men and women with a new form of relationship, which I have been calling affiliation but which is also a new system" (19). If *Orientalism*'s account of affiliation became observable as an intertextual and relational process of constituting an analyzable formation, or a field of inquiry, it later becomes a new order for Said, understood in contradistinction to the extant order of filiation. For this book, I take up an approach to intertextual reading as affiliation in contradistinction to a model of filiation that would establish authors or literary texts as derivative of canonical European predecessors. Instead, affiliation brings into view the agency of selection, innovation, and transformation involved in intertextual strategies.

My work is also significantly shaped methodologically by María Josefina Saldaña-Portillo's work on discursive regimes in the paradigm of development, Brent Hayes Edwards's investigation of the intertextual and intralingual work of diaspora as a practice, Bruno Latour's process-driven rather than product-driven "actor-network" theory, and Édouard Glissant's theories of "relation" (*Poetics*). Affiliation ultimately serves as a model for the consequences of regional or archipelagic thought in this book, a mode of thinking that is necessarily generative of new forms of relation.

The chapters that follow develop a query about the relationship between Caribbean literary magazines and the function of location writing as a strategy in tension with the material and ideological constraints of empire. I proceed by establishing location writing as a decolonial approach with literary, social, and (geo)political consequences in chapter 2, "Locating a Poetics of Freedom in *Tropiques*." The sociopoetic theoretical works of the Césaires and Ménil offer an Afro-diasporic Antillean location in *Tropiques*. Location writing in *Tropiques* brings into view a potent decolonizing practice wherein the structure of desire is the poetic excavation of the layers of a colonial episteme that emerges upon posing the question "qui et quels nous sommes (who and which are we)"? Chapter 3, "*Gaceta del Caribe* v. *Orígenes*" in Cuba: Black Aesthetics as Battleground," challenges the supposition that Caribbean-located writing would be a necessary or obvious approach for a literary magazine. I demonstrate how locating the Caribbean in *Gaceta del Caribe* works both to enunciate anti-imperial solidarity with the region and position the magazine through the reclamation of an Afro-diasporic position. In both direct and indirect opposition to *Gaceta del Caribe*, I argue that *Orígenes* included hemispheric-, Atlantic-, and Havana-centered forms of location writing without consolidating a location for itself outside the dislocated realm of literary practice that it prioritizes. The implications of this move would be to unseat the Afro-diasporic location of Cuba's literary and social image that *Gaceta del Caribe* promoted. As I examine in chapter 4, "*Bim* Becomes West Indian," *Bim* would feature fictional location writing that set the tone for regional literature as a predominantly anticolonial practice. At the same time, this literary work would be predominantly about how the region has been produced *as colonial*, so that anticolonial critique, rather than nationalism, would comprise the primary paradigm it offered. Whereas chapters 2 through 4 are composed by slow reading practices, chapter 5, "Polycentric Maps of Literary Worldmaking," engages forms of distant reading. The chapter offers a theoretical approach to location writing as central to the medium of the literary magazine in comparison to the medium of the map, arguing for the Caribbean literary magazine as a cartographic technology. In this chapter I add that this set of Caribbean magazines construct locations in explicitly literary ways and offer polycentric maps that reconfigure world literary space.

CHAPTER 2

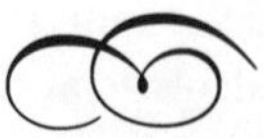

Locating a Poetics of Freedom in *Tropiques*

Fort-de-France, Martinique. April 1941.[1] The emergence of the literary magazine *Tropiques* (Tropics) at this time coincided with the third year of World War II. France, along with most of its empire, was occupied by Germany and governed by a collaborationist Vichy regime under the leadership of Marshall Phillipe Pétain. General Charles de Gaulle, along with 35,000 French soldiers, defected upon the armistice between Nazi Germany and France in 1940 and continued his alliance with Britain against the Nazi army. Pétain sought to safeguard the French Empire from British conquest and augmented the presence of the global war in the French Caribbean colonies.[2] Although many high-ranking colonial officers and governors sided with de Gaulle, both Martinique and Guadeloupe were blockaded by the British Royal Navy and ruled defensively by Pétainist regimes. Jennings argues that in the French Empire under Vichy "the years 1940 to 1944 contributed to decolonization" (*Vichy in the Tropics* 2). While *Tropiques* certainly serves as evidence of a decolonizing intellectual transformation that strategically intervened in Vichy ideology, this literary magazine would more broadly contribute to fashioning a regional Antillean locus of enunciation for a poetics of freedom.[3]

From the vantage point of *Tropiques*, the potential to forge literary and cultural decolonization out of this escalated colonial regime within a war-torn world was not self-evident. Instead, *Tropiques* indicates that the potential for change first had to be imagined to become possible, and for its editors and primary contributors, poetry became the arsenal of choice for sociopolitical and aesthetic transformation. The theories of poetry and culture that *Tropiques* circulated from 1941 to 1945 demonstrate, moreover, that something beyond nationalism would suit their vision, for their work poeticized the regional reinvention of the colonial Antilles.

The debut of *Tropiques* marks one of many Caribbean instances of the *petit revue*, the French manifestation of the modernist "little magazine."[4] The six entries of the first issue totaled seventy-five pages in length, and the issue sold for twelve francs. One thousand copies are reported to have circulated (Leiner ix). *Tropiques* shared its typeface with the local weekly newspaper, *Courier des Antilles*, whose printing press was employed to produce *Tropiques* until 1943, when the press was nationalized.[5] The magazine was a collaborative venture that saw Martinique through its subjection to Vichy under Admiral Georges Robert and continued to run until 1945. The poet-politician Aimé Césaire first conceived of *Tropiques* and edited it with the close collaboration of the other two principal contributors, philosopher René Ménil and playwright and cultural theorist Suzanne Césaire.[6] *Tropiques* can be understood as an affiliate of other magazines that Aimé Césaire and René Ménil had been involved with in France: *Legitime Défense* (Legitimate defense), the magazine Ménil had edited in Paris with Martinican poet Etienne Léro in 1932; *L'Etudiant noir* (The Black student), the magazine of Afro-diasporic cultural politics that Aimé Césaire edited with Léopold Senghor of Senegal and Léon-Gontran Damas of Guiana for three issues from 1934 to 1935; and *L'Etudiant martiniquais* (The Martinican Student), the magazine that covered issues relevant to Martinican students studying in Paris that predated *L'Etudiant noir*, for which Césaire wrote as a student (Véron and Hale 15–17).[7] Although Haitian literature rarely entered *Tropiques*'s manifest discourse, its presence was latent. For example, *Tropiques* resonates strongly with the highly influential literary magazine, *Revue Indigène* (Indigenous review) (1927–1930).

Tropiques ran three times a year until Vichy censors blocked it temporarily on charges of "racism" and "sectarianism" in 1943. As Ménil would explain in his retrospective testimony on *Tropiques* under Vichy, its pages become increasingly more aggressive as the Nazi army loses ground in Europe, and the ultimate censure would be no surprise ("Sous l'amiral" 147).[8] Allied and Free French forces toppled Robert's regime several months later, after which the magazine re-emerged in October 1943. The last half of the magazine, like the first, continues to be predominantly dedicated to poetry, though more overtly political works were more frequently included. In sum, between 1941 and 1945 *Tropiques* consisted of eleven issues.[9] In its period of circulation, the target audience was primarily local, consisting mostly of Lycée students (Ménil, "Pour une lecture" xxv), but the magazine also traveled to other parts of the Caribbean (at least to Cuba, Haiti, and Curaçao),[10] and news of it appeared in contemporaneous magazines in New York, Buenos Aires, Santiago de Chile, and Algiers.[11]

The end of the magazine, in 1945, gave way directly to Aimé Césaire's political career as the mayor of Fort-de-France and a representative to the French National Assembly. The following year Césaire would lead the French colonies in the Antilles to "departmentalization," the neologism that Césaire created for this transition from colonial status to statehood (Bonilla 52–53). As Césaire explained retrospectively, upon France's liberation from Germany, the "cultural combat" of the magazine venture gave way to "political combat" (Leiner viii). *Tropiques* became more overtly politicized after the liberation, but its commitment to poetry and to Black and Antillean-located discourse remained strong throughout. Although the immediate urgency of the Vichy regime prompted the *Tropiques* group to what Césaire has called cultural combat, in addition to its poetic resistance to Vichy, the magazine provided a theoretical foundation and model for socially and geographically located poetry that bears a sustained influence in the Francophone Caribbean.

Tropiques has received substantial critical attention, but scholarship has primarily focused on *Tropiques* as a source for something else: Aimé Césaire's poetics, Suzanne Césaire's essays that have recently become highly influential, surrealism, or the Francophone poetic movement focused on interrogating the colonial experience of Black identity known as "négritude." For some critics, *Tropiques* served as a Martinican locus for international surrealism. Although it is often assumed that *Tropiques* was a hub for the négritude movement, this view has been questioned by some critics due in part to coeditor Ménil's critique of the mythologizing potential of négritude elaborated as an ideology.[12] I offer a reading of the homegrown magazine-cum-"thought office" the Césaires and Ménil generated that highlights an intertextual theory and practice of Antillean-located poetry as a method of literary and social liberation.

My reading of *Tropiques* examines the cultural combat its editors sustained against the Vichy regime, literary marginality, and the internalized racism they diagnosed in Antillean society. *Tropiques* consisted of an interdisciplinary approach to poetry, cultural theory, and politics, constructing for itself a networked locus of enunciation, one that articulated multiple affiliations through which to excavate a critical and regional literary voice. The magazine's name is at issue here, for "Tropiques" is a choice that refers to a broad geopolitical location and affiliation. Furthermore, it is a fitting name for a literary magazine so devoted to poetry, for *Tropiques* demonstrates much concern for theorizing and engendering literary *tropes*. *Tropiques*, in addition to speaking from and through the tropics, as its name indicates, lays claim to and, in so doing, constructs a Caribbean locus of enunciation. At times the region as a whole is invoked in its pages—*le Caraïbe*—but primarily it delivers a critical voice to the French-ruled territories in and around the Caribbean Sea, *les Antilles*. The editors and main contributors of *Tropiques* additionally refer specifically to Martinique as their locus of enunciation, and often they refer interchangeably to Martinique and *les Antilles*. Often, as is more well known, they also locate themselves in the space of Black internationalism.[13] Furthermore, while they repudiate the imitation of French aesthetics, they by no means repudiate France but instead affiliate themselves selectively to a revolutionary French literary and political tradition.

Tropiques's networked locus of enunciation demonstrates that its editors' anticolonial enterprise was not about fomenting nationalism; on the contrary, they availed themselves of a belonging-in-relation, through every possible, available affiliation. Each affiliation bears on their theories and practices of poetry that were at once locally situated, regionally oriented, and transcolonially resonant.

Thus multiply situated, the *Tropiques* group understood the practice of poetry as a liberating method that would combat the colonial condition with which they diagnosed Antillean society and engender new ways of imagining the self in the colonial Antilles. James Clifford uses the term "a poetics of cultural invention" to describe Aimé Césaire's poetic oeuvre, but the idea applies well to the direction of "cultural combat" in *Tropiques* (176). Through their collective offering of a located poetics of freedom, Aimé Césaire, Suzanne Césaire, and Réne Ménil poeticized the region's freedom from colonially imposed cultural alienation.

Poetic Resistance: *Tropiques* against Vichy and Literary Marginality

Critically assessing *Tropiques* requires understanding the two historical axes that constrained its writers and inspired its difficult and sometimes obscure collection of texts: the literary marginality of colonial Martinique and the duress of the Vichy regime. Predating the constraints imposed by the war, the literary marginality of Martinique was produced through the intellectual work of colonialism in the Caribbean that Paget Henry calls "communicative inequality," or prioritizing the dissemination of European intellectual traditions at the expense of African, Indigenous, and Asian traditions that also comprised the cultural inheritance of island inhabitants (9).[14] But this inequality was not simply ideological. It was based on, carried out, and extended by the French Empire's publishing economy. To this day, metropolitan France primarily dominates the publishing of French-language books, but in the years before and during *Tropiques*'s run, independent publishing was extremely rare. *Tropiques* thus generated the possibility of semiautonomous publishing for local writers associated with its publication. Another result of the colonial publishing divide was that the circulation of books on the island was minor when compared to its metropolitan counterpart. Fort-de-France's library, the Bibliothèque Schoelcher, housed a small selection of books approved by the colonial administration, and several small bookstores sold a modest selection of books sent from the metropole, but books—European books—were already precarious on the island, becoming all the more precarious when Martinique was blockaded by the Allies in 1940. As Aimé Césaire explains,

> nous *n'avions pas de livre*! A la Martinique, c'est incroyable, mais il n'y avait pas un *seul* Mallarmé, par exemple. Nous n'avions pas de textes. Nous ne

> recevions rien de France; les libraries martiniquaises étaient extrêment pauvres. Quant à la Bibliothèque Schoelcher, c'était une petite bibliothèque coloniale. (Leiner vii)

> we *did not have any books*! In Martinique, it's incredible, but there was not a *single* Mallarmé, for example. We did not have any texts. We did not receive *anything* from France; Martinican bookstores were extremely poor. As for the Bibliothèque Schoelcher, it was a small colonial library.

The circumstances for literary production and consumption in which *Tropiques* intervened suggest that for Martinique, communicative inequality exceeded beyond subjugating non-European traditions and limiting extremely the publishing possibilities for colonial intellectuals. It also meant restricting access to European cultural production. Césaire's correspondence with Henri Seyrig, cultural attaché for the Free French, reveals that they coordinated to address the lack of French books on the island. In a letter addressed from New York dated December 15, 1943, Seyrig accounts for his efforts: "D'autre part je fais envoyer à la bibliothèque Schoelcher un premier envoi des livres; d'autres suivront" (In other news I have sent to the Schoelcher library a first shipment of books; others will follow) (Seyrig). This effort would only partially redress the lack of books at the library, but its record corroborates Césaire's concern with the limited circulation of books to Martinique.

Césaire perhaps best explains the result of literary marginality for literary culture as follows: "J'ai toujours été frappé par le fait que les Antilles souffrent d'un manque. Il y a aux Antilles un vide culturel" (I was always struck by the fact that the Antilles suffered from a lack (*manque*). There is a cultural void in the Antilles) (Leiner v). A critical understanding of *Tropiques* hinges on the relationship between Césaire's diagnosis of *un manque* in Antillean culture and the kind of writing that the magazine published. "*Manque*" refers to a lack or an absence but also has an agricultural usage much closer to the telluric discourse that emerges in texts published in *Tropiques* by all three of its main editors: "*Espace non labouré, non planté*," an untilled, unplanted space, as in fallow land ("Manque"). When *manque* is read this way, *Tropiques*, more than filling a void, may be seen to be tilling the fallow space of Martinican cultural production. In effect, the erudite texts published therein proliferate literary print culture.

I emphasize an agricultural reading of *manque* in order to suggest how the *Tropiques* group contributed to publishing infrastructure and literary print culture in Fort-de-France as well as to highlight its interaction with the ideology of the Vichy regime, the other historical axis out of which the magazine emerged. If *Tropiques* resisted Vichy, its resistance was deployed through Pétain's ideological frame, which included an agricultural nationalism.[15] As Jennings suggests in *Vichy in the Tropics*: "The Vichy regime quite unwittingly set in motion several forms of opposition in its "loyal colonies." It did so on two levels; first by hardening an already ruthless colonialism; second, and more ironically, by introducing to the empire Pétain's cherished themes of authenticity, tradition, and folklore" (3). Jennings's study serves a critical reading of *Tropiques* well. On the one hand, the Vichy regime employed a more conservative (read: more racist) colonial policy than its French republican predecessors, as it overturned assimilationist policies for colonial subjects and promoted essentialist policies of racial exclusion that were favorable for extracting imperial booty for the Nazi government with which it collaborated (Jennings 2–30). On the other hand, as Jennings contends, the Vichy regime replicated Vichy nationalism throughout the empire ironically *in order* to promote loyalty to Pétain's National Revolution in the colonies, thus facilitating the proliferation of nationalist discourse against the empire in the *very language* that Vichy used to justify itself (21–23). In the case of *Tropiques*, the language of Vichy served the magazine's work but in a somewhat different way than Jennings suggests. Instead of glorifying Martinique in nationalist terms, the editors employed a self-repudiating language of critique aimed interchangeably at Martinique and the Antilles more broadly. As Ménil would go on to explain, one could politically and culturally operate within Vichy's permitted purview by taking blame for France's terrible condition ("Sous l'amiral" 144). This position allowed the group a limited opportunity to be permitted to diagnose the cultural maladies of the island and the French-ruled region more broadly. The agricultural emphasis of Vichy ideology also provided the *Tropiques* group an excuse to center their poetics on agricultural rather than urban tropes. In effect, *Tropiques* did not directly endeavor to ruin Vichy's colonial-nationalist crops; instead, the magazine's texts planted decolonizing seeds in the *manques*, or fallow fields, Vichy overlooked.[16]

As Ménil hints, because of direct Vichy censorship and the self-censorship it encouraged until 1943, the critical reader of *Tropiques* must read between the lines ("Pour une lecture" xxv). During this period its writers often wrote in an obscure, sometimes wholly abstract style that often made definitive singular interpretations impossible: "Terre muette et stérile. C'est de la nôtre que je parle" (Mute and sterile land. It is of ours that I speak) (5). This dramatic, condemnatory statement is the first line of the opening "Presentation" text of *Tropiques*'s first issue, by Aimé Césaire. It is customary for magazines to begin with an introductory presentation piece, but this piece, a little over one page of poetic prose, does not directly address the magazine's texts or goals. Instead, it models the kind of poetic resistance to Vichy the magazine would perform. It begins by invoking land in a deficient state of sterility and personified as mute, presumably as a metonymic stand-in for a mute people. The sterility and silence censured in these lines could be read between the lines as a condemnation of the island's lack of productivity, as implicit blame for the demise that led to France's defeat by Nazi Germany. At the same time, these lines may also be read as resistance to the silence and sterility resulting from colonialism more broadly and from Vichy's particular version of it. René Ménil has also suggested that this presentation text opens itself up to a double reading, one that responds to the silencing fascism of the Vichy regime and one that refers to the history of colonialism ("Sous l'amiral" 145).

Césaire continues by establishing *Tropiques*'s Caribbeanist locus of enunciation as a network of affiliations to Europe, Africa, and Asia: "Et mon ouïe mesure par la Caraïbe l'effrayant silence de l'Homme. Europe. Afrique. Asie. J'entends hurler l'acier, le tam-tam parmi la brousse, le temple prier parmi les banians. Et je sais que c'est l'homme qui parle" (5) (And my hearing measures by the Caribbean the frightful silence of Man. Europe. Africa. Asia. I hear the steel howl, the tam-tam in the bush, the temple prayer among the banyans. And I know that it is man who speaks). The silence poeticized across the Caribbean is not a total silence but rather one positioned as belonging to universal "Man," capitalized. As the passage develops, it passes through the sounds of Europe, Africa, and Asia and juxtaposes to capitalized "Man" an uncapitalized particular "man." By implication the poetic voice Césaire locates to introduce *Tropiques* is multiply located in the particular sounds left in the silence of "man" as a universal ideal, a silence that more than lamented is frightening. Through the continents from which the Caribbean region draws its population, Césaire's poetic prose, in typical Césairian fashion, opens up onto several simultaneous readings.[17]

First, in the lines that follow Césaire continues to carry out a thesis of cultural silence and emptiness in the Caribbean. Europe, Africa, and Asia may indicate, in contradistinction, those places of cultural fulfillment, each continent's culture grounded by what follows: Europe's howling steel, Africa's tam-tam in the bush, and Asia's temple among banyan trees. In this sense, Europe is portrayed as the producer of steel—indicating both industry and weaponry, Africa as the producer of rhythm and ritual, and Asia as the producer of prayer and the sacred. Second, although Césaire continues to indict cultural vacuity in the Caribbean in this passage, the markers of Europe, Africa, and Asia indicate the sources of the Caribbean's mixed ethnic heritage from which its cultural productions may draw. Third, Europe, Africa, and Asia furthermore signal the primary fronts of World War II at this time. The French Empire under Vichy also ruled over and fought to maintain sovereignty over territories in all of those continents. Fourth, Europe's inclusion allows for the tropical anti-imperial solidarity that the passage also underwrites to pass unnoticed, a solidarity implied in the image of the banyan tree. Although the passage that ends in "parmi les banians" directly refers to the temple that lines up with the reference to Asia above, all of the tropics, from at least the Caribbean to Southeast Asia—the tropics under Vichy rule and pillaged by Vichy to sate the Nazi government—favor the growth of the banyan tree.[18] Any tropical locus of resistance to imperialism would therefore be, quite literally, among the banyan.

As the piece draws to a close, a rejection of fascist imperialism returns in Césaire's daring assertion, "Pourtant nous sommes de ceux qui disent *non* a l'ombre" (But we are among those who say *no* to the shadow) (6). This statement positions the editors of *Tropiques* as the "nous" (we) resisting the shadow—of fascism—that overtook the world during the war. And before the end of the piece, Césaire adds ominously "L'Ombre gagne" (the Shadow is winning). The presentation piece testifies obliquely to a bleak, worldwide political situation, to which it makes a humble, poetic offering of resistance: "Et vainement sur cette terre nôtre la main sème des graines" (And in vain on our own land the hand scatters some seeds) (5). This agricultural metaphor indicating how limited the small-scale infrastructure of a magazine may be emerges after the infrastructurally robust forms of knowledge produced elsewhere: science, philosophy, and aesthetics. A literal reading of this passage renders Martinique completely agricultural and as such lacking the supercultural productivity occasioned elsewhere. However, the image also serves as a metaphor for the poetic germination of the magazine project it introduces not only against the encroaching shadow of Vichy but also in the shadow of universal "Man." *Tropiques*, produced far away from the infrastructure of French cultural productivity, was financed independently by a group of middle-class intellectuals with little hope of making a political impact on the dire colonial situation of their island or any other part of the world.

André Breton has testified how much it impacted him to read the boldness of this piece. During his short stay in Martinique on his way to New York, he famously encountered *Tropiques* at a local bookstore run by René Ménil's sister and went on to become acquainted with the *Tropiques* group. As Breton describes his first reading of *Tropiques* in his introduction to Césaire's most famous poem, *Cahier d'un retour au pays natal* (Notebook of a Return to the Native Land):

> Je n'en crus pas mes yeux: mais ce qui était dit là, c'était ce qu'il fallait dire, non seulement du mieux mais du plus haut qu'on pût le dire! Toutes ces ombres grimaçantes se déchiraient, se dispersaient; tous ces mensonges, toutes ces dérisions, tombaient en loques: ainsi la voix de l'homme n'était en rien brisée, couverte, elle se redressait ici comme l'épi même de la lumière. ("Martinique" 119–120)
>
> I could not believe my eyes: what was being said was exactly what needed to be said, not just in the best way but with the greatest force! All those mocking shadows were torn aside and dispersed; all the lies and derision fell in tatters. It was proof that, far from being broken or stifled, here the human voice rose up like the very shaft of light. ("A Great Black Poet" 191–192)

The multiple affiliations and defiant resistance that *Tropiques* established would not fall unto deaf ears. This passage moved Breton, who was among the small number of fortunate Jewish people able to escape France via a

Marseille–Fort-de-France boat route (so long as the island was not their final destination).[19] Through his poetry and his *Manifestes du surréalisme*, Breton had already become an important reference point for *Tropiques*, and he would also facilitate many international connections for the group, extending their reach internationally, along with that of Aimé Césaire's poetry. Breton's reception also indicates that *Tropiques*'s first poetic editorial demonstrates in practice the poetic cultural combat it would offer to Martinique, the Caribbean, and the world.

Location Poetics as Cultural Combat

In his essay "Negritude in Retrospect," Léon-Gontran Damas draws on work René Ménil published in *Tropiques* in 1945. Damas had collaborated with Aimé Césaire and Leopold Senghor from Senegal on the short-lived publication *L'etudiant noir* when they were all students in Paris and became, along with his two collaborators, a leading poet of the literary movement known as "négritude" and a leading politician. Damas draws on Ménil's work from *Tropiques* in his retrospective essay to convey a located insight pertaining broadly to the French colonized Antilles. The regional resonance Damas ascribes to Ménil's ideas demonstrates the legacy of the regionally located discourse in *Tropiques*. Ménil's insights serve as one of the theoretical culminations of the dialogue he participated in with Suzanne Césaire and Aimé Césaire in *Tropiques*. As this dialogue highlights the importance of locating poetry, it also serves to interrogate what their location, presented as Afro-diasporic and interchangeably as Martinican, Antillean, and Caribbean, has been, could be, and would become. Damas refers to Ménil's essay "Situation de la poésie aux Antilles" but at the same time indirectly summarizes the Antillean-located social malady that the *Tropiques* dialogue diagnosed and sought to remedy: "The fact was that this West Indian elite . . . had doubtless become a victim of an inferiority complex. René Menil, a Martinican philosopher, explains this in historical terms as a consequence of replacing the repressed African spirit with slave consciousness, a representative entreaty of the master, an entreaty instituted at the base of the community and which was to watch over it like a garrison" ("Negritude " 4).[20] In Damas's terms, more than in Ménil's, the focus of the problem is the Black and mixed-race "West Indian" elite suffering from an "inferiority complex."[21] Ménil would prefer "bourgeoisie" to "elite," but in any case, Damas indicates accurately that it is the educated sector of French-colonized Antillean society where *Tropiques* locates its social and poetic intervention. Ménil, in dialogue with the Césaires, would gradually develop his located ideas until the culmination of a theory of the historical progression out of slavery of Black and mixed-race Antilleans, the first two steps of which Damas recalls in his essay, translating almost exactly Ménil's terms. Indeed, Ménil understood these first two steps together to be "ce qui explique le complexe d'inferiorité du peuple antillais" (that which explains the inferiority complex of the Antillean people) ("Situation" 132). The premise of this "inferiority complex" would be the primary site at which he and the Césaires would seek to poetically revise Antillean-located selfhood throughout *Tropiques.*

Ménil's first offering to this cause in *Tropiques* would be his essay "Naissance de notre art" (Birth of Our Art) (*Tropiques* 1, 1941), in which he catalyzes a located poetics.[22] Ménil opens up a path toward the possibility of cultural renovation in this essay by rewriting a colonial conception of culture with an anticolonial one:

> La culture—nous ne parlons pas de l'idée de la culture, innocente conception de l'esprit mais de la culture réelle qui est faite d'un ensemble vivant des conditions déterminées (sol, race, formes économiques, etc.) . . . —est *nécessaire* c'est-à-dire qu'elle échappe à la fantaisie de ceux-là mêmes qui la vivent. Elle est, par là même, *intransmissible.* (55)

> Culture—by which we do not mean the idea of culture, an innocent intellectual conception, but real culture, which is made from a living ensemble of determinate conditions—soil, race, economic forms, etc.) . . . —is *necessary,* meaning that it exceeds the fantasies of the very people who live it. It is, thereby, *untransmissable.*

This work thus rejects a definition of culture that would permit Antilleans to view themselves as or seek to become products of French culture as transmitted to them through colonial government and education. Ménil stresses, to the contrary, the importance of lived realities in the makeup of culture. Ménil thus calls culture home to the Antilles against the cultural "*dépaysment*" experienced by the distance of France as a cultural center. In this sense, Ménil assimilates *Tropiques* to the project of reversing cultural unhoming or "*dépaysment.*"[23] Ménil also antilleanizes the problem of cultural alienation posed as the practice of ignoring lived realities—and in particular the lived reality of racial difference—in favor of an existentially inauthentic assimilation to French culture.[24] To be located in the culture of lived reality emerges as the authentic remedy to *dislocated* cultural alienation. He positions this problem in relation to aesthetic creation, arguing that the universality of art is only achieved through the rooting of the artist in a particular context: "Et l'universalité est atteinte, non par la suppression de ce que l'artiste porte en lui de plus particulier mais par l'expression des particularités dans le language adéquat" (And universality is attained not by suppressing those unique particularities the artist carries within, but by expressing those particularities in the right language) ("Naissance" 58).

The goal of poetic production in these terms, to express the universal, becomes simultaneously about expressing the particular.[25] The key to achieving the universal through the particular, however, requires the right language to express the particular *in such a way* that it will be able to attain the status of the universal. Ménil proposes these as definitions at large, but they are also critical guidelines for the kind of located literature he advocates for throughout *Tropiques*. Of the three main contributors to *Tropiques*, he appears the most wedded to a universalist conception of art, as he proposes located aesthetic production as an avenue for accessing an otherwise foreclosed terrain of the universal.[26]

Ménil also poses selfhood as a question that hovers around the locus of enunciation, clearing space for a practice of location writing that could poeticize a reinvention of Black Antillean selfhood:

> Qui parle ici?—Des Martiniquais, vivant sur la ligne des Tropiques, entre les deux Amériques, partageant avec la France les chances de sa culture impériale, et qui s'interrogent aujourd'hui sur leur destin. . . . Nous avons LU la culture des autres. . . . La culture est ailleurs. La vie aussi, du reste. Le vente passe . . . ("Naissance de notre art" 59)
>
> Who speaks here? The Martinican people, who live below the border of the Tropics, between the two Americas, who share with France the fortune of its imperial culture, and who ask themselves today about their destiny. . . . We have READ the culture of others. . . . Culture is elsewhere. So is life, incidentally. The winds turn . . .

Here, Ménil carefully designates the locus of enunciation for himself by establishing many of the coordinates at stake: a tropical alignment, the in-betweenness of the Caribbean between the two Americas, the in-betweenness of French imperial culture and the revolutionizing transformation of Western culture—the latter part we may read as an indirect reference to both Marxism and surrealism that could also pass by the censors as a reference to Pétain's national revolution. Location and affiliation seem to be here the only accessible answer to the "*qui*" or "who" question, suggesting their importance to the sociogenic mission embedded in *Tropiques*.

Ménil also positions the locus of enunciation he proposes against a disembodied "elsewhere" that refigures a passage of Breton's first surrealist manifesto. Lamenting Antillean absorption by foreign cultural productions, Ménil suggests, "La culture est ailleurs. La vie aussi, du reste" ("Naissance" 59). Breton ends his manifesto with a contiguous statement: "L'existence est ailleurs" (Existence is elsewhere) (60), which in turn rewrites Arthur Rimbaud's famous poetic suggestion "La vrai vie est absente" (Real life is absent) (68–69). In Breton's rendering, elsewhere functions like the impossible arrival of the surrealist pursuit. Existence, beyond *just* living and dying, becomes equivalent in this statement with surrealism. In Ménil's statement, the object sought through poetic practice—culture, surrealist or not—remains *ailleurs*. It is a vision of culture that, in his own terms, may also be equated with existence insofar as existence pertains to defining the self as expressed through lived, or experienced, reality.[27]

The irony that hangs in suspension in this *ailleurs* pertains to the reality of colonial hybridity that Ménil's essay cannot simply wish away: French culture, geographically produced elsewhere, has also become embedded in local culture. Of course, this situation is also not simply ideological: the hoarding of French infrastructure for literary production in the metropole, often reliant on resources and labor extracted from the colonies, is the material base of this colonial malady. The *Tropiques* group carved out a distinction between locally imposed French culture and values and the kind of self-abnegation that would refuse to recognize and valorize a local way of being that also already existed. Ménil accuses Martinican art of perpetuating the latter when he denounces its achievement of European forms without engaging Martinican realities. In his terms this kind of art produced a downward spiral of cultural vacuity. In other words, aesthetic production responding exclusively to the European elsewhere, even if produced locally, would continue to produce the sense of culture as elsewhere. The point was not to undo French culture but instead to break down its singular supremacy as the formative factor of local existence and as such of local aesthetic production. *Ailleurs* also marks, however, the limits of accessing the "we" the *Tropiques* group aimed to poeticize into being: in Ménil's and the Césaires's writings part of this "we" remains inaccessible, beyond location, seeming to reside for Ménil in his concept of "lived culture" but not yet attainable.

Suzanne Césaire's later essay "Misère d'une poésie" (An impoverished poetry) (*Tropiques* 4, 1942) critiques the history of Martinican poetry in dialogue with Ménil. Lamenting the poetry she calls literary tourism that has been written by colonial poets about Martinique and other parts of the Americas, Césaire echoes Ménil's echo of Breton with "Allons, la vraie poésie est ailleurs" (Come on, true poetry is elsewhere) (50). If Ménil echoes Breton's statement to focus more specifically on culture, Césaire's echo of his echo focuses specifically on "authentic" poetry, the kind that through Ménil we can read as grounded in cultural realities; she adds to this "*Allons*," calling on her readers to reroute their work to a new elsewhere, that of "true" poetry. For the purposes of *Tropiques*'s poetics, to interpret in these echoes a set of equivalences between existence, culture, and poetry would not be too far-fetched.

Suzanne Césaire's prognosis for this true poetry follows suit in the same essay with the famous proclamation "La poésie martiniquaise sera cannibale ou ne sera pas" (Martinican poetry will be cannibalized or it will not be), which in turn Ménil repeats with a twist in his essay "Laissez passer la poésie," one of many instances of the magazine's intertextual moves (50). Ménil's version reads "La poésie martiniquaise sera virile. La poésie martiniquaise sera cannibale. Ou ne sera pas."[28] As Jennifer Wilks argues, Suzanne Césaire's call for literary cannibalism plays on the trope of Caliban (126). Ménil would concur, and Aimé Césaire would go on to more famously follow suit in his revision of William Shakespeare's *The Tempest*.

Several essays in *Tropiques* further explore cultural alienation, a malady interchangeably ascribed to Martinique and to the Antilles more broadly. After the fall of Vichy, cultural alienation took center stage as the raison d'être of the review, as the site of struggle for poetic liberation. In *Tropiques* 5, two essays in particular—Suzanne Césaire's "Malaise d'une civilization" (A Civilization's Discontent) and René Ménil's "Laissez passer la poésie" (Let poetry pass by)—raise the stakes of their critique of local-regional cultural alienation. Césaire's essay diagnoses all of Antillean society with the malaise of cultural alienation. In this essay, she historicizes cultural assimilation in the region by referring to its prohibition under slavery and explaining how, out of prohibition, assimilation had been conceived as an avenue for freedom (46–47). She suggests, however, that this path has led Antilleans astray, away from their true selves. The tragic result of cultural alienation as she portrays it is that the Antillean "*ignore* sa véritable nature, qui n'en existe pas moins" (does *not know* his true nature, which nonetheless exists) (48).

The "true nature" Césaire insists on nonetheless remains elusive in this essay. She considers similarities between Martinicans and the peoples that ethnographer Leo Frobenius theorized as "homme-plante" ("Malaise" 46). Pace critiques of essentialism, Césaire suggests that the passivity of this "Ethiopian" condition in Martinicans results from a cultural exhaustion imposed by slavery. Furthermore, in her readings and considerations of Frobenius's notions of the "homme-plante" and "homme-animal," the two amount to little more than differing biorhythms. Césaire analyzes them as apertures for Antillean culture, but by no means does she make totalizing propositions. Rather, they function as heuristics for critiquing the postslavery colonial condition of the island. In her earlier essay "Leo Frobenius and the Problem of Civilization" (*Tropiques* 1, 1941), she defines his philosophy as poetry, which suggests that her engagement with his work should also be approached poetically instead of as categorically defining moves (36). Against assumptions that Frobenius influenced her or Aimé Césaire as a source for African essences to be inscribed onto the Caribbean, I contend that Suzanne Césaire glossed his cultural categories poetically as methods of cultural invention.

In "Malaise d'une civilization," far from defining the "true nature" of Antillean identity, Césaire proposes it as a problem for the reader—and imagined writer of the future—to tackle: "Nous voici appelés à nous connaître enfin nous-mêmes, et voici devant nous les splendeurs et les espoirs. Le surréalisme nous a rendue une partie de nos chances. A nous de trouver les autres. A sa lumière" (We have been called to know ourselves at last, and we find splendor and hope before us. Surrealism has returned part of our luck to us. It is up to us to find the rest. By its light) (48). Just as Ménil only partially answered the question "Qui parle ici?" (Who speaks here?), Suzanne Césaire indicates that she can offer only partial self-knowledge by exploring Frobenius's civilizational categories but noting their limitations along with those of surrealism for providing the answers.

Ménil's essay from the same issue, "Laissez passer la poésie" (Let poetry pass by), both continues and contracts the critique of Antillean society Suzanne Césaire levels in "Malaise d'une civilisation." In Ménil's take, the biggest problem posed to Martinican-Antillean society was its petty bourgeoisie; in other words, for him it was this class that was most culturally alienated, posing a stumbling block for the transformation of society as a whole:

> Dans la grande cuve Caraïbe bouillonne la vie, violente. . . . Ici, les grandes steppes bleues de la mer, là les criques claires au pied des falaises en dérive, loin dans les terres, la folie convulsive des plantes rejoignant le rêve gelé de la lave et du morne. Et sur cela, sur cette vie déchaînée et incompréhensiblement fixée dans son mouvement, voici que s'avance, cauteleux, l'homme le plus "réussi" de la région: le petit-bourgeois antillais. Risible rencontre. (21)

> In the great Caribbean cistern life bubbles, violently. . . . Here, the great blue steppes of the sea, there the clear coves at the foot of the drifting cliffs, deep into the earth, the convulsive madness of plants meets the frozen dream of lava and the hills.[29] And on top of that, onto that unrelenting and incomprehensibly fixed life in its movement, here he comes, wily, the most "successful" man in the region: the petty bourgeois Antillean. Laughable encounter.

In this surrealist image of a cistern-Caribbean, Ménil portrays the region's petty bourgeois class as an element completely out of place in the landscape, an intruder, obviously unaligned with the natural elements, laughably out of place. As the essay proceeds, Ménil sets up this class as an enemy target for *Tropiques*'s poetic enterprise (24). At the same time, he clarifies in a footnote attached to the title of the essay that it addresses only that segment of the bourgeoisie "de bonne volonté" (of good faith), or those Ménil conceived of as transformable. It should therefore be understood that he targets this class *insofar as* he considers its members transformable.

Ménil suggests that this class is threatened by a potent—but literary—danger: "Constatant ce que vous êtes, comme par une savante projection géometrique, nous ferons profiler sur l'écran caraïbe ce que vous n'êtes exactement pas" (Certifying what you are, like a knowing geometric projection, we will profile you on the Caribbean screen as that which you are not quite) (28). The flagrant animosity of this essay, replete with literary threats, may be partially attributed to a poor reception of *Tropiques* among the local middle class, but it also bespeaks what Dalleo calls *Tropiques*'s "contest with the professional class" (*Caribbean Literature* 115). The disdain Ménil projects on the petty bourgeoisie is embedded in a critique of imperial capitalism including, as Dalleo has indicated, the overvaluation of instrumental reason associated with the bourgeoisie at large (115).

In "Situation de la poésie aux Antilles" (Situating Poetry in the Antilles) (*Tropiques* 11, 1944), Ménil would offer his culminating analysis—social and literary—of the past, present, and possible future of both Black and mixed-race Antilleans and the literary movement in which he situated *Tropiques*. Although he explains the importance of surrealism as a method for this movement and locates its social implications specifically for Black and mixed-race Antilleans, neither surrealism nor négritude would be his choice for naming it. Instead, he called it "Romantisme antillais" (Antillean Romanticism) and suggested that it combined a variety of approaches, including surrealism, psychoanalysis, ethnography, and historical materialism (133). Ménil notes that this movement had begun with the literary magazine he had coedited in Paris, *Légitime Défense*, and culminated in Aimé Césaire, its signature poet. Although Ménil's critical proposition of Antillean Romanticism did not become the canonical way for literary criticism to memorialize Antillean literature between *Légitime Défense* and *Tropiques*, as surrealism and négritude have instead become the primary critical categories used for this literature, it is important to account for his Antillean-located proposal.

A Poetics of Freedom

The intertextual dialogue on poetics established between the Césaires and Ménil was as concerned with establishing the importance of location in poetic discourse as it was with constructing a vision of poetry's potential as a freeing medium endowed with the power of undoing the racist cultural paradigms imposed by French colonialism and slavery in the Caribbean. The urgency of the difficult task the *Tropiques* group set to poetry was compounded by the exigencies of the moment. As Fanon has analyzed these changes in Martinique at the time, the extenuating circumstances of the period uncloaked French racism for Martinicans:

> Before 1939, there were about two thousand Europeans in Martinique. . . . Now from one day to the next, the single town of Fort-de-France was submerged by nearly ten thousand Europeans having an unquestionable, but until then latent, racist mentality. . . . The four years during which they were obliged to live shut in on themselves, inactive, a prey to anguish when they thought of their families left in France, victims of despair as to the future, allowed them to drop a mask which, when all is said and done, was rather superficial, and to behave as "authentic racists." ("West Indians and Africans" 22)

In other words, the illusion that cultural assimilation could produce equality between the metropolitan French and Antillean colonials was shattered by the racism revealed by the multitudes of displaced French sailors and civilians during the war. In this essay, Fanon attributes to Aimé Césaire alone a task that necessarily involved *Tropiques*: transforming literature and racial consciousness in Martinique. As Fanon explains the shift, "Before Césaire, West Indian literature was a literature of Europeans. The West Indian identified himself with the white man, adopted a white man's attitude, 'was a white man.' . . . The West Indian of 1945 is a Negro" (26).[30] Fanon repeats a move here that was typical of *Tropiques*: to describe circumstances specific to Martinique and assume they are generalizable more broadly as Antillean. He also repeats the doubling of *Tropiques*'s literary-cultural project of bringing into being an authentically Antillean literature and transforming Antillean racial consciousness, even if he ascribes these achievements to Aimé Césaire alone. There is no necessary connection between innovating in literature and altering consciousness, but the poetics offered by *Tropiques* endeavored to transform poetry and consciousness together. In dialogue with each other—and at times passing through Bretonian or their own deviant takes on Bretonian surrealism—Aimé Césaire, with Suzanne Césaire and René Ménil, developed a poetics of freedom.

The *Tropique*-al theory of poetry as freedom received its first treatment by Ménil in his essay "Orientation de la poésie" (Orienting Poetry). In this essay he suggests that poetry offers a temporary freedom from the constraints—though not the facts—of lived reality (13–21). In a poignant conclusion to his essay on the role of poetic freedom he suggests, "L'homme délivré un instant de la dictature des choses, conçoit de la vie et de la vérité un idéal qui cesse enfin d'être dérisoire. C'est le temps de la liberté d'esprit" (When man has been momentarily released from the dictatorship of things, he can conceive out of life and truth an ideal that finally ceases to be ridiculous. This is the time of the freedom of the mind) (21). The poetic image delivers freedom here from a "dictatorship of things," but of course, in the middle of the Vichy regime, the actual dictatorship cannot help but be implicated in this turn of phrase. It is not that the work of poetry is escapist but instead that the poet's critical confrontation with reality yields a spiritual freedom from the confinement of lived—and present—realities toward a critical poeticization of reality. In other words, the freedom offered by poetry results from its critical engagement with reality. For Ménil, poetry makes this possible "étant commentaire des choses et non leur présentation" (as commentary on things and not their presentation) (20).

Suzanne Césaire, the only one of *Tropiques*'s main contributors who advocated explicitly for surrealism in her theories on poetry, presented surrealist poetry in particular as a medium for freedom. As her now famous essay "1943: Le surréalisme et nous" (1943: Surrealism and Us) proclaims, "Mais, lorsqu'en 1943 la liberté elle-même se trouve menacée dans le monde entier, le surréalisme . . . se veut résumé tout entier en ce seul mot magique: liberté" (But in 1943, when freedom finds itself threatened throughout the world, surrealism . . . may be summed up in a single magic word: freedom) (15). Césaire directly invokes here the Vichy regime that has just ended in Martinique along with Nazism and other forms of imperial domination that she positions against freedom in 1943. Surrealism, *as* freedom, reads in her terms like an antidote to fascism. Although the *Tropiques* group was clearly influenced by Bretonian surrealism, they deviated from it extensively. They drew from many sources, most of them presurrealist, in order to construct a particularist, located poetics.

Even when they advocated for surrealism directly it was already a transformed, situated surrealism oriented toward freedom. Suzanne Césaire, for example, in "1943: Le surréalisme et nous" uses the language of evolution to explain how they transformatively deploy the surrealist movement. She references the global scope of surrealism by drawing on a list of locations—New York, Brazil, Mexico, Argentina, Cuba, Canada, Algiers—and qualifies how surrealism interacts with each location and gives the voices that rise out of them access to timbre and resonance they would not have without the movement (14). In her essay, surrealism functions to name and transnationally affiliate locally situated poetic resistance rather than a precise or strict philosophy or movement. Surrealism's internationalist scope also provided a broad threshold of visibility for *Tropiques*. As Césaire makes sure to stress, however, its breadth did not mean that surrealism had spread throughout the world as an unchanged and static form or philosophy. On the contrary, she explains, "Mais, signe même de sa vitalité, le surréalisme a évolué. Evolution, mieux, épanouisement" (But surrealism has evolved: the very sign of its vitality. It would be more accurate to say it has blossomed) (15; "1943: Surrealism" 124).

In one of her most potently poetic and political moments, Césaire proclaims in the same essay that millions of Black hands will revolt: "Délivré dun [*sic*] long engourdissement, le plus deshérité de tous les peuples se lèvera, sur les plaines de cendre" (Delivered from a long slumber, the most dispossessed of all people will rise up across plains of ashes) (18; "1943: Surrealism" 126, with my modification of "dispossessed" for "deshérité"). For Suzanne Césaire, the liberating quality of surrealism necessarily translated into Black international uprising; her vision of surrealism was not just revolutionary in itself but could also catalyze a revolutionary consciousness leading to concrete political changes.[31] Her radical and transformative vision of surrealism would be an important precursor to Alejo Carpentier's critique of surrealism's distance from the surreal realities or, in his terms, the "marvelous real" imbued by the history of the Americas.[32]

"Poésie et connaissance," Aimé Césaire's signature treatise on poetics, builds on the idea of poetry as a freeing form of expression. Importantly, although this text has sometimes been read for understanding his take on négritude or surrealism, it is more broadly a synthesis of his understanding of poetry as a form of knowledge. At no point in this essay does Césaire advocate surrealist practice in poetry even if his ideas on poetic knowledge draw from Breton in addition to Breton's own predecessors in French poetry. This essay was published in the final issue of *Tropiques* (no. 12, 1945) but had been presented the year before at a philosophy conference in Haiti.[33] In the essay Césaire conceives of the freedom involved in poetry as the freedom of signification, granted to words between the poet's writing and interpretation, a freedom that gives rise to meaning-making in contextual terms, which Césaire refers to as the word's "free associations" in the following: "Et parce que dans tout poème vrai, le poète joue le jeu du monde, le poete [*sic*] vrai souhaite abandonner le mot à ses libres associations, sûr que c'est en définitive l'abandonner à la volonté de l'univers" (And since in every true poem the poet plays the world's game, the true poet wishes to release the word to free association, with the certainty of definitively releasing it to the will of the universe) (164). Although this is an obscure passage by itself, I understand it—in terms of the rest of the essay about the kind of knowledge offered by poetry—to mean that in true poetry, the poet wishes to free the word to take on the associations to which it gives rise, as directed by the context of the poetic universe of the poem, but also abandoning it beyond that. The word, in this sense, is freed from any fixity of meaning it may acquire in language outside of poetry.[34]

In this essay, Césaire diagnoses the poverty of scientific rationality as the problem that poetic knowledge indirectly combats. "La connaissance poétique nait dans le grand silence de la connaissance scientifique" (Poetic knowledge is born in the great silence left by scientific knowledge) (157). Analogous to the way I have conceived the magazine's cultural work as poetically tilling the fallow terrains (*manques*) of Antillean culture, Césaire portrays the knowledge produced by poetry as that which is born in the silent space left behind by scientific knowledge.[35] In his terms, scientific methods are inadequate methods of perception for the contiguous realities of existence. Poetic knowledge, for Césaire, contains the key to understanding the intricacies of context, contiguity, and association. This concept of poetic knowledge is central to poetic practice as a liberating method for both the Césaires and Ménil. Césaire explains the methodological possibilities of producing poetic knowledge best in "Poésie et connaissance" as follows: "Si je précise que dans l'émotion poétique, rien n'est jamais plus près de rien que de son contraire, on comprendra que jamais homme de paix, que jamais homme des profondeurs ne fut plus rebelle et plus pugnace" (If I specify that in poetic emotion nothing is ever as close to anything as to its contrary, you will understand that no man of peace, no man of depth, was ever more rebellious and pugnacious) (164). The radical potency of poetry in this theory lays in its ability to produce contiguity between opposites, an idea that dovetails with Breton's writings on surrealism, which Césaire engages indirectly in the building of his own view throughout the course of this essay. In Breton's writings, the surrealist image works best when what it brings together is most disparate (*Manifestes du surrealisme* 49). Césaire's essay pushes further to suggest that the poetic method of bringing opposites together speaks to a truth that scientific knowledge cannot accommodate.

Césaire goes on to elaborate the underlying poetic principle of this essay that is of the utmost importance for understanding his own poetic practice. For him, the creative play involved in poetry (or its method) allows for the same word to stand for "itself" and its "opposite" *at the same time*. As he elaborates, in a poetic image, A can be A and –A at the same time ("Poésie et connaissance" 166). As Césaire would also explain, "Et parce que l'arbre est stabilité, l'arbre est aussi abandon" (And because the tree is stability, the tree is also abandon) (162). This proposal is not supposed to appeal to instrumental reason but instead to poetic thought, or the associative, contextual thinking that occurs in the mental fields *untilled* by science. Aimé Césaire's practice of this principle is perhaps more complex than his description, for what is important about his advocacy of poetic knowledge is the capacity to signify multiply and even contradictorily in lyric composition. In this description Césaire relies on the abstract possibility of contradictory ways of poeticizing a tree, but as he clarifies early in the essay, context gives rise to the possibility of coexistence between contradictory meanings in poetry; what would allow a tree to signify as stability as well as abandon would be the context—or location—of the poetic image that gives meaning to the tree.

Ménil in turn more specifically locates poetry's methodological potency for freedom. The dualities he diagnoses in the Martinican present serve for him as potential for a new aesthetic, one that would resolve the duality of the present ("Naissance" 62). Ménil would elaborate that the duality he refers to is the form-without-content of contemporary art and poetry in Martinique on the one hand and the living content of Martinican realities on the other. He thus suggests an aesthetic resolution of the seeming contradiction between French aesthetic forms and Martinican realities. In his approach to these dualities he seeks future aesthetic resolutions.

Suzanne Césaire would empower surrealist poetry, beyond expressing dualities or resolving them, to transcend them. In particular, she refers to surrealism's potency to transcend the "sordides antinomies actuelles: blancs-noirs, européens-africains, civilés-savages" (sordid contemporary antinomies of black / white, European / African, civilized / savage) ("1943: Le surréalisme" 18; "1943: Surrealism" 126). If, as Aimé Césaire explained, poetic knowledge can conceive of the coexistence of opposites even in the same term, the surrealism Suzanne Césaire appropriates in her essay can work poetic "magic" on the dichotomies that govern racist ideologies toward transcending them. Drawing on her terminology, Aimé Césaire would go on to suggest that the poetic image's dialectic transcends antinomies ("Poésie et connaissance" 167). In an intertextual conversation with each other these writers constructed a vibrant debate on the potential freeing power of a *located* poetry.

Poetics in Practice: Aimé Césaire's Antimanifesto

Aimé Césaire's poetry was such a consistent presence that it served as one of the fundamental pillars of *Tropiques*. His poems are either directly or indirectly invoked in many of *Tropiques*'s theoretical texts, and the social and philosophical questions raised in them in turn directly affect the evolution of his poetry during this time.[36] During the *Tropiques* period he incubated the collection of poems that would be included in his first book, *Les armes miraculeuses* (Gallimard, 1946); his first play, *Et les chiens se taisaient*; and two new and distinct editions of his highly acclaimed book-length poem *Cahier d'un retour au pays natal*. By "incubate" I mean that he published from these works in *Tropiques* as well as other magazines during the period in which he edited *Tropiques*, that his publications during this period often included early drafts of works that would undergo revision later, and that the works he sent out for publication during this period and after were highly enriched by the theoretical dialogue on poetics observable in *Tropiques*.

While Césaire drafted later installments of *Cahier d'un retour au pays natal* that would follow from the first 1939 version featured in the French literary magazine *Volontés*, he published in *Tropiques* one piece that would feature prominently in the two distinct 1947 entries of the poem and partially, but significantly, in the 1956 entry: "En guise de manifeste littéraire" (In the guise of a literary manifesto).[37] I use "entries" to refer to what might otherwise be called "versions" of the poem to account for my understanding of the multiple versions over the years as one poem-journal with multiple installments or entries that we might situate historically as an aesthetic, political, and theoretical evolution through a fecund period of Césaire's poetic and political life.

"En guise de manifeste littéraire," which I understand as an antimanifesto, would in fact yield significant passages for the critical appraisal of *Cahier d'un retour au pays natal*.[38] For example, one poetic moment that Gregson Davis refers to as the most explicit in its "stark formulation of the problem of identity" (36) comes directly out of the poem: "Qui et quels nous sommes? Admirable question!" ("Who and which are we? Admirable question!) (8). This moment that opens up identity as a question for literary examination was emblematic of the theoretical exploration of a located poetics for the Antilles in *Tropiques*.

The antimanifesto operates as *Tropique*-al poetics in practice insofar as it is both highly located *and* brings location into view as a problem and a process more than an achievement or a fact. "En guise de manifeste littéraire" is also historically located in the Vichy regime, as it appears in the second-to-last issue of *Tropiques* before the end of Robert's Vichy rule in Martinique (*Tropiques* 5, 1942). This would be the same issue that includes Suzanne Césaire's essay critiquing cultural assimilation in the Antilles, "Malaise d'une civilisation," and Ménil's essay that attacks the Antillean petty bourgeoisie, "Laissez passer la poésie." "En guise de manifeste littéraire" may be productively read in dialogue with these works, the located theories of poetry they offer, and the critique they lodge at the colonial bourgeoisie.

It is quite fitting for Césaire, as a proponent of poetic knowledge as the realm of multiplicitous and even contradictory forms of signification, to offer instead of a manifesto a poem perfomatively *disguised as* a manifesto. "En guise de" (In the guise of) announces the work of dissimulation whereby Césaire's poem takes the place of a manifesto and as such operates *as if* it were one, thus offering poetic knowledge on the genre of the manifesto instead of serving as one. If anything is "manifest" here, it is a poetics-in-practice; if it is a call for a kind of literature, it calls *as* a model. Of course, the genre of the manifesto was first a political genre before it became aesthetic, and therefore the residue of the political is always present in the genre (Obszyński 1). Although there are important political implications in Césaire's antimanifesto, it is precisely his turning upside down the *political* terms of the genre that engenders both aesthetic and political interventions.

The poem, read through the paratextual work of its title, thus breaks down, par excellence, the generic structure of the manifesto, which seems to operate by establishing one locus of enunciation by rejecting another, or to construct a "we" in contradistinction to an "other." As Kaiama Glover argues in her evaluation of the "Pour une littérature monde" (Toward a "World Literature" in French) manifesto (2008), "manifestos in general risk misrepresenting *belonging* by leaving out important voices" (109). Glover also suggests that manifestos practice "reterritorializing demarcations of *us* and *them*" (109). Indeed, the manifesto as a genre of literary politics seems more oriented toward the construction of a normative "we" that begs the reterritorialization of a "them" as other. As Sylvia Wynter suggests in "Ethno or Socio Poetics," in popular culture of the African diaspora a "we that needed no OTHER to constitute their Being" has been produced through a radical assumption and redeployment of "otherness" (85). It is precisely because Aimé Césaire's text radically assumes and redeploys otherness, both staging and bringing into question the radical oppositionality of "us" and "them" embedded in the manifesto form, that I read it as an antimanifesto and understand the relational breakdown of alterity in it through the terms that Wynter would go on to theorize.[39]

The antimanifesto operates through an antagonism that is both reinforced and undermined by the uncertainty it establishes between who fits into the oppositional categories of "nous" (we) and "vous" (you), clarified by the production of an "I" between them. The introductory verses set up the principal antinomy of "nous" and "vous" that Césaire both works with and through in this piece:

> Inutile de durcir sur notre passage, plus butyreuses que des lunes, vos
> faces de tréponème pâle.

> Inutiles d'apitoyer pour nous l'indécence de vos sourires de kystes suppurants. (7)
>
> Futile, to harden your faces of treponema pallidum
> creamier than moons, as we pass by.
>
> Futile, to pity upon us the indecency of your smiles of suppurating cysts.[40]

The relational actions undertaken by "vous," whose faces are compared to the agent that causes syphilis (treponema pallidum), are figured as futile. Although the introductory verses abstract the relation between "vous" and "nous," they ground the image of "vous" in illness and ugliness without describing "nous." At the same time, the tension portrayed suggests that "vous" attempts to act both defensively and condescendingly toward "nous." The resulting irony is that the defensive and pitying gaze is returned to "vous" with disgust and what will go on to be revealed as hatred.

The "nous" and "vous" of the piece do not remain strictly opposed, however; their perspectives are curiously entangled in a manner exemplary of Césaire's poetics and interventions in racist ideology:

> Parce que nous vous haïssons, vous et votre raison, nous nous réclamons de la démence précoce, de la folie flambante, du cannibalisme tenace. ("En guise de manifeste" 7)
>
> Because we hate you, you and your reason, we call upon
> precocious dementia, blazing madness, tenacious
> cannibalism.

By this time in the piece hatred is figured to propel "nous" to lay claim to the presumed opposite of the reason "belonging" to "vous." What propels the action is not decrying the injustice of being represented malignantly by "vous" through madness or cannibalism. Instead, the poetic voice assumes and deploys the otherness embedded in what might otherwise be the racist accusations of madness and cannibalism as veritable weapons. The piece proceeds by continuing to invoke madness in many forms and proclaiming fallacies, such as "that 2 plus 2 is 5," before proceeding at last to characterize "nous" by way of the now canonized question for its later role in Césaire's *Cahier*: "Qui et quels nous sommes? Admirable question!" (Who and which are we? Admirable question!) (8). The answer emerges in a series of nouns that demand an ambivalent reading in accordance with Césaire's theory of poetic contradiction in "Poésie et connaissance": "Haïsseurs. Bâtisseurs. Traitres. Hougans. Hougans surtout" (8) (Haters. Builders. Traitors. Vodou priests. Vodou priests especially). Here, ambivalence works in each term. First, *haïsseurs* is usually followed by an object (*haïsseurs de . . .*), so in this moment the hating ascribed to "nous" has an unclear object. On one level it picks up the residue of meaning left by the hating of the previous page, wherein "vous et votre raison" is the object of hate, but here this reading can only be partial. What renders the ambivalence of the series most strongly is the use of "Hougans" (priests of Vodou). The irony of defining "nous" as "hougans" is reinforced with the comical emphasis of "*surtout*."[41] But this usage is only ironic if you know that Césaire did not understand Vodou to be widely practiced in Martinique at this time, not the way it was, for example, in Haiti. As he remarked in his interview about the *Tropiques* years with Jacqueline Leiner, "Il n'ya pas de vaudou à la Martinique come réligion constituée, mais il existe à mon avis, comme tendance. . . . Les gens doivent faire un peu de vaudou sans le savoir. Peut-être que ce vaudou est laïcisé dans des crises de colère, dans certains comportements, dans des choses très bizarres" (There is no Vodou in Martinique as a constituted religion, but it exists, in my opinion, as a tendency. . . . People must practice some Vodou without knowing it. This Vodou is probably secularized in fits of anger, in certain behaviors, in very bizarre things) (Leiner xviii). This interpretation identifies Vodou in Martinique as a cultural trace and not an actual religious practice. As such, "Hougans" does not operate as a completely straightforward representational proposition in answer to the question about who (and what) "nous" could be. There is nothing completely referential in the entire series. On one level, the series probably enunciates the internalized reflection of a racist colonial gaze that became all the more acute during the Vichy period, an enunciation that cannot be repeated without some irony. But the series evolves into a possibility deeply in line with Césaire's poetics of excavating the wounds of slavery's history and salvaging the traces of African cultural traditions under erasure in the French-dominated Caribbean. Césaire goes on to gesture to something like—"en guise de"—a spiritual ritual.

Car nous
voulons tous les démons
Ceux d'hier, ceux d'aujourd'hui
Ceux du carcan ceux de la houe
Ceux de l'interdiction, de la prohibition, du marronage

et nous n'avons garde d'oublier ceux du négrier . . .
Donc nous chantons. ("En guise de manifeste" 8)

For we
want all the demons
Those of yesterday, those of today
Those of the stocks those of the hoe
Those of the ban, of prohibition, of marronage

and how could we forget those of the slave ship . . .
So we sing.

In the guise of an *hougan*, Césaire calls on a series of demons here, demons he associates with assorted guises of slavery, its tortures, and its victorious defeat in resistance. The segment's ending, "Donc, nous chantons," evokes that wishing to stir the demons that live in the infrastructure of slavery and its ending as impetus for song, including of course the song of poetry, staged throughout this piece as a collective endeavor.

The collective wish to sing up the demons of the past reads ambivalently. On the one hand, it is an appropriation and therefore a resignification of otherwise imposed otherness, an enactment of what Sylvia Wynter calls the "*poetical / political* assumption of *Otherness*, an assumption at once heretical and revolutionary" ("Ethno or Socio Poetics" 79). For Wynter, this assumption "can negate the *we / they* dichotomy and restore to *ethnos* its original integral meaning—of *we*" (79).

At this point in the antimanifesto, the piece has not yet broken down its "guise" of a manifesto, however. It has both poeticized an antagonistic we / they dichotomy and assumed and therefore intervened in the screen of Otherness as it demonstrates a processual and even ritualistic movement through Wynter's dictum. In this moment of the ritual what we see is a *working through*—in a psychoanalytic sense—the demons of slavery's past and the legacy of imposed otherness written onto blackness in its wake. Fred Moten, as if he were referring precisely to this moment in Césaire, writes: "There is an open set of sentences of the kind blackness is x and we should chant them all, not only for and in the residual critique of mastery such chanting bears but also in devoted instantiation, sustenance and defense of the irregular" ("Preface," viii).[42] For Moten, devoted chanting, such as that instantiated by Césaire in this piece, is both critique and defense.

By the end of the piece, "vous" has shifted, "nous" has parted, and the poetic "je" remains in a different kind of dialogue with a transformable "vous" called upon as a target audience for this piece. Just before the end, it reads:

> Vous
> ô vous qui vous bouchez les oreilles
> c'est à vous, c'est pour vous que je parle, pour vous qui écartelerez demain
> jusqu'aux larmes la paix paissante de vos sourires, (Césaire, "En guise de manifeste" 12)

> You
> oh you who cover up your ears
> it is to you, for you that I speak, for you who will tomorrow
> quarter to tears the passing peace of your smiles,

"Vous" becomes both the audience and the entity for whom the poetic "je" seeks to speak or, in other words, represent. Whereas before "nous" necessarily implied the pertinence of the poetic "je" and therefore the locus of its enunciation, here the locus of "je" has indirectly shifted, for it does not claim pertinence to "vous" as much as a relational "speaking for." What follows is an invocation for "vous" to transform from refusing to listen to carrying out the poetic voice's instruction to self-mutilate. The piece's "je" completes the manifesto genre's undoing in this moment, for it calls upon the supposed oppositional group and prophesies the group's self-inflicted and violent transformation but also unsettles the neatness of a poetic "je" on the side of a "nous" that is discretely dislocated from an oppositional "vous" by crossing the purported lines of the divide, by addressing "vous" as a transformable body.

The entreaty to this later "vous," especially when the piece is read in the intertextual domain of *Tropiques*, in which again and again it is the Black and mixed-race Antillean bourgeoisie who is at turns under attack and also called upon to transform, suggests that there is a poetic reason for the abstraction of "vous" from any clear segment of the population. When the Black and mixed-race bourgeoisie deigns to propel racist discourse to denigrate their poorer and darker-skinned would-be compatriots, they become confusable with the antagonizing "vous" that might otherwise be read on the side of the Vichy regime and racist French soldiers. The problem with the dichotomy, of course, is that siding with "vous" does not allow one to escape the condescension and othering that is blanket-applied to those Césaire identifies as "nous." The Black and mixed-race bourgeoisie is necessarily doubled in this sense. Even the unalienated and race-proud member of the Black and mixed-race Antillean community, however, would presumably be able to access the intersubjective double consciousness produced by countenancing an anti-Black racist gaze. By "double consciousness," I refer to Du Bois's concept for the intersubjective tension produced by the awareness of being misapprehended as "other" (37–39).[43] Césaire's antimanifesto calls for a violently radical transformation, one that may be readable as the violence of revolutionary war but is also readable as the violence of partial self-destruction necessary in the process of disalienation, which may in turn be read as the anterior work of movement building or the revolutionary transformation itself. The poetic "je" performs such a self-inflicted violence as a model of sorts:

> Je force la membrane vitelline qui me sépare de moi-même.
> Je force les grandes eaux qui me ceinturent de sang (10)

> I force open the yolk membrane separating me from myself.
> I force open the great waters that wrap me in blood

The violence in this moment, which appears after the claim that the poetic "je" is a speaking cadaver, is also readable as the violence of birth, such that what the antimanifesto enacts and calls for is a transformation so radical it is assimilable to both enduring a death and violently forging a new birth. The violence of quartering one's own smile of so-called peace is readable into this domain of figuring an intersubjective disalienation as a self-imposed violence of transformation.

"En guise de manifeste littéraire" as a *Tropique*-al production would thus sharpen the intersubjective dimension of the process of disalienation from anti-blackness, colonialism, and bourgeois mores in Césaire's *Cahier* for its future of installments. It is fitting that this intersubjective piece would emerge in *Tropiques*'s corpus given that the theoretical dialogue it featured among the Césaires and Ménil would regularly recur to a Black Marxist and Antillean "we" that targets a "you," most often readable as the Black and mixed-race Antillean bourgeoisie.

As a *Tropique*-al poetics-in-practice, this piece demonstrates how complicated it may be to confront Antillean reality poetically as Ménil proposed it, how difficult it is to articulate, even poetically, a "nous" overdetermined by racist colonial ideologies. There is no clear sense of who the enemy "vous" may be or to what extent the enemy gaze is internalized within the ranks of the "nous." Just as Ménil's answer to the question "Qui parle ici?" ends in the resigned affirmation that culture and life are "elsewhere," and just as Suzanne Césaire suggested that surrealism has only provided part of the answer of local self-knowledge, Aimé Césaire's response to the question "Qui et quels nous sommes?" is self-consciously limited. Instead, it offers a polyvalent proposition that implicitly critiques the history of colonialism and slavery and performs an intersubjective disalienation that would clear space for new ways of answering such a question.

To *Créolité* and Beyond: Rerouting Black Consciousness

Lacking local infrastructure contributes to the perfect environment for reducing and undervaluing the nonetheless foundational literary and philosophical output of Black Martinicans such as the Césaires and Ménil in a magazine of limited circulation such as *Tropiques*. In Menil's reflection on how the single issue of *Légitime Défense* he produced with Étienne Léro and others in Paris in 1932 was forgotten, he faults the colonial censorship that halted the magazine for the conditions of its forgetting. But he also indicts a more amorphous phenomenon of colonial blindness: "Mais plus encore la cause de ce qu'il faut bien considérer comme un rejet réside dans la conscience sociale elle-même dont la distorsion en régime colonial est telle qu'elle s'aveugle elle-même aux vérités de son drame devant le miroir" (But even more the cause of what may well be considered a rejection resides in social consciousness itself where the distortion of the colonial regime is such that it blinds itself to the realities played out in the mirror) ("Légitime défense" n.p.). Ménil approaches here the density of the matrix formed by the interplay between infrastructural scarcity for cultural production and the colonial ideology that a priori devalues the creativity emergent from a colonial context. His analysis of this matrix results in identifying a distortion of vision, one his earlier literary-theoretical work in *Tropiques* sought to redress but nonetheless persists into the future beyond the magazine. In my reading of *Tropiques*'s place in Francophone Antillean literary history, its legacy appears to have been explicitly obscured and distorted and implicitly appropriated and extended.

The ideas the Césaires and Ménil produced in *Tropiques* have often been enervated and repackaged through a thin appraisal of négritude. In the highly acclaimed 1989 manifesto by Jean Bernabé, Patrick Chamoiseau, and Raphaël Confiant, *Eloge de la créolité*, many of the *Tropiques* group's ideas appear reworked under the multiracial rubric of "*créolité*" centered around the Creole language. In the multiracial push and centering of Creole they certainly differentiate the theoretical parameters of the *créolité* manifesto from the Afro-centric positions sustained and elaborated by *Tropiques*. What is troubling, however, is the reduction of the *Tropiques* contribution to a distorted projection of négritude alongside key and uncited influences present in the *créolité* text that if attributed would demonstrate how imbricated the work in *Tropiques* has been to the development of "*créolité*." While I maintain that the infrastructural limitations of circulating *Tropiques* are central factors to account for the appearance of rupture between them, the theoretical universe of *Tropiques* resonates vividly in the pages of the later manifesto.

The silent legacy of *Tropiques* in *Eloge de la créolité* is evident from its first pages. Just as René Ménil and Suzanne Césaire diagnosed Antillean art as alienated from lived and located reality, the manifesto writers make the related claim that the truth of Antillean life remains hidden, as they explain why "Caribbean literature does not exist." In their words, "our truth found itself behind bars, in the deep bottom of ourselves, unknown to our consciousness and to the artistically free reading of the world in which we live" (76). They go on to echo Suzanne Césaire and René Ménil's proclamations that both reality and true literature have remained "elsewhere" when they explain, "this determined a writing for the Other, a borrowed writing, steeped in French values, or at least unrelated to this land, and which, in spite of a few positive aspects, did nothing else but maintain in our minds the domination of an elsewhere" (76). As in *Tropiques*, the trope of aesthetic *dépaysement*, or the positioning of art as "elsewhere," persists later in the manifesto: "What we accept in us as aesthetic is the little declared by the Other as aesthetic. The noble is generally elsewhere. So is the universal . . . for our idea of aesthetics was elsewhere" (86). The literary alienation posed by the *créolité* manifesto over forty years later is very close to its positioning throughout *Tropiques*, so close that the manifesto writers engage almost the same language to pose it. Mamadou Badiane indicates that in Suzanne Césaire's essay "Malaise d'une civilisation," she set the stage for the debate about cultural identity that Glissant and the *créolité* manifesto writers would later explore as she indicates therein her disinterest in a return to Africa and the past or an essentialist conception of race (841–842). I would expand this view to the whole of *Tropiques*.[44] Like the *Tropiques* group, the *créolité* group sought to renovate cultural production along with selfhood in the Antilles. Whereas the *Tropiques* group led the way to transformation with a theory of located poetry and the promulgation of Black consciousness, the *créolité* group promulgates "interior vision" and Creole consciousness.

Although the writers of the *créolité* manifesto pay their respects to Aimé Césaire, proclaiming "we are forever Césaire's sons," the "we" they advocate for emerges against the "other" of a distorted view of négritude that they attribute to Césaire. Although they never define what they understand as négritude they position an amorphous and damaging version of it as the substance of Césaire's contribution: "Negritude did not solve our aesthetic problems. At some point it even might have worsened our identity instability by pointing at the most pertinent syndrome of our morbidities: self-withdrawal, mimetism, the natural perception of local things abandoned for the fascination of foreign things, etc., all forms of alienation" (Bernabé, Chamoiseau, and Confiant 82). This criticism suggests that the critique embedded in the authors' idea of négritude may have been damaging precisely for pointing out symptoms of alienation, even though the manifesto opens precisely by pointing out almost the same symptoms. In another surprising move, the manifesto suggests that "indeed the prodigious power of Negritude was such that it could do without a poetics. Its brilliance shone, marking out with blinding signs the space of our blinkings" (81). It is as if what emerges in *Tropiques* were not indeed theoretical works on poetry, as if Aimé Césaire had not penned his now lauded treatise on poetics, "Poésie et connaissance." Although the *créolité* writers advocate for an Antillean literature grounded in the Creole language and criticize the insufficiency of "Negritude" for understanding Antillean reality, they nonetheless recognize Césaire's foundationality for the region's literature.[45]

To clarify, *Tropiques* offered no definition or official proposition of négritude, and in fact the word appeared only twice in the entire magazine. It first appears in an unsigned introduction to an essay by the German ethnographer Leo Frobenius, "Que signifie pour nous l'Afrique?" (What does Africa Mean to Us?) and later returns in Suzanne Césaire's essay "Le Grande Camouflage." In my reading of *Tropiques*, "Négritude" (capitalized) as a philosophy, is not what drives the magazine.[46] Instead, *Tropiques* participated in "négritude" (uncapitalized), as a practice of naming, reclaiming, and exploring the dimensions of Black identity that was both part of and on the edges of the local-regional poetics developed in its pages. The task of *Tropiques,* to interrogate the postslavery colonial existence in the French colonies of the Caribbean, to explore poetry as an avenue for liberation from this condition, and to offer a located poetics from which to project a possible future of decolonization, certainly included a practice of "négritude" on the edges.

Instead of proclaiming a mythical vision of blackness, the *Tropiques* group's practice of "négritude" primarily consisted of a strategy of employing and claiming identification with the word "*nègre*" as part of their project of undoing what they critiqued as an Antillean brand of cultural alienation. As Natalie Melas has presented Césaire's employment of "négritude" in *Cahier d'un retour au pays natal*, "the neologism *négritude* seizes the improper colonial name *nègre*, seeking to transvalue denigration and alienation instead of positing something completely anterior to colonial history" (569). The adoption of this term in Martinique constituted the primary transformation in consciousness that Fanon has attributed to Aimé Césaire, and *Tropiques* was certainly involved in that transformation ("West Indians and Africans" 26). As Fanon explains, the word "*nègre*" for "Black" had been previously associated derogatorily with Africans. This word was primarily used on the edges of *Tropiques*, for example, in relation to the so-called *nègre-americain* poets of the Harlem Renaissance, the *conte nègre-cubain* of Afro-Cuban folklore written by Lydia Cabrera, African art, a history of the slave trade, Frobenius's ethnographic writings on African civilizations, and Martinican folklore. In one illustrative example of the status of the word "*nègre*" in *Tropiques*, Ménil footnotes his own use of the word to indicate a constituting facet of reality to be addressed in Antillean literature:

> Je sais! Les Antillais veulent qu'on les disent mulâtres pour avoir le droit de mépriser les Africains. N'est-ce pas, que deviendrait-on, en ce monde hiérarchisé de si infecte façon, si l'on n'avait personne à mépriser? Et c'est ainsi que les nègres antillais ont le bonheur d'avoir des nègres plus nègres qu'eux. ("Situation de la poésie aux Antilles" 133)
>
> I know! Antillean people insist on being called mulattos in order to have the right to despise Africans. What would become of us, in this world made hierarchical in such a corrupt way, if there was no one to despise? How fortunate that Antillean negroes have negroes who are more negro than they. ("The Situation of Poetry in the Caribbean" 133, with my modification of "Antillean" for "*Antillais*" instead "Caribbean")

Ménil spells out perfectly here the context for the project of deploying the word "*nègre*" in *Tropiques*—it is a choice to identify with Black Africans against Black denigration in all its forms.

The work of the magazine that contributed to the transformation in racial consciousness that Fanon both marvels at and critiques in "Africans and West Indians" was thus primarily achieved in framing gestures and on the edges of other discourses such as Ménil's footnote. These framing practices can be understood as the group's way of achieving two related goals: naming African heritage both accomplished and relegated to erasure through the French versions of slavery and colonial administration of power in the Caribbean and connecting Black and mixed-race Antilleans to Africans and the African diaspora, or participating in Black internationalism. Brent Hayes Edwards's analysis of earlier appropriations of the word "nègre" to forge Black internationalism illuminates the force of similar choices evinced in *Tropiques*. As he explains the implications of "claiming" and "deploying" the term "*nègre*," they are "*framing* gestures . . . positioning, delimiting, or extending [the term's] range of application; articulating it in relation to the discursive field, to a variety of derived or opposed signifiers (*homme de couleur, noir*); fleshing out its history of use; and imagining its scope of implication, its uses, its 'future'" (38). The regular use of "*nègre*" on the edges of *Tropiques* thus articulated the cultural politics of the choice to claim the word to the discursive field of the rest of the magazine. In *Tropiques*, "négritude" was part of the postslavery colonial condition to be expressed, a way of stating African heritage in the French-ruled Antilles, a way of claiming the lived experience of blackness against its record of abnegation. Use of the term aligns with the later work of the *créolité* group insofar as it pertained to the literary quest for Antillean reality.

The *créolité* group continue to lament the same cultural alienation that is the target of *Tropiques*'s cultural combat. And the solution they propose for it is also quite in tune with their literary forbearers: "Only poetic knowledge, fictional knowledge, literary knowledge, in short, artistic knowledge can discover us, understand us and bring us, evanescent, back to the resuscitation of consciousness" (Bernabé, Chamoiseau, and Confiant 99).[47] The *créolité* movement owes more to *Tropiques* than its authors account for in their homage to négritude; their entire theoretical apparatus is structured by the theories of poetry in *Tropiques*. It is a repetition with an important difference, however. They would propose a much less provisional answer to the question that Aimé Césaire first posed in *Tropiques*: "Qui et quels nous sommes? Admirable question" ("En guise de manifeste littéraire" 8). The hybrid linguistic structure of the Creole language is their response to the question; *créolité* is their answer to the question of Antillean being and expression—it is what they see living beneath French in the still French-ruled Antilles. Their proposition is nonetheless rooted in many of the local-regional premises for the relationship between literature and culture—including but not reducible to the contribution of négritude—which *Tropiques* established almost fifty years before.

Conclusion: Poetic Vision against Colonial Blindness

Suzanne Césaire's "Le grande camouflauge," the final essay of *Tropiques*'s final issue, poetically reflects on the entire Caribbean region, articulating it as a constitutive contradiction, a conglomerate of beautiful landscapes camouflaging its social problems. As she describes her own experience of perceiving the "intolérable beauté" (unbearable beauty) of the Caribbean, first from the top of Mount Pelée in Martinique and later from Kenscoff in Haiti, she reflects on the difficulty of seeing beyond that beauty even as she describes her own ability to do so: "Mon regard par delà ces formes et ces couleurs parfaites, surprend, sur le très beau visage antillais, ses tourments interiors" (My gaze, going beyond these perfect forms and colours, catches by surprise the torment within the Caribbean's most beautiful face) (269; "The Great Camouflage" 157, with one modification of "Antillean" for "*antillais*" instead of "Caribbean"). She describes the torment of the Antilles as a surprise, for it is not *actually* visible; she just knows how to see it, hidden behind the natural beauty. Toward the end of the essay she reframes the beauty of the region as a literary problem:

> Ici les poètes sent chavirer leur tête, et humant les odeurs fraîches des ravins, ils s'emparent de la gerbe des îles, ils écoutent le bruit de l'eau autour d'elles, ils voient s'aviver les flammes tropicales non plus aux balisiers, aux gerberas, aux hibiscus, aux bougainvilliers, aux flamboyants, mais aux faims, aux peurs, aux haines, à la férocité qui brûlent dans des creux des mornes. (272–273)

> Here poets feel their heads reeling and, imbibing the fresh odors of the ravines, they seize the spray of the islands, listen to the sound the water makes around them, and see the tropical flames no longer revive the canna, the gerbera, the hibiscus, the bougainvillaea and the flame trees, but instead the hungers, the fears, the hatreds and the ferocity that burns in the hollows of the mornes. ("The Great Camouflage" 161)

This passage transfers onto poets the overwhelm inspired by the natural beauty of the Antilles, and as that beauty is burned by a tropical (*Tropique*-al?) fire, their gaze shifts beyond the burning beauty to the torments hidden within the burning landscape.

Implicit in the poets' seemingly magical ability to see the affects of social disorder behind the terrestrial beauty of the land, however, is the very real probability of *not* seeing these at all, as Césaire had accused previous poets of in "Misère d'une poésie." What makes poetic social vision possible—beyond the terrestrial beauty that would otherwise hide it—is the fire that brings out the social torments of the place. Implicit in this passage is the shifting task of the local-regional poet that *Tropiques* ventured to direct, away from reflecting the telluric beauty of the Antilles and toward engaging with the troubled social circumstances that would otherwise remain hidden from view, camouflaged.

"Le grande camouflauge" suggests both *Tropiques*'s achievement and unfulfilled goals. The essay lit a fire under what in "Misère d'une poésie" Césaire calls "literary tourism" (50), a form of poetry that had focused on the Antilles as beautiful scenery for touristic enjoyment. The *Tropique*-al fire redirected the vision of local-regional literature to the social conditions created by postslavery colonialism, to the torments unapprehendable through the poetic inscription of beautiful landscapes. It is precisely through rerouting local-regional literature toward the lived reality of colonialism in the wake of slavery that *Tropiques* reinvented the Antilles.

The fragility of the power embedded in this shift, however, the fragility of the power of *Tropiques*'s propositions to reach their addressees at the local, regional, and international levels, may be seen in Césaire's conclusion to "Le grande camouflauge": "si mes Antilles sont si belles, c'est qu'alors le grande jeu de cache-cache a réussi, c'est qui'il fait certes trop beau, ce jour-là, pour y voir" (if my Antilles are so beautiful, then the great game of hide and seek has succeeded, and that day was certainly too beautiful to be seen) (273). The power, both of the Antilles's natural beauty and of their overdetermined discursive and literary representation, continues to loom heavily over the kind of vision that *Tropiques* aimed to illuminate. That power overdetermined even the readability of their own work, as can be seen, for example, even in the exoticist title of Breton's own essay on Aimé Césaire, "Martinique charmeuse de serpents" (Martinique Snake Charmer). *Tropiques* did not go so far as to transcend the "sordid antinomies" that Suzanne Césaire proposed, and its pages never definitively answered the question "Qui et quels nous sommes?" that Aimé Césaire posed or "Qui parle ici?" that Réne Ménil posed. The revue's generative task, however fragile, was to offer a located poetics of freedom centered on these questions.

CHAPTER 3

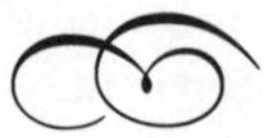

Gaceta del Caribe v. *Orígenes* in Cuba

BLACK AESTHETICS AS BATTLEGROUND

In the spring of 1944 when opposing Cuban literary magazines *Gaceta del Caribe* and *Orígenes* were both inaugurated in Havana, the future of the world hung in the balance. While Allied and Soviet troops had made major offensives that would lead to their victory in World War II, their victory was by no means inevitable at this time. The following year would usher in the end of the war, global decolonization, and most notoriously the start of the Cold War. These futures were as unvisible from the spring of 1944 as the prospect of Pan-Caribbean unity. In Cuba, 1944 was also a decisive presidential election year: Carlos Saladrigas was running for the Partido Socialista Popular against ex-president Ramón Grau San Martín.[1] They both sought to succeed Fulgencio Batista, who would return to the helm from 1952 until the 1959 revolution.[2] Eleven years prior in 1933, a less famous countrywide revolution had brought down the regime of dictator Gerardo Machado, achieving many reforms that were institutionalized in the new Cuban constitution of 1940.[3] From the vantage point of the presidential election in 1944, the widespread corruption to come, including selling swathes of the country to the U.S.-based mob, were not inevitable, and it was still possible that the 1940 reforms would lead to the governing of a more equitable and just society. At the same time, the global war both directly and indirectly impacted Cuba. For example, food shortages resulted from the naval blockades in the Atlantic Ocean and the Caribbean Sea, and the fascist movement was on the rise in Latin America with a strong presence in Cuba.[4] The United States continued the economic and political domination of Cuba that had begun with its imposition of the Platt Amendment to the Cuban constitution in 1901, which established its ability to intervene in Cuban affairs and the U.S. naval base at Guantánamo Bay. Since 1940, the takeover of military bases by the United States throughout the Caribbean region also strengthened its imperial stronghold.

In the midst of global war, the heightening of U.S. imperial power in the Caribbean, and a national presidential election in Cuba, *Gaceta del Caribe* and *Orígenes* waged a battle over the terms that would shape the present scope and later character of Cuban literature. National politics, both Stalinism and Nazism, as well as U.S. empire and the contested racial and geopolitical location of the Cuban nation would overdetermine this magazine battle over how to govern Cuba's literary terrain both internally and on the world stage. In my reading of this battle for critical dominion over Cuba's literary field, I highlight how both magazines do covert, unexplicit work on the Eurocentric ideologies fueled by highly limited literary infrastructure and illuminate the strategic confluence between Caribbean location and Black aesthetics in Cuba.

Gaceta del Caribe and *Orígenes* advocated opposing theories of literature, and their critical opposition is instructive for understanding the ramifications of location writing, or the practice of writing locations into international legibility that I argue for throughout this book. Whereas *Gaceta del Caribe* modeled an antiracist and anti-imperial sociopolitical project in tandem with an explicit commitment to historicism and social realism, *Orígenes* renegotiated the terms of imperial literary influence from Spain and the United States in a formalist and poeticist approach to fomenting Cuban literary power. I argue that the Caribbean location enunciated by *Gaceta del Caribe* functioned strategically to covertly orient the national literary canon and the Communist Party in Cuba away from a Eurocentrist orientation toward the politics and aesthetics located in Black popular culture. *Orígenes*, I argue, disavowed Caribbean location as part of a covert project to relegate Black aesthetics to a minoritarian—as opposed to central—position in its cosmopolitan projection of Cuban arts and letters.

This magazine battle overdetermined by the legacy of slavery and empire in Cuba took place in an intellectual field with a high volume of magazines in comparison to other Caribbean locations including Martinique and Barbados, where *Tropiques* and *Bim* would emerge. Writers and intellectuals had produced cultural magazines, or *revistas*, in Cuba since at least the 1820s, when Félix Varela edited the magazine *El Habanero*. Roberto Esquenazi-Mayo records 558 *revistas* between 1902 and 1958 (xi). The number of literary periodicals would be much lower, but this figure indicates the abundance of cultural periodicals, beyond the news-focused medium, in Cuba's republican period. By 1941, however, magazine production had significantly declined (Esquenazi-Mayo xii).[5] I would venture that the decline was likely due to the paper shortages resulting from World War II. Although the history of Cuban magazine production was rich, the overall decline in cultural magazine production during the 1940s, combined with the probable decrease in the importation of books due to the global war, likely drew a disproportionately large number of intellectuals and other literary aficionados to publications such as *Gaceta del Caribe* and *Orígenes*.

The significance of literary magazines such as these relates directly to the state of literary book production. Although a comparatively high *volume* of literary titles were printed in Cuba in the period leading up to the 1959 Cuban Revolution, the *scale* of book production during this period much more closely approximated the rest of the Caribbean than has been widely understood. Limited editions of typically hand-printed books, of five hundred or less copies, appears to have been the standard (Smorkaloff 27). Furthermore, a high number of eventually canonized literary works produced during the 1930s and 1940s were actually published abroad in Mexico, Argentina, or Spain including, for example, one of the most canonical works of the period, Alejo Carpentier's *El reino de este mundo* (*The Kingdom of This World*), published in Mexico in 1949. In a 1965 article for the Argentinian literary magazine *Sur*, Carpentier would assert that there were no publishing companies (*empresas editoriales*) in Cuba (Esquenazi-Mayo xix). Pamela Maria Smorkaloff corroborates this assertion in her suggestion that the book production process remained largely unchanged from the nineteenth century into the first half of the twentieth century in Cuba (27). This process consisted of either self-financed runs or the selling of subscriptions to finance each book. In other words, it was rare for presses to offer capital to back book production. In my estimation, the overwhelming lack of capital investments in book production determines the proximity in scale of Cuba's publishing field to that of the Caribbean archipelago at large.[6] Both Smorkaloff and José Ricardo also note that U.S. companies dominated the production of materials used by printing presses (Smorkaloff 27; Ricardo 149–150). To what extent did U.S. material domination of the publishing field impact the nature of published works? In any case, local book publishing had an extremely limited reach and was prohibitively expensive for many Cuban authors.

As alternatives to expensive books, magazines occupy a central role in the development of the Cuban literary and intellectual field. As Smorkaloff has argued, "The history of Cuban literary production in the Republic has its most reliable sources not in the bibliographies of the period but in the *tertulia*, the cultural societies and groups, the journals and publishing experiments which together served as the only viable, although fragile, literary infrastructure in an inhospitable environment" (49). In fact, literary magazines were usually tied to the *tertulia*, or literary salon, and to book publishing ventures. Although small-scale and fragile as infrastructure, the literary magazine form may be regarded as the primary institution of Cuban literary development and circulation at home and abroad.

The most well known of the magazine institutions remain the Havana-based *Revista de avance* (1927–1930) and *Orígenes* (1944–1956).[7] *Avance*, as it is usually called, was the leading avant-garde literary magazine of its time in Cuba and would additionally publish a series of boutique books. Because of its influential prominence, many scholars assume that although *Orígenes* was published much later, it operated in opposition to *Avance*. However, the "post-*Avance*" group of Communist Party–affiliated poets and critics who first produced *Mediodía* (1936–1937) and later *Gaceta del Caribe* (1944)—Nicolás Guillén, José Antonio Portuondo, and Mirta Aguirre—actually carried out the direct opposition to the work of *Orígenes*, the magazine and the group around it that has been known as the "grupo *Orígenes*." This group, led by leading poet, novelist, and critic José Lezama Lima, included the poets Cintio Vitier, Fina García Marruz, Eliseo Diego, Gastón Baquero, and Lorenzo García Vega; the art critic Guy Pérez Cisneros; and *Orígenes* coeditor, critic, and literary translator José Rodriguez Feo. Printed at the independent boutique press Ucar, García y cía., *Orígenes* was the culmination of a series of literary magazines, most of which José Lezama Lima coedited: *Verbum* (1937), *Espuela de plata* (1939–1941), *Clavileño* (1941–1943), and *Nadie parecía* (1942–1944). *Orígenes*'s (expensive) high-aesthetic quality, longevity, heavy inclusion of U.S. American writers and critics, and long list of translated works are all attributable to Lezama's partnership with the young and wealthy José Rodríguez Feo, who had studied at Harvard and personally funded the magazine. During the eleven-year run of *Orígenes*, the *Editorial Orígenes* literary series they sponsored at Ucar, García y cía., published twenty-three books, primarily of poetry by writers also featured in its magazine pages (Smorkaloff 60).

Gaceta del Caribe had aspired to the kind of institutionality achieved by *Avance* and *Orígenes*. The *Gaceta* group sought to sponsor a book series and hold events, but due to its untimely termination by the leaders of the Communist Party that sponsored it, it did not reach the level of prominence and stability enjoyed by *Orígenes*.[8] There is evidence of one book produced by *Ediciones Gaceta del Caribe*, Nicolás Guillén's essay *Estampa de Lino D'ou* (1944). *Gaceta del Caribe* was, however, published by Arrow Press, the same press that published the books produced by *Páginas*, a prominent leftist publishing enterprise, that ran from the early 1940s until the 1950s (Smorkaloff 61–62). *Páginas* was unique as an editorial project insofar as it financially backed the books it produced at Arrow Press and a number of magazines, including the eponymously named *Páginas*, *Dialéctica*, and *Fundamento*. Even though *Gaceta del Caribe* did not reach the kind of prominence held by *Orígenes*, it was connected to these leftist intellectual projects that were surely impacted by its interventions in Cuban literary, intellectual, and political culture.

The complex ideological battle waged between and around *Gaceta del Caribe* and *Orígenes* has received only cursory attention, even though *Orígenes* has been the subject of many critical works in recent years.[9] Attention to the battle between *Gaceta del Caribe* and *Orígenes* has the potential to illuminate and redirect a split in Cuban literary scholarship focused on the republican period before the 1959 revolution. One camp of scholars has tended to focus on *afrocubanismo*, the literary movement focused on the experience and forms of expression of Black Cubans that began in Cuba during the 1920s and was participated in by white-presenting, mixed-race, and Black-presenting Cubans, or *negrismo*, which the same movement is sometimes called, articulating it to a broader tendency of Afrocentric verse produced throughout the Spanish-speaking Caribbean.[10] The other camp of scholars has primarily focused on the high-modernist group of writers associated with *Gaceta del Caribe*'s rival literary magazine that originated at the same time, *Orígenes*. This critical split is not at all total but does indicate the fracture of a polemical tension that constituted both the Black-located poetics of Cuban *negrismo* (or *afrocubanismo*) and the antilocation poetics of *Orígenes*. My reading of *Gaceta del Caribe* in its embattled dialogue with *Orígenes* offers a critical gateway into that tension.

The literary-critical battle they waged hovered around *Gaceta del Caribe*'s unspoken project to canonize and extend *negrismo*, or *afrocubanismo* (late 1920s–1930s) and *Orígenes*'s unstated project of forging a rupture with this movement in order to redirect Cuban letters away from Black popular culture and toward a high cultural formation in dialogue with U.S. American and Spanish authors and critics. This literary battle illustrates a longstanding divide in Cuban literary history on the canonical positioning of Black aesthetics, which I understand in the Cuban context to comprise works by Black and mixed-race authors as well as works by white authors that self-consciously centered African aesthetic and religious traditions as well as Black Cuban popular culture.[11] As Miguel Arnedo-Gómez has described the tension between the *Orígenes* group and *afrocubanismo*, "Members of the movement in Cuban poetry that succeeded poetic *afrocubanismo*, the Grupo Orígenes, became critical of the poetry of the previous generation and moved toward a type of literature that avoided 'localisms' and 'folklorisms'" (2). In other words, the *Orígenes* camp steered Cuban literature away from localized Afro-centric and "social" literature toward what Roberto Fernández Retamar called its "transcendentalism," or a poetics with a will to spiritual power that sought to overtake instead of reflecting or engaging reality (86–87). *Gaceta del Caribe* intervened, both directly and indirectly, in the *Orígenes* occupation of literary culture by redirecting Cuban literature, including its *negrista* elements, toward the Caribbean.

Gaceta del Caribe: Caribbeanizing Cuba as Nationalizing Blackness

Under the aegis of the Communist Party (the Partido Socialista Popular), in March 1944 a group of prominent poets and literary critics released *Gaceta del Caribe* (Caribbean Gazette), a literary magazine with a Caribbeanist positioning. Its mixed-race editorial committee included the acclaimed poet Nicolás

Guillén along with the poets and literary critics Mirta Aguirre, Angel Augier, and José Antonio Portuondo.[12] Guillén was the most prominent figure in this group, but the letters they exchanged do not suggest that his voice superseded those of his comrades. Even so, his highly influential books of poetry and especially *West Indies, Ltd.* (1934) align with the stated and unstated work of *Gaceta del Caribe*. Like *West Indies, Ltd.*, *Gaceta del Caribe* names—and constructs—a Caribbean locus of enunciation with a Cuban inflection. The book of poems includes several of Guillén's most well-known and evocative poems that unsilence the past and persisting violence of slavery in Cuba and the Caribbean, such as the poem "El Apellido." At the same time, the book of poems, most notably its titular poem, "West Indies, Ltd.," elaborates a clear critique of imperial and racial capitalism in the contemporary Caribbean inflected by the poet's Marxist position. *Gaceta del Caribe* would reposition the coordinates Guillén lays out in this book by forwarding antiracist, Black-affirmative, and anti-imperial discourses along with Caribbean solidarity.

Socially engaged literary criticism and a methodically selected corpus of editorials and essays that ranged from exclusively political to literary-political, short fiction, poetry, and practical criticism consisting of reviews of books, theater, visual art, and music by women and men from Cuba and abroad would comprise the pages of *Gaceta del Caribe*. Approximately the size of a newspaper and thirty-two pages long, this black-and-white with spot-color publication printed at Arrow Press in Havana lived to see only nine issues, released semimonthly, between March and December 1944. Notably, *Gaceta del Caribe* ran no advertisements and did not directly declare its ties to the Communist Party, but it regularly featured articles and editorials that advanced party positions and backed its presidential candidate. *Gaceta* grew to circulate as many as 1,000 copies of each installment and boasted readership across the Americas: namely in Haiti, Brazil, Venezuela, Uruguay, Argentina, Mexico, and the United States ("Pedimos la palabra" 31). Its pages were sprinkled with articles by and about writers and critics from around the Caribbean and Latin America, most notably Jacques Roumain from Haiti, Juan Bosch from the Dominican Republic, Luis Lloréns Torres from Puerto Rico, César Vallejo from Peru, Pablo Neruda from Chile, and Alfonso Reyes from Mexico. At the same time, the *Gaceta* projected ties to Europe, especially a strong solidarity with antifascist Spain and cultural producers of the Soviet Union.[13] Its nine issues evince an effort to direct socially and politically engaged literary production in Cuba and to another less obvious goal: to extend the work of the *afrocubanismo* cultural movement. As Robin Moore has explained one of the most important achievements of that movement, "The arts of socially marginalized blacks, for centuries ignored or dismissed by Cuba's middle classes, took on new significance as symbols of nationality" (2). Moore sums up this project's achievement as "nationalizing blackness," which I understand as the rendering of Black representation *as* national representation. In

Gaceta del Caribe, the Caribbeanist location of the magazine functioned implicitly in order precisely to extend the nationalization of blackness in Cuba.

The strategies that the magazine would undertake can be understood through several pathways, all highlighted in this first opening editorial offered by the magazine's editors: projecting socially engaged literature and literary criticism, diagnosing the state of Cuban literary culture as deficient, advocating for better national cultural policies to support the flourishing of the nation's literature, and defining a Caribbean regionalist perspective with broader affiliations. An epigraph attributed to Beethoven introduces it: "La libertad y el progreso son la finalidad del Arte como son de la vida entera" (The purpose of Art, as well as the purpose of life, are freedom and progress). The famous Romantic composer's words forward an aesthetic position centered on the social values of freedom and progress. In what follows, the editorial personifies the magazine, suggesting that it "cree en el Arte por el Hombre" (believes in Art for the sake of Man) and asserting "its" belief in the purity of art, qualifying that art can serve "Man" *and* be simultaneously pure.

The editorial clearly indicates that *Gaceta del Caribe* would not be lighthanded in its approach. T. S. Eliot, in his essay and editorial note for *Criterion,* the magazine he edited in London, "The Idea of a Literary Review" (1926), elaborated on the difference between magazines that formulate a "programme" and those that advance a "tendency." Although these terms lack precision and come from an aesthetic-political position much closer to that elaborated by *Orígenes* than that of *Gaceta*, they are helpful for parsing the distinctions between both magazines. In Eliot's terms: "the ideal literary review will depend upon a nice adjustment between editor, collaborators, and occasional contributors and that "such an adjustment must issue in a 'tendency' rather than a 'programme'" (3). According to Eliot, programs for literary reviews were fragile, their fragility increasing with their dogmatism. Conversely, as he put it, "a tendency will endure, unless editor and collaborators change not only their minds but their personalities" (3). *Gaceta*'s first editorial, for example, is unabashedly programmatic and dogmatic: "Por eso, esta revista, . . . combatirá sin excesos, pero sin descanso, a cuantos huyen, a la hora de crear, de todo contacto con el alma y la sangre del pueblo" ("Primeras palabras" n.p.) (Therefore, this magazine, . . . will unexcessively but unceasingly fight those who, at the time of creation, flee from all contact with the soul and blood of the people). Although the *Gaceta* editors directly identify social evasionism as their target "enemy," the oblique reference to race in the idea of "the soul and blood of the people" is as direct as their editorials become about the antiracist combat waged by this gazette. For the editors of *Gaceta del Caribe*, "socially evasionist" writers were dangerous and assimilable to the fascism they overtly fought and the postcolonial and neocolonial racism they combated.

Whereas Aimé Césaire posteriorly reflected that *Tropiques* had been created for "cultural combat," *Gaceta del Caribe* directly presented itself for a literary battle. If fascism and a colonial context structured by racism were the targets of *Tropiques*'s cultural combat, *Gaceta del Caribe* was embattled with a relatively independent Cuba still structured by a loosely enforced racist social order in a terse relationship to U.S. empire governed by white supremacy. In the antifascist continuation of a "popular front" political strategy, *Gaceta del Caribe* was positioned to intervene in the liberal and left-leaning intellectual class with an inexplicit but legibly Marxist aesthetic code. As Vincent Leitch surmises about this strategic form of Communist Party approaches, it was a "softened" form of political activism designed to garner the support of "liberals of many persuasions" (3).[14]

In the course of their opening editorial, the *Gaceta* editors make underhanded references that clarify to those in the know which group of writers they positioned themselves against combatively: the *Orígenes* group. Curiously, their most vicious attack on this group ensues in the same paragraph as the description of the democratic and broadly inclusive nature of *Gaceta*'s pages: "el mensuario aspira a tener una anchura en la que pueda entrar todo, salvo lo que no deba entrar" (the monthly aspires to a breadth in which everything may be included, except that which should not enter) ("Primeras palabras" n.p.). This proposal indicates the quest to unite the literary and the political as well as lettered and popular culture at both national and international levels. From the outset, however, they announce exceptions to the unity they seek, proclaiming the exclusion of "what should not enter," or those intellectual adversaries who have also in turn excluded politicized literature from their own platform. As the editors elaborate this position, they indirectly insult the "enemy camp": "Aquí, dicho sea sin alusiones, todo el mundo parece lo que es, y nadie necesita de plateadas espuelas para hacer andar a Pegaso. El narcisismo intelectual, pues, no cabrá en GACETA DEL CARIBE" (Here, said without allusions, everyone appears as they are, and nobody needs silver spurs to make Pegasus go. Intellectual narcissism will not, then, have a place in GACETA DEL CARIBE).

This is an underhanded blow at Lezama Lima and his literary associates. The two previous magazines Lezama edited, *Nadie parecía* and *Espuela de plata*, are alluded to directly here in a quip that differentiates Lezama's group from the *Gaceta* group on two counts: first, for the difficulty of their opaque poetic language, and second, for their hidden homosexuality—as they play on the Cuban expression "Mejor serlo y no parecerlo que parecerlo y no serlo" (It is better to be it and not appear it, than to appear it and not be it) about being and appearing gay. This quip normatively polices the borders of the magazine, exiling Lezama (and his group) from its pages, illustrating the *Gaceta*'s "portrait of the artist as enemy": socially disengaged, incoherent, narcissistic, and secretly gay.

The passage thus sets up an equivalence between a hidden homosexuality and the hidden meaning of difficult writing. The rhetorical violence of this attack was, to quote Eagleton's description of the nasty polemics that took over literary criticism in Victorian England's public sphere, "wracked by a fury which threatens to strip it of ideological credibility" (37). It is highly unfortunate to confront this thinly veiled homophobic joke on the very first page of a magazine that also produced a noteworthy intervention into the coloniality of the Cuban literary canon, but it is also an important discourse to highlight, for this is the same ideological structure that will emerge in postrevolutionary Cuba's state policy to persecute those who deviated from normative gender presentations and heterosexual codes.[15]

The opening editorial also stakes out the territory for *Gaceta de Caribe*'s literary battle against the *Orígenes* camp: literary criticism. The magazine would serve as a venue for their goal of promoting Cuban literature around the Americas and the world and contribute to "la obra crítica de que carecermos" (the critical oeuvre that we lack). If in Martinique Aimé Césaire understood there to be a "*manque culturelle*," or a void (or fallow field) of cultural production and consumption, in Cuba the cultural lack, or "*carencia*" that Nicolás Guillén et al. of *Gaceta del Caribe* observed, lay more specifically in cultural criticism. It is likely that the emphasis on lacking criticism in *Gaceta* as opposed to a missing or lacking literature or cultural productivity writ large results from Cuba having a more voluminous cultural field, observable in the abundant circulation of magazines and the higher volume of printing presses and book publications, even if this publishing occurred on a contiguous infrastructural scale to that of Martinique. In other words, if developing a literary field is the hard work of an underdeveloped and colonial cultural terrain, developing a *literary-critical* field may be the task of a postcolonial, minimally developed literary field.

What work, then, did the magazine's name, asserting a Caribbean locus of enunciation, do for its literary-critical project? *Gaceta del Caribe* was primarily concerned with national culture, yet it projected a nationality rooted in regional as well as international affiliations. Moreover, by directly invoking the Caribbean in the magazine's name, *Gaceta del Caribe*'s editors made a deliberate choice to foreground its Caribbeanist aspirations. Because names, as Michel-Rolph Trouillot demonstrates, "set up a field of power" (115), the choice to highlight "Caribe" in the magazine's name demarcates a field of intervention in a dominant European-identified form of Cuban nationalism.

As Alejandro de la Fuente suggests, during this period "planters, merchants, and many intellectuals in Cuba" considered that "Africanness equaled savagery and symbolized backwardness. Even those who subscribed to the ideal of a racially fraternal nation agreed that Cuba should be predominantly white and culturally European" (45). *Gaceta del Caribe* thus participated in a resistant strain of Cuban intellectual history against the tendency to over valorize white people and European culture. As José Buscaglia indicates about the myth of a "European ideal" around which Caribbean societies have been historically organized, "In the history of the Caribbean, every-body that wanted to be some-body has had to measure itself against that ideal" (xiv).

Locating a Cuban literary and arts magazine in the Caribbean, I argue, is the symbolic indicator of its embattled position against the European ideal. Since 1910 Cuba had been importing, en masse, sugarcane workers from other islands of the Caribbean, who were known as "*los antillanos*" (the Antilleans). The presence of these workers was decried in dominant discourse, and "the whole notion of 'undesirability' applied to the Antilleans was racially defined" (de la Fuente 47). The Caribbeanist stance taken by this magazine sidesteps altogether the presumed exceptionalist differentiation between Cuba and the rest of the Antilles.[16]

Although nationalist discourse also flows through this magazine, it is not, like its contemporary avatar, named *Gaceta de Cuba*. The naming in this case enacts a merger between nationalism and regionalism that symbolically offsets—or mutates—the national myth: "arrancando desde lo hondo de esta Isla nuestra, centro geográfico del mar de las Antillas, queremos dar el latido pleno del archipiélago dentro del ámbito continental, pero con una alerta conciencia de universalidad" (starting out from the depths of this Island of ours, the geographic center of the Antillean Sea, we wish to produce the booming pulse of the archipelago within its continental setting, but with an alert conscience / consciousness of universalism) ("Primeras palabras" n.p.). Cuba stands out here as the privileged locus of a Caribbean enunciation. In this period, it is no small or obvious move to locate Cuba in the Caribbean—as opposed to the Atlantic or Latin America. In continuation, the editors further inflect the archipelagic community imagined in their title, invoking their solidarity with "los pueblos con los que estamos hermanados en el Caribe" (the peoples with whom we are fraternally tied in the Caribbean). Importantly, the regional solidarity thus established manifests as a fraternal affiliation (*hermandados*) to the peoples of the Caribbean. It is precisely through this claim to fraternity with the peoples of the Caribbean, understood to invoke a population whose majority is of African descent, that *Gaceta del Caribe* erodes the European Ideal as a bulwark of Cubanness.

The editors' explanation of the name also claims a universal *conciencia* (which in Spanish means both "conscience" and "consciousness"). The universal conscience / consciousness articulated here operates as a border figure accompanying the locus of enunciation. This universal may function as the universal of Marxist internationalism, but it notably replaces what one might otherwise expect to find here that is suggested in the introductory editorial of *Tropiques* in 1941: a reference to Europe, Africa, and Asia as the multiple cultural and ethnoracial origins of Caribbean peoples. Furthermore, universalism is posited as neither the goal nor the larger sphere within which *Gaceta del Caribe* functioned; its presence edges into the magazine platform, hovering on the contours of its goals. This foundational discourse is not a critique of the false "Europeanness" of the universal, nor is it a platform for a universal humanism. Instead, *Gaceta del Caribe* lingers—consciously—on the edge, between universalism and its critique.

From this border position on universalism and through a Cuban-Caribbeanist locus of enunciation, *Gaceta del Caribe* carried out a critique of empire, the historical recovery of important Black Cuban intellectuals, and an antiracist critical program. A closer look at works featured in its first two issues from March and April 1944 demonstrates precisely what kind of magazine it set out to be. The first article after the opening editorial is "11 Síntomas" (11 Symptoms) by Lino Novás Calvo. The essay elaborates a critique of the role of empire on the Cuban literary field by diagnosing the marginality of Cuban letters as an economic and cultural (ideological) malady. The Spanish-Cuban fiction writer had authored *El negrero* (The slave trader), a biographical novel critical of the transatlantic slave trade that was first published in Madrid (1933) and later in Buenos Aires (1944).[17] Having opted to publish his own literary creations abroad, Novás Calvo understood well the dearth of Cuban publishing infrastructure.

In Novás Calvo's assessment, if the insufficient outlets of publication make up the underdeveloped economic base of literary production in Cuba, then a "colonial mentality," or a perception of the superiority of foreign writers, from Spain and the United States, functioned as its ideological symptom, or superstructure: "Aquí se combinan y complementan dos fuerzas ajenas, una del pasado y otra del presente. La del pasado fue creando en el público eso que se llama mentalidad colonial, y que puede ser también complejo de inferioridad; la del presente aprovecha ese mismo complejo" (Here, two external forces are combined and complemented, one from the past and the other from the present. The one from the past began to create in the public that which is called a colonial mentality and that may also be an inferiority complex; the one from the present takes advantage of this complex) ("11 Síntomas" 3). Importantly, Novás Calvo suggestively indicts the Spanish and U.S. empires that have dominated Cuba (the external—imperial—forces from the past and the present) for the production of a "colonial mentality." In his analysis, the material unevenness between the foreign and the local feeds the "colonial mentality" afflicting the Cuban reading public. The close reading of Cuba's marginal position through its relationship to the Spanish and U.S. empires distinguishes Novás Calvo's analysis from the tenor of critical works published in *Orígenes* that would appear to ignore the imperial character of U.S. and Spanish influence.[18]

Cuban playwright José Antonio Ramos also invokes the legacy of colonialism in Cuba when he laments about the older generation of writers in an essay from *Gaceta del Caribe* 2, "Nosotros debimos liquidar, y no liquidamos, el pasado colonial" (We should have liquidated, and did not liquidate, the colonial past)

(10). Ramos's essay reflects on the intellectual work of undoing the colony that his postindependence generation did not achieve: "Y la nave del pasado sigue ahí, donde siempre, encallada, pero intacta. Y legalmente cubana además, con todos los derechos" (And the ship of the past remains there, where it has always been, run aground, but intact. And legally Cuban, too, with every right)" (11). The image serves as a useful metaphor for what Aníbal Quijano has described as "the coloniality of power." The form of power exercised by a colony, like a ship lodged into an island, may remain intact after the end of formal colonialism, rebranded, incorporated into the national body politic but still deploying a defunct distribution of racialized power.[19]

A series of works dedicated to honoring the nineteenth-century mixed-race Cuban poet Gabriel de la Concepción Valdés, or Plácido, was also central to *Gaceta del Caribe*'s project. Plácido was executed by the Spanish Crown on charges of participating in conspiracy to organize a revolt against slavery, known as the Ladder Conspiracy, one hundred years earlier, in 1844. In addition to publishing his poems, the first issue of *Gaceta* included one essay by Sergio Aguirre and one by José Antonio Portuoundo, both about him. Aguirre's "Hubo Conspiración de la Escalera?" (Was there a ladder conspiracy?) suggests that the Ladder Conspiracy had been officially denied in Cuba and that Plácido's "innocence" has also been officially maintained (12–13). Aguirre questions his innocence, however, demonstrating an investment in recovering Plácido's heroic role in organizing politically against slavery. Portuondo's essay, "Plácido, 1844," praises Plácido as the eminent incarnation of his age, corroborating the thesis that he was indeed an antislavery agitator. Portuondo's homage is a mix of biography and Marxist-inflected literary criticism. About Plácido's poetry, Portuondo distinguishes between his "pre-Romantic" verses in which he disguised his antityranny sentiments and the "real Plácido" of his more popular verses (22–23). *Gaceta* 2 would continue this series with a short story by Carlos Montenegro, "Doce Corales" (Twelve Corals), that fictionalizes Plácido's life. In his story too, Plácido is "guilty" of conspiring for freedom, but instead of being killed by a firing squad, he escapes. Tributes to Plácido such as these would continue throughout *Gaceta*'s run.

In addition to recovering Plácido historically, *Gaceta del Caribe* would feature tributes to Juan Gualberto Gómez and poetry by Juan Francisco Manzano. Gómez, also a mixed-race Cuban, continues to be underserved by official Cuban history. He collaborated with Martí for Cuban independence from Spain and, as an elected member of Congress, would have one of the votes opposing the U.S.-imposed Platt Amendment of the Cuban constitution in 1901. *Gaceta* 2 features an essay by Gómez, "Martí y yo" (Martí and me) in which he reflects on their collaborations. Manzano, a poet and nonfiction writer, is the author of the famed slave narrative *Autobiografía de un esclavo* (1837), which was first published in England and in English translation to fuel the abolition movement but would not be published in Cuba until 1937. His poem "La cocuyera" would appear in *Gaceta* 4.

Caribbean solidarity, antiracism, and recuperating Black history would come together in two articles featured by Dominican writer and politician Juan Bosch and one by Haitian poet Jacques Roumain. Bosch would go on to briefly be president of the Dominican Republic (in 1963) and to pen one of the most important regional treatises of the Caribbean, *De Cristobal Colón a Fidel Castro: El Caribe frontera imperial* (1970). During this period, however, he was in exile from the Trujillo regime in Cuba. Bosch's first article, "Cien años" (One hundred years) commemorates the end of the Haitian takeover of the territory that became the Dominican Republic, from 1821 to 1844. Against the anti-Haitian antipathy that had fueled the Trujillo-led mass assassinations of Haitians and Black Dominicans on the border between the two countries in 1937, Bosch's article bestows great praise on the Haitian Revolution. Bosch calls it "la revolución más completa que conoce la historia" (the most complete revolution in history) (19). Jacques Roumain, the highly acclaimed Haitian poet, novelist, and founder of the Haitian Communist Party, who had befriended Nicolás Guillén at the 1937 conference of writers against fascism in Spain, authored a treatise that would appear in *Gaceta del Caribe* before appearing in his home country, "La poesía como arma" (Poetry as a Weapon). Roumain advocates in this piece for the role of poetry as a political "weapon." His essay dovetails well with *Gaceta del Caribe*'s opening editorial and establishes a trans-Caribbean solidarity for a Marxist approach to literature. The choice to feature Roumain in the opening issue of *Gaceta del Caribe* is further central to its expressed project to expound a Caribbean-centered venue for literary politics and its unexpressed practice of recovering and promoting Black intellectuals.[20]

Gaceta del Caribe's project would be cut short by January 1945. Having lost the presidential election, the Partido Socialista Popular changed policies and cut its funding. In a letter announcing *Gaceta*'s demise to Portuondo, who worked on the magazine from Mexico City for much of its run, Guillén attests to the labor of love among friends who were like family that the magazine effort had consisted of: "En cierto modo, ésta es una de esas cartas que se escriben a los parientes fuera del país cuando hay novedad en la familia. Efectivamente: tenemos un enfermo grave, muy grave. No te diré que lo haya desahuciado el médico, pero hay una junta de eminencias clínicas para ver qué carajo tiene . . . Como comprenderás, me estoy refiriendo a nuestra amadísima *Gaceta* (In a way, this is one of those letters that are written to the relatives away from the country when there is news in the family. In fact, one of ours is gravely ill, very grave. I will not say that the doctor has condemned him to death, but there is a meeting of preeminent clinicians to figure out what the hell is wrong . . . As you will understand, I refer to our beloved *Gaceta*) (Romero and Castillo 135). Guillén personifies the magazine as a sick relative in this passage but also writes in a code, keeping secret what for political reasons becomes unsayable.[21] How much of *Gaceta del Caribe*'s work remains unsayable? What would it mean to interpret its work from the perspective of its editorial pages, the most common methodology among critics of literary magazines, instead of examining its carefully curated contents more closely? In the pages of this magazine, the Caribbean as a locus of enunciation becomes a cypher for an antiracist project added to the social realist drive of the magazine's Marxist-inflected aesthetics against the anti-Caribbean positioning of the *Orígenes* group.

Book Reviewing Cuba into the Caribbean

The book review contributed significantly to *Gaceta del Caribe*'s practice of Caribbeanizing Cuba and nationalizing Cuban blackness. The reviewers, always members of the editorial committee, positively assessed books that appear carefully selected for promotion as they advanced the literary periodical's mission. For example, a review of Fernández de Castro's 1943 book *Tema negro en las letras de Cuba* (Blackness in Cuban letters) (*Gaceta* no. 1), an anthology of Black Cuban literature from the nineteenth century to the present of the publication, forwarded *Gaceta del Caribe*'s project of nationalizing blackness and extending the reach of the *afrocubanista* movement. The significance of this choice was reinforced by other publications in the magazine, such as the series of articles dedicated to the nineteenth-century mixed-race Cuban poet Plácido (*Gaceta* no. 1, no. 2, and no. 5), an article on Black characters in the work of highly influential Baroque Spanish poet Góngora (*Gaceta* no. 2), and a selection of Nicolás Guillén's own poems that both portray Black and mixed-race characters and engage Cuba's history of slavery (*Gaceta* no. 8). The book review served as an opportunity to promote creative projects that aligned with the gazette's unstated mission of decolonizing Cuba's intellectual and literary record.

Two reviews in particular, of important poems published in Havana as limited edition books in 1943, practice Caribbean location writing in their criticism, or criticism that serves to "Caribbeanize" Cuba. The poetry reviews I refer to are Angel Augier's review of Afro-Martinican poet Aimé Césaire's *Cahier d'un retour au pays natal* (Notebook of a Return to the Native Land), translated by Euro-Cuban writer and ethnographer Lydia Cabrera and published as *Retorno al país natal* (Return to the Native Land) with illustrations by Afro-Chinese-Cuban artist Wifredo Lam, and Mirta Aguirre's review of Euro-Cuban and openly gay poet Virgilio Piñera's poem *La isla en peso* (The Weight of the Island). Aimé Césaire, coeditor of *Tropiques*, would go on to become highly acclaimed as a poet who fomented Black consciousness for the Antilles and the diaspora at large, and this poem has been central to his great influence in that regard.[22] The 1943 Cuban publication of this book was made possible by Wifredo Lam, whose stopover in Martinique in 1941, along with André Breton, on his return to Cuba from studying painting with Pablo Picasso in France, would inaugurate a long-term friendship and collaboration with Césaire. Lam would also develop a long-term friendship and collaboration with Lydia Cabrera, who was chosen to translate this text after her great success as an ethnographic writer was established with her first highly acclaimed book, *Los cuentos negros de Cuba*.[23] Virgilio Piñera in turn would become a highly influential poet, playwright, novelist, and critic in Cuba. In 1943 in his own short-lived literary review *Poeta*, Piñera had included his own translation of Césaire's poem "Conquête de l'aube" (Conquest of a Dawn), translated to "Conquista del alba," indicating the circulation of Césaire's poetry to Cuba beyond the *Cahier* as well as suggestive of his impact on Piñera. Although Piñera the playwright might have earned him the greatest notoriety, the poem *La isla en peso* was monumental in its influence. His poem criticized longstanding colonial structures in Cuban society with a special emphasis on the role of European conquest, slavery, and Catholicism in overdetermining the taboos of Cuban sexuality.[24] It picks up on many of Césaire's motifs but is replete with images of sexuality, investing in sexual desire the possibility of something like liberation. Like Césaire's "Cahier," Piñera's *La isla en peso* is set on an unnamed but obviously Caribbean island. It was so heavily influenced by Césaire's poem that some critics considered it not to engage with Cuban realities. The *Gaceta del Caribe* reviews of Aimé Césaire and Virgilio Piñera respond indirectly to reviews of both poems penned by "Origenista" poet Gastón Baquero in the 1943 state-sponsored cultural review *Anuario de la cultura cubana*.

In the period just before either magazine in question appeared, members of the *Orígenes* group had taken over a new state-sponsored platform for circulating national arts at home and abroad, the *Anuario cultural de Cuba 1943* (The cultural yearbook of Cuba 1943), published by the Office of Cultural Relations at the Cuban Ministry of the State. The *Anuario* would emerge in Havana in February, just before the debut of both *Gaceta* and *Orígenes*. The stated purpose of the publication was to circulate Cuban literary, artistic, and scientific activities abroad through the channels of diplomacy ("Propósito" n.p.). Guy Pérez Cisneros, a principal contributor to *Orígenes*, coedited this volume and authored its visual arts section. Gastón Baquero, another principal contributor of the group, penned the literary section. Baquero's review of the state of Cuban literature presents it between the opposing paths of historicism and poeticism: "se está llegando, por dos caminos opuestos: uno, la investigación fervorosa, amorosamente revisora del siglo XIX, y otro, la obra de creación que se asoma y alimenta en fuentes de metafísica, de religiosidad, de búsqueda penetrante en las zonas más ocultas de la vida espiritual" (we are arriving by two opposing paths: one, the zealous and loving revisionist investigation of the nineteenth century, and another, the emergent creative oeuvre that is nourished by metaphysical, religious sources, in a penetrating exploration of the most occult zones of spiritual life) ("Tendencias" 266). In the bifurcation of Cuban literature Baquero describes here, he favors the new path of metaphysical, religious, and spiritual poetry over the social engagement of historical literature. Whereas *Orígenes* would emerge to ground the literary path against history and toward the metaphysical that Baquero describes, *Gaceta del Caribe* contested the representativeness of Baquero's essay by circulating an explicitly politicized vision of Caribbeanist Cuban literature.

Baquero's review of Césaire, while generally positive, ceremoniously dismisses its connection to Cuba: "Para todo amante de la poesía contemporánea, este 'Retorno al país natal' de Aime Cesaire [*sic*] constituye uno de los puertos indispensables de parada y admiración" (For all lovers of contemporary poetry, Aimé Césaire's 'Return to the Native Land' constitutes an indispensable port to stop and admire) ("Tendencias" 282). His note does not in any way engage with the anticolonial or antiracist subject matter in the poem; instead, as he does throughout his essay for the 1943 cultural yearbook, Baquero banalizes any material that could be politically potent in the poem. But his note on Césaire exceeds banalization: Baquero recommends the poem as an object to consume in literary tourism, as if instead of poeticizing a Caribbean island it were an "exotic" object from a faraway place.[25] Much later, Baquero would exceptionalize Césaire's Afrocentric poetry in relation to the Spanish-language *negrista* movement: "En América, hasta la aparición de Aimé Césaire, se llamaba poesía negra a una de las más penosas e hipócritas formas del racismo antinegro. Ahora, cuando la obra de Césaire se ha expandido, y cuando se ha comenzado a conocer la poesía africana, comprenden muchos que había algo podrido, extraño, en aquella cosa que llamaban poesía negra en América Hispana" (In America, until the apparition of Aimé Césaire, what was called Black poetry was one of the most embarrassing and hypocritical forms of anti-Black racism. Now that the work of Césaire has expanded and African poetry has begun to be known, many understand that there was something rotten, strange, in that thing they called Black poetry in Hispanic America) (*Darío* 210). Although Baquero would retrospectively pay tribute to Césaire in the context of deriding the poetry of the *negrista* and *afrocubanista* movement as racist forms, from the vantage point of 1943 in the capacity of official literary reviewer, Baquero would not contextualize his reticence to acknowledge Césaire's value in what was likely to be his deeply held antagonism against literary *negrismo*, a view that was consistent among many of those associated with *Orígenes*. Although this later view adds important context to Baquero's 1943 review, he nonetheless dismisses Césaire's poem from the Cuban context at this time.

Having distanced Césaire from the Cuban context, it follows that in his 1943 review Baquero would find the closeness of Piñera's poem to Césaire a problem. Baquero's review distances Piñera's poem by suggesting that the Caribbean location it constructs is veritably un-Cuban: "Esta Isla que Virgilio Piñera ha levantado en el marco de unos versos inteligentes, audaces, a veces deliberadamente llamativos y escabrosos, en desconexión absoluta con el tono *cubano* de expresión, es Isla de una antillanía y una martiniquería que no nos expresan, que no nos pertenecen" (This Island that Virgilio Piñera has raised up through the frame of intelligent and audacious verses, sometimes deliberately flashy and risqué, absolutely disconnected from the *Cuban* tone of expression, is an Island of an Antilleanness and a Martiniquery [*Martiniquería*] that do not express us, that do not belong to us) ("Tendencias" 278–279). As official gatekeeper of the Cuban literary field, Baquero resisted a critical portrayal of Cuba assimilable to Césaire's portrayal of Martinique so much that he pushed Piñera's poem in dialogue with it out of Cuban letters. Piñera's poem was worse than derivative for Baquero—its affiliation with the *other* Antillean islands rendered it too Caribbean to be Cuban. His review exiled the poem from Cuban literature onto the shores of other islands, such as Césaire's Martinique. Although Piñera published occasionally in *Orígenes*, he maintained a distance from the group. As Duanel Díaz points out, with *La isla en peso*, Piñera asserts his fundamental dissidence from the aesthetics Lezama Lima would promote (122). According to Díaz, what would most make Baquero reject his poem is that it presents "un territorio en las fronteras de Occidente" (a territory on the borders of the West) (126). Although projecting Cuba's pertinence to Western culture would not be an explicit goal of the *Orígenes* magazine project, it would certainly be one of its implicit goals, one Piñera's poem clearly detracted from and to which *Gaceta del Caribe* seemed veritably indifferent.

Baquero's reviews disavow the possibility of intra-Caribbean vision potentialized in Césaire's poem and fomented by its Cuban circulation, which is precisely what Angel Augier's *Gaceta* review of Césaire's poem recovers. Angel Augier's review recontextualizes Césaire's work in order to position its relatability to the Cuban context: "Una desbordada fuerza lírica y una angustia humana en su más dramática plenitud, son las características de este gran poema, en el que intervienen, con la misma intensidad, la vegetación poderosa y alucinante de nuestras islas, y el hombre que en ella sufre dolores seculares del más diverso origen" (An overflowing lyrical force and a human anguish in its most dramatic plenitude are the characteristics of this great poem, in which the powerful and amazing vegetation of our islands intervenes, with the same intensity, and the man who, in its midst, suffers secular pains of the most diverse origins) ("*Retorno*" 30). Here, the claim staked by "*nuestras islas*" (our islands) opposes Baquero's distancing of Césaire's poem. It is not some faraway island but rather one of "ours," Augier indicates, that produces the anguish of the poem. "Ours" raises the possibility that the people of Martinique in Césaire's poem suffer "secular pains" akin to those suffered in Cuba. Augier goes on to offer a suggestive reading of Césaire's affiliations to other poets of the French language who, like him, were born across the Atlantic from France. Augier also remarks that Césaire's writing intimates the writing of Jules Supervielle and Comte de Lautréamont.[26] On the one hand, Augier thus positions Césaire in a transatlantic genealogy of French writers. In affiliating him to two South American–born French poets, Augier also evokes Alex Gil's understanding of Aimé Césaire as a hemispheric poet ("Aimé Césaire" n.p.). Césaire's participation in the lyrical "essence" of the "subconscious" is not the affiliation to his writing that Augier seeks to establish for *Gaceta del Caribe*, however. It is Césaire's closeness to what Augier calls "reality" that makes his poem exemplary and aligned with the *Gaceta del Caribe* project. According to Augier, "lejos . . . de evadirse de la realidad, la refleja en vigurosos trazos y deslumbrantes imágenes" (far . . . from evading reality, he reflects it in vigorous strokes and dazzling images) ("*Retorno*" 30). Césaire's poetry, as Augier presents it, fulfills the magazine's stated goals of approximating human reality. Augier rewrites the distance Baquero imposes on the poem from Cuba, suggesting that Césaire is instead "far" from the evasion of reality, which is an indirect characterization of those Cuban poets *Gaceta del Caribe* opposes—Gastón Baquero included. In his assessment, Augier also establishes the literary-theoretical affinity between Césaire's *Tropiques* and *Gaceta del Caribe*, observable through prioritizing social engagement in literature based on a confrontation of reality. Instead of elaborating on the specific social and political critiques of Césaire's poem to its readers, however, Augier's use of "*nuestras islas*" suggests that what they read in Césaire may be closer to their reality than Baquero would admit.[27]

Mirta Aguirre's *Gaceta* review of Virgilio Piñera's long poem *La isla en peso* linked its widespread dismissal as "un-Cuban" with the accusation that it is influenced by Césaire: "Se ha señalado que este poema tiene su antecedente en *Retorno al país natal*. Ciertamente hay puntos de contacto, sobre todo en lo que respecta al andamiaje arquitectónico entre esta obra de Piñera y la de Aimé Cesaire [*sic*]. . . . ¿ [E]s acaso en esas cosas en las que vale la pena detenerse cuando se va a juzgar el valor intrínseco de una realización artística?" (It has been indicated that *Return to the Native Land* is this poem's antecedent. There are certainly points of contact between this work of Piñera's and that of Césaire's, especially in what concerns the architectural structure. . . . [I]s it worthwhile after all to focus on such things when judging the intrinsic value of an artistic creation?) (30). Aguirre acknowledges the "point of contact" between Piñera and Césaire's poem but questions why Césaire's influence would be used against Piñera to disqualify his oeuvre. In her review, Aguirre conversely applauds Piñera's accuracy of vision: "*La isla en peso* es un cambio de rumbo, el inicio de un camino. Virgilio Piñera ha vuelto los ojos hacia nuestro país y lo ha percibido, de golpe, en toda su belleza física. La Cuba de agua y tierra, de animales y flora, de blancos y negros, salta por todos sus poros" (*La isla en peso* is a change of course, the initiation of a path. Virgilio Piñera has turned his eyes toward our country, and he has perceived it, suddenly, in all of its physical beauty. The Cuba of land and sea, of animals and flora, of whites and blacks, jumps through all of its pores). For Aguirre, Piñera's poem perceives Cuba rather well and indicates an important literary turning point. In the conclusion of her review she uses what has become a very famous quote from Piñera's poem to conclude her tribute to it: '"el peso de una isla en el amor de un pueblo'" (the weight of an island in the love of a people) (30). And she continues with a play on that verse: "El peso de una isla en el amor de un poeta que comienza a verla" (The weight of an island in the love of a poet who begins to see it). It is somewhat condescending that Aguirre implicitly accuses Piñera of previously not seeing the island, but even so, in the context of a magazine that advocates aesthetic engagements with "the blood and soul of the people," Piñera receives her stamp of approval for achieving just that.

The problem Baquero and others found with the affiliation between Piñera's poem and Césaire's is not that Piñera's version was derivative and thus lacking in quality but that, like Césaire's version, Piñera's was vociferously socially engaged and anticolonial with a local-regional locus of enunciation. Furthermore, Piñera's poem engaged with a Black-and-white Cuba that culturally resonated with other parts of the Caribbean and implicitly distanced Cuba from the European ideal. Baquero's reviews, representing a dominant view that extends well beyond him, instead constructed Cuba as an extension of Europe, far from the Afro-Caribbean he locates elsewhere. Aguirre's review responds to Piñera, as Augier responds to Césaire, with an oppositional project integral to *Gaceta del Caribe*'s achievements: forging a decolonizing turn of the nation toward itself and the Caribbean at the same time.

Orígenes: The Ideology of the Literary and Postcolonial Eurocentrism

Orígenes premiered at almost exactly the same time as *Gaceta del Caribe*, in the spring of 1944.[28] Like *Tropiques*, *Orígenes* was funded privately; like both *Tropiques* and *Gaceta del Caribe*, with the exception of occasional advertisements for books or other magazines, *Orígenes* did not run commercial advertisements as *Bim* would. As Lezama Lima's coeditor, José Rodríguez Feo, posteriorly mock-boasted, *Orígenes* was made possible by alienating capital from the laborers of his family's factories (*Mi correspondencia* 7).[29] The vastness of his wealth, compared to that of the middle-class schoolteachers who made *Tropiques*, can in part explain the uniqueness of its design and the high aesthetic quality of its printing. *Orígenes* was released seasonally and was circulated internationally in the Spanish-speaking world, in the United States, and beyond.[30] Smaller in size than *Gaceta del Caribe* but larger than both *Tropiques* and *Bim* (almost the dimensions of a square, at twenty-three by twenty centimeters), each issue printed at the Ucar, García y cia., press was longer than any of these other magazines, over fifty pages long. *Orígenes* ran in black and white with spot color, with covers featuring paintings by famous Cuban artists and inserts of paintings and photographs. Spot color displayed the magazine name on its cover, varying colors for each issue, like *Gaceta del Caribe*. Running for twelve years, until 1956, *Orígenes* greatly outlasted *Gaceta del Caribe*.

Like *Gaceta del Caribe*, *Orígenes* also appears to be primarily a literary-critical project, though the formalist and idealist theory of literature it espoused is far from the Marxist social realism of its literary magazine opponent. *Orígenes* regularly featured texts of formalist literary criticism in addition to poetry, short fiction, and reviews of literature, music, and visual arts that also practice formalist analysis. In addition to publishing numerous Cuban creative writers and critics, *Orígenes* regularly featured translations of work from English and French by José Rodríguez Feo and others. The Cuban writers and critics featured during its first two years of circulation included those considered part of the *Orígenes* group who hovered around Lezama: the poets Cintio Vitier, Fina García Marruz, Eliseo Diego, Gastón Baquero, and Lorenzo García Vega and the art critic Guy Pérez Cisneros. Among those Cuban authors not affiliated with this group whose work also appeared in the magazine during this period are Lydia Cabrera, Alejo Carpentier, Lino Novás Calvo, Virgilio Piñera, and the visual artists Mariano Rodriguez, Amelia Pelaez, and Wifredo Lam. There was also a preponderance of work published by creative writers and critics from the United States and Spain in *Orígenes*.[31] U.S. American writers featured during the first two years include Francis O. Matthiessen, George Santayana (a Spanish American philosopher), Theodore Spenser, William Carlos Williams (of partial Puerto Rican heritage), T. S. Eliot, Walter Pach, Harry Levin, Katherine Anne Porter, Elizabeth Bishop, and Anaïs Nin (who was born in Paris to Cuban parents). Spanish writers and critics published in the first two years include Juan Ramón Jimenez and Maria Zambrano, both of whom spent time with the *Orígenes* group in their exile from the Franco Regime in Havana; Jorge Guillén; and Pedro Salinas. While the number of Spanish writers and critics is lower, these four would appear repeatedly. *Orígenes* would also publish writers from other parts of Europe and other parts of Latin America. It is worth noting the volume of women published in *Orígenes*. *Gaceta del Caribe* would also regularly publish women alongside men, but the number of women contributors to *Orígenes* would be higher. Furthermore, although it would be rare for *Orígenes* to feature writers from other parts of the Caribbean, Aimé Césaire's poem "Batuc" would appear in the summer issue of 1945, one year after Angel Augier's review for *Gaceta del Caribe* rehabilitated the relevance of Césaire for the Cuban context.

Orígenes has been located by critics in national, Hispanist, and Latin Americanist terms, but my investigation of its first eight issues (those published before the end of World War II) between 1944 and 1945 demonstrates that the magazine editors expressly avoided asserting a clear locus of enunciation for the magazine. In this sense, my reading of *Orígenes* is close to Jaime Rodríguez Matos's reading of "the formless" in Lezama Lima's work through a "less formalized place of enunciation" (18). Although forms of location writing enter the pages of *Orígenes,* its editors appear to avoid locating the project as much as possible in order to project their magazine *as an instance of* a theory of literature that necessarily evaded a social or geographic location as both a productive literary origin and a constructive object of literary production. Expounding a theoretical vision very close to that of the New Criticism school, which was on the rise in the United States at this time, *Orígenes* seemed to seek an approach to aesthetics and the literary magazine as a force *within* the act of creation, which seemed to accompany underemphasizing and putting into question the value of location as an element of literary production.[32] Leitch's description of the ideological embattlement between Marxist literary critics and the formalist New Critics in the United States resonates strongly with the antagonism between *Gaceta del Caribe* and *Orígenes*: "The politics of New Critical formalism, like that of Marxism, deplored the disorder and dislocation, the human alienation and loss of community, and the 'commodification' of work and leisure that typified capitalist life during the interwar period. While literary Marxists tried to bring politics consciously to bear on poetry, New Critics sought to ban politics from poetics and to provide an aesthetic purity, a safe haven, for literature and criticism" (18). In accordance with New Critical philosophies, Lezama Lima and Rodríguez Feo positioned their magazine and the aesthetic realm it represented as a refuge from a corrupt social and political order, one that would exceed, or presume to transcend, a social or geopolitical locus of enunciation.[33]

Therefore, instead of positioning *Orígenes* from Havana, Cuba, or the Caribbean, in the spring 1944 introductory editorial, its editors locate their magazine in the practice of literature, explicitly stating the magazine's lack of interest in proposing a program, national, regional, or otherwise. Whereas Frank Collymore, the main editor of *Bim*, simply does not propose a literary program, the editors of *Orígenes* dispelled a program while proposing and orienting literary theory for their magazine. In this sense, both the editors of *Orígenes* and *Bim* likely sought to follow T. S. Eliot's suggestion that a literary review would do better to elaborate a "tendency" rather than a "programme."[34]

It is possible, however, that in the case of *Orígenes*, the theoretical specificity the editors grant the realm of the literary may itself have exceeded Eliot's notion of the "tendency," for in his terms a literary review could also enervate "by sticking too closely to a narrow conception of literature" (2). As Lezama Lima and Rodríguez Feo begin their opening editorial note, "No le interesa a ORÍGENES formular un programa, sino ir lanzando las flechas de su propia estela. Como no cambiamos con la estaciones [*sic*], no tenemos que justificar en extensos alegatos una piel de camaleón. No nos interesan superficiales mutaciones, sino ir subrayando la toma de posesión del ser" (ORÍGENES is not interested in formulating a program, but instead seeks to shoot the arrows of its own wake. As we do not change with the seasons, we do not need to justify chameleon skin with extensive allegations. We are not interested in superficial mutations, but rather to stress taking possession of being) (5). Although they project the magazine antiprogrammatically, what they propose is perhaps more ambitious or sweeping than a program would have been, for they seem to build on the very name of the magazine so that *orígenes*—origins—would become the work of the magazine itself. The manifest work of "origins" would refer in this editorial to the origins of creativity, or the birthplace of art, positioning the magazine as a source of creativity, writ large. This would be the broad sense of projecting a future wake of launched arrows, but in the context in which this project would have the most purchase, the Cuban literary context with Havana at its center, the project would materialize as establishing an originary influence on the future of Cuban literature. The other latent sense of "origins" would then implicate the magazine project of curating the influences, primarily from Spain and the United States, that would "originate" the new literature.

Like *Gaceta del Caribe*, *Orígenes* presents itself for literary battle from its opening editorial. The first three opening sentences set up the magazine's project in opposition to a negation, and it is not until the fourth sentence that a positive project begins to be suggested. The tendency to define the magazine oppositionally would repeat multiple times throughout the editorial. Furthermore, like *Gaceta del Caribe*, *Orígenes* would be personified, forwarded as if the magazine itself exercised agency and power.[35] One of the most bellicose propositions the editorial forwards is the magazine's aim to occupy, or take possession "del ser" (of being). This proposition is indeterminate and difficult to read out of context. Irlemar Chiampi forwards a reading through an essay by Martin Heidegger on Friedrich Holderlin's poetry published the previous year (1943) in *Clavileño*, one of the magazine prequels to *Orígenes*, in which Heidegger suggests that poetry takes possession of being or, put another way, that poetic time may anticipate historical time (7). This reading dovetails well with my view that one of the most striking features of *Orígenes* as a magazine is its projection *as* poiesis, for in their refiguring of Heidegger's theory of poetry as a force that may occupy being as the purpose of their magazine, the editors unite the magazine with poetry and endow it with poetic power. Salah Dean Assaf Hassan would describe the stakes of the magazine in related terms, as an investment in "the capacity of artists and writers to produce images that historically transcend the confines of their period and have the potency to fuse with the images of subsequent generations" (52).

Orígenes resembles *Tropiques* in its theoretical richness and poetic indeterminism perhaps more than any other magazine of the region at this time, but its aversion to literary location deviates significantly from the located theory of literature espoused by the *Tropiques* group.[36] *Tropiques*, like *Orígenes* was deeply invested in poiesis, but for the editors of *Tropiques* the multiple fronts of location writing, including an Antilles-located Black consciousness, were united with their aims of socioliterary genesis. To the contrary, the editors of *Orígenes* propose the magazine's aim as the occupation of being precisely *in opposition to* the idea of "superficial mutations," which in the context of Lezama Lima's prior work suggests their rejection of ethnological theories of aesthetics that had been quite influential in Cuba or, in other terms, a rejection of the ethnoracial location of literature.

In Lezama Lima's famous and highly influential text "Coloquio con Juan Ramón Jiménez" (Colloquium with Juan Ramón Jiménez) (1936), he rejects applying to literature a theory of "transculturation," by which I refer to Fernando Ortiz's concept for what we might also call creolization, the process whereby two cultural forms mutually transform, or mutate, through contact and exchange (Ortiz 98). An ethnic conception of literature fueled the earlier *indigenista* literary movement in Latin America, the earlier Haitian *indigenisme* movement represented by the highly influential literary magazine *Revue Indigène* (1927–1931), *afrocubanismo*, and the broader Spanish-language Afro-centric Caribbean literary movement known as *negrismo* that Lezama specifically engaged in this essay. Although in "Coloquio con Juan Ramón Jimenez" Lezama notes that *afrocubanismo* or *negrismo* and its "incorporación de la sensibilidad negra" (incorporation of black sensibility) had constituted Cuba's greatest poetic achievement (36); he also suggests in not so uncertain terms his disdain for any ethnic conception of the literary: "Una realidad étnica mestiza no tiene nada que ver con una expresión mestiza. Entre nosotros han existido mestizos que han intentado expresarse dentro de los cánones del parnasianismo, y gran parte de la poesía afrocubana, en cambio, es de poetas de raza blanca. Se ve que una cosa es el mestizaje y otra abogar por una expresión mestiza. Una expresión mestiza es un eclecticismo artístico que no podrá existir jamás" (A mestizo ethnic reality has nothing to do with a mestizo expression. Among us there have been mestizos that have sought to express themselves within the canons of Parnassianism, and a great part of Afro-Cuban poetry, in turn, is by poets of the white race. Clearly, one thing is mestizaje and another is advocating for mestizo expression. A mestizo expression is an artistic eclecticism that could never exist) (41). In this same text Lezama twice employs the term "sensibilidad negra," as if an ethnic or racialized sensibility does indeed exist, but he nonetheless suggests that a mestizo or racially mixed aesthetic form could not exist. Although Lezama's disqualification of ethnoracial aesthetics is heavy-handed and somewhat contradictory, he makes an important qualification in his argument when he points out that the majority of *negrista* writers in Cuba have been white and that mixed-race writers are included among the "Parnassian" poets, by which we might consider the mixed-race Origenista poet Gastón Baquero the exemplary figure.

In contradistinction to an ethnoracial conception of literature, Lezama offers an "undertow aesthetics" for an "insular" context such as Cuba's, which as Ben Heller has suggested we might understand to signify "a receptivity that does not result in wholesale imitation of imported artifacts, but rather in the acceptance and transformation of foreign influences" (398).[37] Against Black aesthetics and a Caribbean locus of enunciation, Lezama would offer this vision of "undertow aesthetics" through a topos of "insularity," a minimal concession to the pressure to locate literature that his position as a Cuban writer—and therefore a marginalized writer in the world literary system—imposed. Lezama's insular "undertow aesthetics," understood as a receptivity to foreign influences and the agency to transform them, seems to capture well the work of *Orígenes*, which functioned as a receptive shore for foreign works, often in translation, as well as the undertow transforming foreign influences into Cuban literature and criticism. The discourse of insularity would not frame the *Orígenes* project, but it is often understood by critics to be central to it. As Arnaldo Cruz-Malavé has noted, however, Lezama offers undertow aesthetics against Black sensibility, which he understood as a superficial tendency dominating Cuban aesthetics (192). What is curious about Lezama's formulation of insularity in relation to the undertow, however, is that it is based on Leo Frobenius's own work comparing coastal and interior cultures in Africa.[38] Not only did Lezama seek to displace the ascendancy of Black aesthetics in Cuba, but he also sought to do so with the aid of a theory of African culture. As the contents of *Orígenes* appear to both embody and promote Lezama's "undertow aesthetics," *Orígenes* would similarly marginalize Black aesthetics.

In the first editorial of *Orígenes*, after rejecting the "superficial mutations" they considered embedded in ethnoracial aesthetics, the editors go on to further a theory of literature that, while it is close to Heidegger as well as the New Critics, instantiates a particularly Eurocentric but nonetheless postcolonial instance of the Caribbean literary magazine. *Orígenes* may even be considered the Caribbean literary magazine's exemplary case of what Raphael Dalleo has termed "the ideology of the literary," also present in many other contemporaneous magazines of this period such as the Dominican magazine *Poesía sorprendida* (Surprised Poetry), *Bim*, and to some extent *Tropiques* (*Caribbean Literature* 107–121). To be sure, Dalleo understands "the ideology of the literary" as pervading the field of Caribbean literary magazines, from the most political to the least overtly political, and I corroborate his view that the literary becomes endowed with a field of power akin to the political in many Caribbean literary magazines. I would, however, categorize *Orígenes* in a literarily-ideological field of its own because of how much its editors elevate the primacy of the literary realm.

Orígenes's editors went so far as to posit a unity between literature and life in the opening editorial's refusal of "false dualism," or anything that would be considered anterior to literary production such as ethnic, racialized, or geographic location: "Sabemos que cualquier dualismo que nos lleve a poner la vida por encima de la cultura, o los valores de la cultura privados de oxígeno vital, es ridículamente nociva [*sic*], y sólo es posible la alusión a ese dualismo en etapas de decadencia" (We know that whatever dualism that drives us to put life before culture, or the values of culture deprived of vital oxygen, is ridiculously injurious, and allusions to such dualism are only possible in times of decadence) (Lezama Lima and Rodríguez Feo 6). They imply the possibility of writing from Cuba a literature of *the world*, or a universal literature. Instead of positioning *Orígenes* in the world or in the service of "Man" like *Gaceta del Caribe*, they locate the magazine in a unified conception of literature as poiesis and in opposition to a dualistic conception of aesthetic practice. The longevity and breadth of circulation of *Orígenes* suggests that this theory of literature appealed to a broad base of readers. In my reading, one of the most compelling elements of the *Orígenes* proposition is its prophesy of the constructive power of aesthetic representation in worldmaking, one of the theoretical premises undergirding this very book. While the attractive elements of the magazine have received significant attention, however, its troubling elements that pertain to the Eurocentrism carried out with and through this theory have received much less attention.

Whereas Novás Calvo would name the coloniality of foreign influence in Cuba in his *Gaceta del Caribe* article, Lezama's elaboration of "undertow aesthetics" does not name the relationship to empire it nonetheless engages. Lezama's idea of the undertow as a mechanism of receptivity to foreign influence relates strikingly to contemporaneous theories of aesthetic "cannibalism" elaborated by Oswald de Andrade in Brazil in the 1930s and by Suzanne Césaire in *Tropiques* in the 1940s. Whereas de Andrade and Césaire would more explicitly index the role of empire in the production of aesthetics in their call to cannibalize Western aesthetics, Lezama would dehistoricize and significantly dislocate his view of the "undertow" as the mechanism of absorbing and refashioning foreign influence. It is likely because Black aesthetics, Caribbean location, and anti-imperialism had become intertwined in Cuban discourse that Lezama's theoretical work against ethnoracial aesthetics would be predicated on a postcolonial aesthetic theory explicitly fashioned independently of anti-imperial discourse and through a topos of the island rather than the locus of the Caribbean.[39] I call Lezama's theory postcolonial, for it appears positioned, like the Brazilian and Martinican theories of literary cannibalism, as a future-oriented aesthetic that would take agency over foreign influences that result from empire in the construction of something new. I employ the term "postcolonial" instead of "decolonizing" or "anticolonial" in reference to Lezama, however, because in my view the work of Lezama's "Coloquio" and *Orígenes* counteracts one part of the colonial episteme while retaining and proliferating Eurocentrism.

Hassan has gone so far as to suggest that *Orígenes* intervened in Eurocentrism through forwarding a "peculiar *americanista* aesthetic" offering the location of the magazine in the Americas (82). Indeed, one form of location writing that enters *Orígenes* in a peculiar way is an "American" discourse that refers to the hemisphere at large and prefigures Lezama's later Pan-Americanist aesthetic treatise, *La expresión americana*. Although the magazine does not lay direct claim to Americanness, its engagement with an Amernicanist discourse works to unsettle the supposed hierarchical difference between the United States and the parts of the hemisphere to its South that have been subject to U.S. imperial designs, setting up instead a shared likeness of "Americanity."[40]

Although the opening editorial of *Orígenes* appears to work hard to locate itself from *within* literature, its reference to "the American" is its only concession to the pressure to locate that its theoretical discourse nonetheless resists: "La libertad consiste para nosotros en el respeto absoluto que merece el trabajo por la creación, . . . dentro de la tradición humanista, y la libertad que se deriva de esa tradición que ha sido el orgullo y la apetencia del americano" (Freedom consists for us in the absolute respect that the work of creation deserves, . . . in the humanist tradition, and the freedom derived from that tradition, which has been the pride and passion of the American) (Lezama Lima and Rodríguez Feo 5–6).

Even in the reference to "the American," the primary weight of the sentence avoids the location expressed, falling instead on their concern with freedom *insofar as* it pertains to the freedom of aesthetic creation. The editors do not, distinctly, utilize any language of pertinence in their offering of "the American" as a proud and passionate humanist. But this "American" takes shape as the magazine progresses. If aesthetic freedom and the humanist tradition characterize "the American" and if *Orígenes* participates in both, then to some degree it exercises this "peculiar" version of an aesthete Americanity, one that is highly limited precisely because of its tension with an ideology of the literary that would extricate—free—creativity from any such constraint, including that of location.

One of the clearest senses of *Orígenes*'s invocation of "the American" pertains to its voluminous publication of U.S. American literature and criticism. Rodríguez Feo's work as critic, translator, and scout for *Orígenes* in the United States cannot be overestimated in the production of *Orígenes*'s engagement with U.S. literary currents. For example, in *Orígenes* 1, Rodríguez Feo contributed an essay on the Spanish American philosopher George Santayana in which his dialogue with the philosopher's work becomes a proposition to the reader. Instead of quoting Santayana as the authority, Rodríguez Feo is the critical authority who makes propositions based on the other's work: "En *Persons and Places* observamos que la soledad es la única salvación para el poeta que busca la belleza en un mundo esencialmente materialista y que al rechazar el ambiente norteamericano Santayana tiene que refugiarse en su vida interior, vida imaginativa y contemplativa"

(In *Persons and Places* we observe that solitude is the only salvation for the poet who seeks beauty in a world that is essentially materialistic and that in rejecting the North American environment Santayana has to seek refuge in his interior life, in his imaginative and contemplative life) (37). Santayana does not by any means represent the ascendancy of an imperial culture but instead critiques its decadence. Rodríguez Feo, the critic of Santayana's critique, proposes implicitly to his primary readers—at home in the decadent milieu of Cuban political corruption overdetermined by U.S. influence—that refuge lies in the interior world of the imagination. This essay would be surrounded by creative works exclusively authored by Cuban contributors, but *Orígenes* 2 would go on to feature work primarily by foreign contributors. Rodríguez Feo provided the translations of Harvard-based literary critic Francis O. Matthiessen's essay on T. S. Eliot and on a work by Paul Valéry. Matthiessen's essay in particular would buttress the magazine's breakdown of literary dualism, for it intervenes in the presumed dualism between Eliot's critical and poetic work (3–17). *Orígenes* 3 would also include Rodríguez Feo's translations of Theodore Spenser's essay on James Joyce's manuscript of *Portrait of the Artist* and of William Carlos Williams's poem "The Bitter World of Spring."

Orígenes 3 appears to equalize Cuban and foreign voices and display a veritably cosmopolitan distribution of voices and topics. An essay by Spanish philosopher María Zambrano in clear dialogue with *Orígenes*'s established literary project defines metaphor as follows: "La metáfora es una definición que roza con lo inefable, única forma en que ciertas realidades pueden hacerse visibles a los torpes ojos humanos" (Metaphor is a definition that grazes the ineffable, the only form in which certain realities can be made visible to clumsy human eyes) (3). Zambrano would emphasize here why metaphor, and by extension literary discourse, would be so important to making certain realities visible. Her arguments align well with Aimé Césaire's in his essay from almost exactly the same time, "Poésie et Connaissance," in which Césaire defines poetic knowledge as the knowledge offered in the gaps left by science and, in particular, the knowledge that makes meaning from context. This issue would also feature Lezama's poem "Pensamientos en la Habana," (Thoughts in Havana), which though located in the city by its title would not, curiously, participate in the form of writing that would construct the city's location as particular or identifiable, for it is the interior space of thought and not the city where the thoughts occur that would make up the poem's primary locus. Fina García Marruz's poetic tribute to Peruvian poet César Vallejo would also be featured in this issue. The review section would include Vitier's essay on Argentinian writer José Bianco's book published by Ediciones *Sur*, the publishing project associated with the eponymously named Argentinian literary magazine to which *Orígenes* had ties, and Rodríguez Feo's essay on Cuban painter Mariano Rodríguez's work. In the map outlined by this table of contents, Cuban poetry and art connect to U.S. poetry and literary criticism, South American poetry and fiction, and Spanish aesthetic philosophy, all presented on the same plane together.

While it is easy to marvel at the postcolonial achievement of worldliness in *Orígenes*'s pages, the magazine nonetheless projects a Eurocentric image of literature and art, one that is as potent as it is conveyed through understatement: after all, it is through silence and indirect discourse that such projections of the universal through the "European ideal" have had their most powerful manifestations. In addition to the overwhelming prevalence of Euro-Cuban voices featured in the magazine, U.S. American writers of European backgrounds would also predominate in its pages. As is usually the case with unstated and understated Eurocentric forms, however, they eventually emit their prejudice. One such emission occurs, curiously, in an essay by the U.S. American art critic Walter Pach, written at Rodríguez Feo's behest, on the exposition of Cuban artists at the 1944 exhibit at the Museum of Modern Art in New York. Pach's essay from *Orígenes* 4, "Problemas del arte americano" (Problems of American Art), symptomatically emits prejudice in two ways. The first is his essay's refusal to engage directly with the Cuban painters of the exhibit and his use of the essay as an excuse to inquire about the state of "arte americano." The use of "American" in his diagnostic essay extends beyond the United States, including Cuba along with the rest of the hemisphere. The most prejudicial work in Pach's essay appears when his discourse all of a sudden becomes racial: "Hemos estudiado el arte oriental lo bastante ya para afirmar que ninguna raza combina los elementos físicos y espirituales con tanta armonía como nosotros" (We have studied Oriental art sufficiently to affirm that no race combines physical and spiritual elements with as much harmony as ours) (20). Pach clarifies that by "nosotros" he refers to Europeans when he continues in opposition to Indian art that "siempre hay otra rama de la familia europea lista para continuar en un nuevo desarrollo la línea que estaba cayendo" (there is always another branch of the European family ready to take the line that was collapsing and continue developing it in a new way) (20). How close is Pach's conception of "American" art to the conception of freedom in the humanist tradition belonging to "the American" in *Orígenes*'s (anti)programmatic first editorial? To what extent does Pach's formulation of American art as European art produced in the Americas translate the otherwise silent Eurocentrism in *Orígenes*, replete with its supremacist notion of European aesthetics? This proclamation of racial aesthetic supremacy operates in a magazine that is otherwise notably silent about race but features European and Euro-American authors alongside a vast majority of Euro-Cuban contributors. It is clear that although *Orígenes*'s Eurocentrism is mutated by a postcolonial intervention that would permit a formalist Cuban magazine to operate in dialogue with European and U.S. American authors and critics, it is nonetheless a project oriented by the practice of European and Euro-descendant aesthetic dominance.

In 1954, Rodríguez Feo and Lezama parted ways and created their own editions of numbers 35 and 36 of *Orígenes*, after which Lezama produced only four more issues until 1956 with the support of the loyal members of his literary coterie. In 1955 just before *Orígenes*'s end, Rodríguez Feo teamed up with Virgilio Piñera and produced a new literary periodical, *Ciclón*, that would last until 1959. Although *Ciclón* in some ways appears to continue the *Orígenes* project in its projection of a Cuban literature in close dialogue with contemporary Spanish and U.S. American authors, it also became progressively more politicized in the years leading up to the Cuban Revolution.

Black Aesthetics as the Battleground of Literary Geopolitics

Far beyond the typical actions that may personify a magazine, in both of these Cuban instances the editors of each literary periodical personify it, suggesting the magazine itself has beliefs, interests, and goals. Their personification pertains to how their editors endowed them with a will to power over the governance of Cuban literature and Cuba's geopolitical image. I understand their differing interventions in Eurocentric ideologies as literary geopolitics. For this concept, I borrow from Adela Pineda Franco's understanding of Latin American *modernista* literary magazines of the late nineteenth century as practicing "a geopolitics of literature" (12). While all the magazines examined in this book participated in some form of literary geopolitics, *Gaceta del Caribe* and *Orígenes* present the particularly acute case of magazines embattled with each other. They projected themselves like competing literary regimes, and with exceptions including Alejo Carpentier, Lino Novás Calvo, and Wifredo Lam, who appear in both periodicals, their editors and coteries seem to have combated each other in order to determine not only the domestic affairs of Cuban literary representation but also its foreign relations. At the center of this battle, which culminates rather than begins with the advent of both magazines in 1944, is how each magazine approached Black aesthetics, *Gaceta del Caribe* forwarding the national character of Black aesthetics and *Orígenes* diminishing its prominence.

The background to the 1944 literary battle goes back at least to 1937. Lezama wrote the essay "Coloquio con Juan Ramón Jimenez" and was already editing the series of magazines that would eventually culminate in *Orígenes*.[41] Amauri Francisco Gutiérrez Coto has suggested that an article by the art critic Guy Pérez Cisneros published in the first magazine Lezama Lima edited, *Verbum*, summarizes how the group associated with Lezama believed that the artist should relate to society (14). I do not wish to reduce the variegated and evolving work of multiple magazines under the helm of Lezama Lima and his associates to Pérez

Cisneros's early article, but the programmatic text indeed illuminates the terms of the impending literary battle between the magazines. The article in question, "Presencia de ocho pintores" (The Presence of eight painters) (1937), elaborates a program for producing art and literature in the service of the Cuban nation. Unlike the opening editorial establishing *Orígenes* as a magazine, this earlier article employed an explicitly national focus. Pérez Cisneros calls for decoupling art and politics, with the exception of the aesthetic-political imperative to fortify the nation: "Derrocar todo intento artístico de tendencia política, pues, en este momento toda tendencia política que no sea estrictamente nacional, está forzosamente equivocada y sólo nos puede conducir a una desaparición total" (Overthrow all artistic attempts of political tendencies, since, in this moment all political tendency that is not strictly national is forcedly mistaken and can only lead us to total disappearance) (66). As he would go on to suggest, in the face of imperial subordination, the political purpose of Cuban art and literature would be to build the Cuban nation, and any other politically motivated aesthetic would otherwise make the nation vulnerable to imperialism. Pérez Cisneros thereby participates in a tendency among writers, artists, and critics to see the work of cultural production as a geopolitical act. His exhortation falls in line with Pascale Casanova's argument for the imbrication of literature and national politics. Casanova suggests that "the quest for political independence brings with it a need to display and increase the nation's literary wealth" (227). Pérez Cisneros seems to suggest in kind that maintaining and increasing national independence should be the priority of Cuban artists. Even if the Cuban nation is not invoked directly in *Orígenes*, this position served as one important backdrop to the battle *Gaceta del Caribe* and *Orígenes* would later fight over how to govern the Cuban literary field.

In Pérez Cisneros's description of the character of art that the project of the nation required, he denounces Nicolás Guillén's poetry as racist for poeticizing the voices and speech patterns of poor Black Cubans. Pérez Cisneros accuses Guillén's poetry of responding to the "unbearable void" of national culture by creating "a racism with no exit" (62). Guillén stands out as the most well known and one of the few Black voices of the *negrista* movement in poetry, and yet it is his approach to this movement that comes under scrutiny here. In this context, the accusation of racism is a double-edged sword.

On the one hand, it indexes an intellectual and political trend in Cuba, beginning at least with José Martí's "Nuestra América," to disqualify racial identification as racist. In what José Buscaglia calls the "keystone that absolutely cannot hold" of that text, Martí formatively declared, "There is no racial hatred, because there are no races" (Buscaglia xii). Although it was a radical move in 1891 to denounce the constructedness of race, Martí inscribed the wish, or the decree, to be rid of racial hatred as if it were an accomplishment that accompanied the myth of racial difference. As Vera Kutzinski notes, these "well-intentioned words" were "at best problematic, at worst hypocritical" just five years after slavery had been abolished in Cuba (6). In a move that encapsulates the lived contradiction between the construction of race on the one hand and racist practices on the other, Martí also denounces the propagation of racial oppositions and hatred as sins against humanity. A violent trajectory would reinforce this trend. In 1912, a large group of Cubans of African descent and African-Cubans formed a political party, the Independent Party of Color, to secure rights for Black and mixed-race Cubans.[42] A law that banned "race-based" political organizing subsequently proscribed the party, and when party members protested this law, the Cuban army massacred 6,000 Black and mixed-race Cubans, most of whom (but not all) were members of the party (de la Fuente 13–14). The massacre violently reinscribed the racial order that the party was formed to shift, and the myth of the raceless nation became visible as a masked discourse for policing the boundaries of an unjust racial order. What the massacre demonstrates, however, is how much violence is behind the Euro-Cuban accusation of Black representation *as* racism.[43] Furthermore, as Arnedo-Gómez explains in dialogue with Aline Helg's work, the massacre meant that Black Cubans would no longer feel safe protesting openly and "adopted more discreet strategies of struggle" (Arnedo-Gómez 24). The discretion that *Gaceta del Caribe* would employ in its antiracist work even decades later belongs to this trend.

On the other hand, Guillén's first published anthology of poems, *Motivos de son* (Son motifs), which poeticizes the speech patterns of poor and working-class Black Cubans as well as the Cuban musical form *el son*, had also been criticized by members of the Black and mixed-race middle class in Cuba as racist for appearing in their view to degrade Black Cubans (Maguire, *Racial Experiments* 108–111).[44] Pérez Cisneros's suggestion that Guillén's poetry indicated a racism with no exit hovered around both of these tendencies, but in the context of a platform for nationalist literature, part of what was at stake was likely a concern that poetry such as Guillén's would become representative of Cuban letters and therefore representative of Cuba. In other words, I am suggesting that part of the concern was that Guillén's poetry, alongside the poetry of his peers of the *afrocubanista / negrista* movement, would represent Cuba to the world as a Black country. In his take on the *Orígenes* group's response to *negrismo*, Jesús Barquet indicates this concern as a fait accompli for the period: "El negrismo invadió, pues, con declarado afán de primacía y exclusiva representatividad nacional, la cultura cubana hasta la segunda mitad de los años 30" (*Negrismo* invaded Cuban culture then, with a declared aim of primacy and exclusive national representation, until the second half of the thirties) (3). Barquet seems to capture the bellicose nature of the resistance to Black representation at this time in his choice of "invasion" to describe the work of *negrismo* in this period. The later *Orígenes* mandate to "occupy being" reads in a terse opposition to the idea of this "invasion."

Lezama clearly signposts the *Orígenes* strategy of displacing Black aesthetics from Cuban letters in his "Coloquio con Juan Ramón Jimenez." In his critique of "black sensibility" in Cuban poetics, he compares it to the role of indigeneity in Mexican letters: "La reserva con que la poesía mexicana, tan aristocrática, acogió al indio, como motivo épico o lírico, contra el gran ejemplo de su pintura, contrasta con la brusquedad con que la poesía cubana planteó de una manera quizás desmedida, la incorporación de la sensibilidad negra" (The discretion with which Mexican poetry, so aristocratic, took in the Indian, as an epic or lyrical motif, against the great example of its painting, contrasts with the brusqueness with which Cuban poetry, in a way that may have been excessive, suggested the incorporation of black sensibility) (35). Here, the operative words are "aristocrática," "acogió," "brusquedad," and "incorporación." There is a case to be made for the problem of "brusque incorporation" in *negrista* literature, especially regarding many of the works written by Euro-Cubans that are exoticizing, culturally appropriative, and ambivalent that have been scrutinized by many critics (Arroyo, *Travestismos* 28–30; Kutzinski 181; Arnedo-Gomez 43–45). As Víctor Fowler's reading of Lezama's poem "Para Llegar a Montego Bay" from this period indicates, Lezama's version of Black representation located in Jamaica for this poem would be to exercise the symbolic violence of denying access to meaning, the will to knowledge, and aesthetic participation in historical evolution (135).[45] In other words, the poem participates in the racist geneaology of white-produced *negrista* poetry by ignoring or negating the interior subjectivities of Black persons. The great irony that renders this poem even more absurd from a Pan-Caribbean perspective is that Jamaica had already become by this period a center of literature and political movements for the English-speaking West Indies. This example is key for Lezama's practice of an "aristocratic" literary approach to Black subjectivity in the Caribbean.

Lezama's interest in an "aristocratic" approach to blackness as "motif" concerns the editorial policy of minoritarian inclusion of Black aesthetics in *Orígenes*. In a minimal way, *Orígenes* does include what Lezama refers to as a Black sensibility, including, for example, paintings by Wifredo Lam on magazine covers (beginning with the spring 1945 cover) and later pieces by and about Lydia Cabrera's literary recuperations of Afro-Cuban folklore and religious practices.[46] Perhaps the best way to understand the style of these inclusions of Afro-Cuban cultural forms may very well be Lezama's following the model of Mexico's aristocratic "discretion" in "taking in" an Indigenous presence. Reading the first editorial of *Orígenes* alongside Lezama's critique of *negrismo* suggests it is likely that the magazine's repudiation of valuing life over literature reads as the wish to underprivilege the aesthetic representation of Black life in particular. At the very least it foments a Latin American imaginary that continues, as Yolanda Martínez-San Miguel has indicated, to privilege "white creole discourse" above all else ("(Neo) Barrocos" 24).

I sustain that Lezama's aesthetic position against the "brusqueness" of Black aesthetic representation feeds the communicative inequality promoted in theory and circulation in *Orígenes*.[47] In other words, I suggest that *Orígenes* enforced an already dominant supravaluation and emphasis on European and Euro-American literary traditions in order to foment an elitist (aristocratic) Euro-Cuban hegemony over Cuban letters, creating a minimal minoritarian space for the "inclusion" of Afro-Cuban and Afro-Caribbean aesthetics without allowing for a shared space of power in the image of the nation's literature.

The *Gaceta* editors in turn were in a "war of position" with socially and politically "disengaged" aesthetic and intellectual production that was also overdetermined by class and racial engagements in literature.[48] Their battle dovetails with one of Nicolás Guillén's central intellectual projects: to write Black culture into Cuban national identity and to eventually achieve what the prologue to his second book of poetry, *Sóngoro Cosongo* (1931), had proposed: a national culture that would assimilate both its Black and white, African and European, elements. As he envisioned it, "Algun día se dirá 'color cubano'" (One day it will be called Cuban color) ("Prólogo" 33). In this earlier prologue, Guillén suggested that this eventual goal would not be reached by "forgetting blackness." To the contrary, Guillén's work and that of *Gaceta del Caribe* would regularly feature work by Black and mixed-race Cubans and offer antiracist discourse. *Gaceta del Caribe* coeditor José Antonio Portuondo also demonstrated his commitment to Black Cuban representation in his critical coverage of *negrismo* as a form of global populism in his book from the same year as *Gaceta del Caribe*'s run, *El contenido social de la literatura cubana* (The Social Content of Cuban Literature). Most of Portuondo's *negrista* canon—including Novás Calvo, Carpentier, and Ortiz—contributed to *Gaceta del Caribe*. In a sense, the magazine brought much of this movement together, a canon-forming gesture.

Furthermore, for Guillén, Black aesthetic representation was a necessary end in itself. In his 1937 speech to the international conference of Writers in Defense of Culture in Spain, published subsequently as "Cuba, negros, poesía," Guillén had claimed that "socially responsible art" spurred Black Cubans' "coming out" into the public. As he understood the contemporaneous literary rise in Black representation, "Para algunos, esa salida es moda, porque no alcanzan el profundo sentido que tiene la aparición del hombre oscuro en el escenario universal, su imperativa, indetenible necesidad; para el resto es, además, modo: modo entrañable de la lucha en que hoy se debaten oprimidos y opresores en el mundo" (For some, that emergence is a fashion, because they do not apprehend the profound meaning of the dark man's appearance on the universal stage, its imperative, undetainable need; for the rest it is, even more, a method: a method intimately connected to the struggle that is waged today between the oppressed and the oppressors of the world) (75). Guillén distinguishes here between the literary representation of Black people as "moda," or fashion, and "modo," or method. But he does not distinguish here between one kind of writer and another. Although Guillén surely understood that some—many—forms of Black representation would indeed reinforce the overvaluation of Eurodescendants in a Euro-dominated world, he nonetheless took a radical stance in favor of inclusion as a method, promulgating with his view the importance of approaching Black aesthetics as a method of aesthetic struggle but not as a fetish. Whereas *Orígenes* would discard Black aesthetics as shallow and proceed to elaborate a discourse and a form of representation that would, as Guillén would put it, "forget blackness," *Gaceta del Caribe* vied to keep Black representation and antiracist discourse at the forefront of the Cuban intellectual milieu and leftist politics.

The Carpentier Peace

Alejo Carpentier's work published in both *Gaceta del Caribe* and *Orígenes* in 1944 instantiates a symbolic peace between both magazine projects. He is one of few writers to be featured and reviewed in both magazines in 1944, the year before he moved from Havana to Caracas. His ability to move freely between camps and to be validated by each side demonstrates the peculiarity of his position in the Cuban literary field: he would be valued by *Gaceta del Caribe* as an avowedly antiracist and anti-imperial writer associated with the *negrismo* movement, *and* he would be valued by *Orígenes* as a difficult and baroque writer highly engaged with themes of religiosity. I argue that Carpentier's writing during this period exemplifies a tension between what Raymond Williams has identified as "alignment and commitment," and it is precisely this tension that demonstrates his ability to move relatively freely between both magazine camps during this period. The tension between Carpentier's alignment with a European perspective and his commitment to overturning European intellectual hegemony over the Americas is evinced in his 1944 works for both magazines that impinge heavily on one of his most important works, the 1949 novel *El reino de este mundo*. In my reading of early out-texts of this novel, I also suggest that this novel functions like a literary peace accord between the magazine projects of *Gaceta del Caribe* and *Orígenes*.

Born in Switzerland, the child of Russian and French parents, before moving to Cuba, Carpentier became one of the most well known and influential of Cuban writers. He has managed to be as central to the canon of Latin American literature as he is to that of Caribbean literature, a centrality achieved through the same monumental novel, *El reino de este mundo*, published in Mexico in 1949. This work is a historical fiction of the Haitian Revolution and the subsequent reign of Haiti's first sovereign, King Henri Christophe, who ruled over northern Haiti, told from the perspective of a fictionalized portrait of a historical figure, Ti Noël, who prominently fought in the revolution and has been memorialized by historians and literary artists alike. The work is a result of Carpentier's travel to Haiti, consultation of historical sources on the revolution, and, of course, fabulation. In Carpentier's rendition of Ti Noël, he participates in major events of the Haitian Revolution, including the uprising led by Makandal and the highly influential incantations by Bouckman. Ti Noël goes on to leave Haiti by force with Lenormand de Mézy, also a historical figure and his slaveholder, only to return to Haiti to be forced into temporary bondage to build the Citadel at La Ferrière for Henri Christophe and to live through the aftermath of Christophe's reign. The fictional work instantiates the historical and imaginative crossing between Cuba and Haiti that necessarily accords *El reino de este mundo* the status of a Caribbean fiction. Carpentier located the work more broadly, however, with a preface that situates it in a hemispheric framework. This preface would become canonical in decades to come, for its exposition of the Americas-located aesthetic of "lo real maravilloso" (the marvelous real) is an important precursor to the label of "magical realism" through which Latin American literature would circulate and accrue value in the world literary system by the 1960s.

It is clear that Carpentier incubated both the fiction and the preface of *El reino de este mundo* as early as 1944, when he published one virtually unknown work, "Capítulo de novela" (Novel chapter), in *Gaceta del Caribe* and one lesser-known short fiction work, "Oficio de Tinieblas" (Service of Darkness), in *Orígenes*. Both short works pertain significantly to the symbolic and geographical terrain of the novel, which takes place between different parts of Haiti and Santiago de Cuba. "Capítulo de novela," as the title suggests, seems to have been intended as a chapter of *El reino de este mundo*, but only fragments of this text enter the novel.[49] This text appears to have been reworked for both the preface to the book and the three climactic chapters that stage the death of Henri Christophe. The text begins as a travel account in the third person, echoing the author's own visit to Sans Souci castle and the Citadel at La Ferrière and morphs into a real-time account of Henri Christophe's death in dialogue with Edgar Allan Poe's short story "The Curse of the Red Death." "Oficio de Tinieblas," a historical short story set in Santiago where part of the later book also takes place, proceeds from the perspective of an enslaved African and relates an outbreak of cholera in the city. Its ominous tone for the future of whiteness echoes the introductory chapter of *El reino de este mundo*, which foreshadows the violent defeat of many members of the white planter and slaveholding class effected by the impending revolution. Anke Birkenmeier has suggested that Carpentier was in a dialogue "marked by silence and distancing" with the *Orígenes* group and had also distanced himself from the version of commitment literature—socialist realism—for which Guillén and those in the *Gaceta* camp would advocate. Her work indicates that instead Carpentier, along with Wifredo Lam, occupied a third position in the literary critical battle between both camps (117–118). In my view of the texts Carpentier published in both magazines, his third position appears to achieve a fusion-intension of both camps. These works and their imbrication in Carpentier's bicanonical book demonstrate, on the one hand, his aesthetic-political commitment to exhuming colonial history and eradicating white power in the Americas that ties him to *Gaceta del Caribe*'s project and, on the other hand, his high modernist aesthetic practice and alignment with the racist gaze of white power that ties him to *Orígenes*'s project.

Williams's understanding of authorial commitment versus alignment provides a framework for organizing the ambivalence of Carpentier's work as a committed antiracist whose sometimes condescending representations of Black characters do not always appear to accord with his sociopolitical commitment. Williams explains that writing is "in an important sense always aligned," incorporating a "specific point of view" that pertains to the author's social position (*Marxism* 199), but at the same time he notes that commitment is "a choice of position" and "conscious alignment" (200, 204). In my reading, Carpentier's alignment as a Swiss-born immigrant to the Caribbean, who by the time of this novel had also lived extensively in France, erupts into a text that is also structured by his conscious alignment as a radical antiracist committed to overturning European social, intellectual, and aesthetic hegemony in the Americas. As Lizabeth Paravisini-Gebert would explain about Carpentier's influence for *El reino de este mundo*, "Carpentier stands in that slightly ambiguous terrain between Price-Mars and Seabrook—committed on the one hand to an alternative depiction of Haitian history that emphasizes the people's enduring faith in Vodou and the lwas, yet not unwilling to fetishize aspects of that faith in his text in his quest for the magic-realist unveiling of that history required by the new literature he envisioned" (118). Natalie Léger would add the charge that although Carpentier's novel attempts to foreground a perspective from below, there is "an imperial bias that the narrator inherits" (92). Paravisini-Gebert and Léger grapple with a Carpentier who on the one hand paid tribute to the Haitian Revolution and the role of Vodou in shaping it and on the other hand seems to repeatedly miss the mark in representations that are at times exoticist and fetishizing and at other times reveal a Eurocentric perspective and banal tropes of antiblackness, in other words a Carpentier shuttling between commitment and alignment. Carpentier's shuttling between commitment and alignment is analogous, I argue, to his ability to shuttle between *Gaceta del Caribe* and *Orígenes*.

"Capítulo de novela," published in *Gaceta del Caribe* 3 (May 1944), fits well into the *Gaceta* corpus. Its engagement with the physical terrain and architecture of Sans Souci castle and the Citadel at La Ferrière from the perspective of a contemporary traveler on a guided tour adheres to some elements of social realism, though the text also exceeds the bounds of realism when it transforms into the narrative of the death of King Henri Christophe. In this sense, the text is more properly classifiable as marvelous realism, which would become Carpentier's theoretical offering to the Latin American canon in the preface to *El reino de este mundo*. As a text by a Cuban-affiliated author engaging the history of Haiti's revolution, Carpentier's extract for *Gaceta* also firmly performs a Pan-Caribbean solidarity. In fact, emphasizing how Cuban nationalism can be synonymous with Caribbean solidarity, the editors of *Gaceta del Caribe* position Carpentier's text as Cuban. The title of the text includes an asterisk that pertains to a footnote in which they state that Carpentier is completing "una novela cubana" (a Cuban novel) that also takes place in Haiti, indicating by implication that the history of Haiti, and in particular the Haitian Revolution, pertains to the novel of the Cuban nation or, read another way, that a Cuban novel can be a novel that pertains to Cuba only peripherally so long as its author is Cuban, a right accrued by lived experience (12). If Carpentier, born abroad, was accorded that right, why not the Haitian workers and those from other parts of the Caribbean who spent much of their lives in Cuba? Tightening the Pan-Caribbean knot of Cuba-Haiti solidarity that publishing this text and presenting it as a Cuban novel also enacts, it is positioned alongside a translation by Nicolás Guillén of a poem by leading Haitian poet Jacques Roumain, "Guinea," which recalls the mythological status of Guinea under slavery as both homeland and heaven.

The highly influential preface to *El reino de este mundo* draws heavily from this earlier text. The preface begins by autobiographically recounting the author's 1943 visit to the remnants of Henri Christophe's kingdom, which Carpentier dramatically evokes from the third-person perspective of "Lucas" in "Capítulo de novela." "Capítulo" recounts Lucas's encounter of Sans Souci castle as a sweeping vision of red: "Ahora se abría ante sus ojos la mole roja de la Ciudadela de Christophe. Rojas las torres; rojas las murallas, bajo un cielo trágicamente cerrado por nubes negras" (Before his eyes now appeared the red mass of Christophe's Citadel. Red towers; red ramparts, under a sky tragically closed by black clouds) (12). The more distant preface would instead theorize what this moment evokes: "Después de sentir el nada mentido sortilegio de las tierras de Haití, de haber hallado advertencias mágicas en los caminos rojos de la Meseta Central, de haber oído los tambores del Petro y del Rada, me vi llevado a acercar la maravillosa realidad recien vivida a la agotante pretensión de suscitar lo maravilloso que caracterizó ciertas literaturas europeas de estos últimos treinta años" (After feeling the all-too-real enchantment of the land of Haiti, finding signs of magic by the sides of the red roads of the central plain, and hearing the drums of Petro and Rada, I was driven to compare this recently experienced marvelous reality with the tiresome attempts to evoke the marvelous that characterized certain European literature of the last thirty years) (*El reino* 5; *The Kingdom* xiii–xiv).

The early chapter draft anticipates Carpentier's theory of "lo real maravilloso" for which the preface is so well known, but with a key difference that would sadly be lost to the preface: "¡Que otros pensaran en el surrealismo! . . . La imprecación de Bouckman volvía a su memoria: 'Arrojen el retrato del dios de los blancos, que tiene sed de nuestras lágrimas; escuchen, en si mismos, la llamada de la libertad.' América no necesitaba hacer grandes esfuerzos para crear cosas sorprendentes, de un terrible valor poético" (Let others think of surrealism! . . . Boukman's call returned to his memory: 'Discard the portrait of the god of the whites, for it is thirsty for our tears; listen, within yourselves, to the call to freedom.' America need not exert great efforts in creating surprising things, of terrible poetic value) (12). This version of his aesthetic theory is embedded in the racial warfare of slavery upheld through a religious hegemony that the Haitian Revolution would combat. Carpentier would, in this text for *Gaceta del Caribe*, render the violence of Eurocentric aesthetics, embodied by surrealism, through Boukman's revolutionary call, forging a unity between the politics of combating slavery with the aesthetics of combating the European ideal. How would Carpentier's theory and novel have differed if the philosophical unity between the revolution that was the first to end slavery and the located aesthetics of the marvelous real been established in the later preface, as it is in this early text? What replaces this passage in the preface instead compares rape to aesthetics: "Hay todavía demasiados 'adolescentes que hallan placer en violar los cadáveres de hermosas mujeres recién muertas' (Lautréamont), sin advertir que lo maravilloso estaría en violarlas vivas" (There are still too many 'adolescents who find pleasure in violating the corpses of newly dead beautiful women' (Lautréamont), unaware of the fact that the truly marvelous would be in violating them while still living) (7; xv). Carpentier thus replaces Bouckman's revolt against Christianity with a metonymical relationship between rape and art that would differentiate between European art and the art of the Americas. The difference between the potently antiracist—but also anti-Christian—first draft and the misogynist final draft is palpable. How would Carpentier's theory and novel be different today if the comparison for the marvelous real had remained a reference to Boukman's call to relinquish the "white god" of Christianity rather than a reference to rape?

The nucleus of Carpentier's later theory also differs structurally in "Capítulo" because it appears within the narrative and not on the prefatory threshold of the historical fiction.[50] It is woven through a character that would not be in the novel: Lucas, who like Carpentier visits twentieth-century Haiti in order, as Léger suggests in her reading of Carpentier, to ignore its present in favor of a glimpse into its revolutionary past (88). How would the inclusion of this contemporary traveler as a character who thinks through the revolution as a historical and geographical other alter this highly influential novel? The early text further establishes the importance of Edgar Allan Poe as an influential reference for Carpentier's novel. Birkenmaier's book on Carpentier demonstrates how important the surrealist movement was to the development of Carpentier's literary aesthetic, even as he critiqued it; Paravisini-Gebert has noted that Carpentier's text was shaped by the influence of Haitian authors Jean Price-Mars and Dominique Hippolyte as well as by the exoticist rendition of Haiti by Seabrook (117); and Frank Janney has noted that Carpentier's early short fiction, in particular his short story "Oficio de Tinieblas" that would be published in *Orígenes*, demonstrates an influence by Edgar Allan Poe (118). The "Capítulo" text confirms both the importance of Poe to his literary imagination and the centrality of Poe's influence to the later novel.

In "Capítulo de novela" Lucas metonymically transitions from taking in the force of the red color of Sans Souci castle and a reminiscence of Poe's "The Masque of the Red Death": "*¡La atmosfera de Edgar Poe!*" (The atmosphere of Edgar Poe), he exclaims, and continues with "¡El castillo de la muerte roja! . . . La ciudad inexpugnable, fuera del mundo, más cielo que barro, donde sólo la muerte pueda penetrar sin permiso del amo" (The castle of the red death! . . . The inexpungable city, out of this world, more sky than clay, where only death might penetrate without the master's permission) ("Capítulo" 12). Poe's literary influence he names becomes the transition for narrating the ominous turn of events that led to Christophe's suicide. As the "Capítulo" text would continue, echoing Poe's story, "Y la muerte había penetrado, en efecto, en la ciudadela La Ferrière. Había penetrado en la propia persona de quien quiso desafiarlo todo, solitario, por encima de las nubes" (And death had penetrated, in effect, in the Citadel La Ferrière. It had penetrated the very person who wished to defy everything, alone, above the clouds). Carpentier aesthetically rehearses here the transitions of the novel that would appear to flow seamlessly from Ti Noël's perspective to the scenes of Henri Christophe's death.

In *El reino de este mundo* Ti Noël's perspective on the city of Cap-Haïtien, or the Cap, would introduce the Poeian curse of death that would lead to Henri Christophe's death: "Pero Ti Noel halló a la ciudad entera en espera de una muerte" (Ti Noël found an entire city waiting for death) (109; *The Kingdom* 88). Instead of the perspective of the foreign traveler Lucas, which approximates the author's own, Ti Noël's perspective personifies the town of the Cap as a city waiting for the impending death of Henri Christophe. "Capítulo de novela" would function as a rehearsal for the scenes surrounding that death, the haunting by Corneille Breille; the confessor who had been ordered to be executed by Christophe, in the mass of the Assumption; Christophe's own paralysis in response; his subsequent return to Sans Souci; and his death there. "Capítulo" reads as an outline of the novel's three chapters that detail Christophe's death, each scene expanded upon significantly in the later text. For example, the culminating scene of the sovereign's death is introduced by almost the same exclamation in both texts: "¡Están redoblando el *manducumán*!" (They're playing the *manducumán*!). The uprising that catalyzes the king's suicide recalls the drums that foretold the uprisings of the Haitian Revolution, demonstrating that once again the people of the Cap would revolt against their ruler. What follows is much more extensive in *El reino* than in "Capítulo," this earlier text much more closely enacting Poe's influence:

> A estos tambores responden otros, y otros, y otros . . . El horizonte se puebla de tambores. Tambores en Haut-le-Cap. Tambores en la llanura que llega al mar. Tambores en los *mornes*. Sobre los tambores crecen enormes llamaradas. El incendio avanza hacia Millot, en redondo, apretando su cerco, levantando trombas de lentejuelas ardientes sobre los sembrados reales. Christophe contempla la noche roja. Rojas son también las torres de la Citadelle. . . . Pero la muerte habla ahora por su propia mano. El estruendo de los tambores apenas si deja escuchar una detonación que repercute largamente por las salas desiertas de Sans Souci. Henry Christophe, rey de Haiti, yace atravesado en una butaca, con la cabeza rota por una bala. Salpicaduras de cerebro se confunden con los arabescos de la alfombra. ("Capítuo" 13)

> To these drums respond others, and others, and others. . . . The horizon is populated by drums. Drums in Haut-le-Cap. Drums on the plain that reaches the sea. Drums on the *mornes*. On the drums grow giant flares. The fire advances toward Millot, in rounds, squeezing its fence, raising deluges of flaming sequins on the royal plots. Christophe contemplates the red night. The towers of the Citadel too, are red. . . . But death speaks now by its own hand. The banging of the drums barely makes audible a detonation that reverberates at length through the deserted halls of Sans Souci. Henry Christophe, king of Haiti, lies across a seat, his head broken by a bullet. Flecks of brain are mixed up with the arabesques of the rug.

Between Henri Christophe's initial exclamation and understanding that a revolt against him ensued and his suicide, the literary time—several pages—as well as the time in the novel—several hours—expands for the published *El reino de este mundo* version. Among the changes, the moment of death is elaborated more directly, less an implied cause of the curse of death and more the actions taken purposively by the king, as he expires thus:

> Casi no se oyó el disparo porque los tambores estaban ya demasiado cerca. La mano de Christophe soltó el arma, yendo a la sien abierta. Así, el cuerpo se levantó todavía, quedando como suspendido en el intento de un paso, antes de desplomarse, de cara adelante, con todas sus decoraciones. Los pajes aparecieron en el umbral de la sala. El rey moría, de bruces en su propia sangre. (*El reino* 123)

> The shot was barely heard because the drums were so near. Christophe dropped the weapon and raised his hand to his wounded temple. His body lurched forward as if to take another step before falling headlong with all his decorations. The pages appeared in the threshold of the hall. The king lay dying, face down in his own blood. (*The Kingdom* 102)

In the novel, Henri Christophe receives greater character development, and greater distance is established between Carpentier's historically engaged fiction and Poe's abstract and dehistoricized fiction. As Roberto González-Echevarría has noted, Carpentier's novel ultimately "recasts" the historical sources he utilizes to structure it, evoking a sense of cyclical and ritualistic time drawn from Christianity: Boukman's rite occurs on a Sunday, and the revolt begins the next day; Henri Christophe's stroke in the church also takes place on a Sunday, and his death catalyzed by revolt occurs the next day. But neither set of dates, pace Carpentier's prefatorial promise of historical accuracy, is temporally accurate (133–139).

Several months after *Gaceta del Caribe* published "Capítulo," Carpentier's short story "Oficio de Tinieblas" would appear in *Orígenes* 4 (December 1944). "Oficio de tinieblas" would not be published in book form until much later, in the second edition of Carpentier's collected short fiction, *Guerra del tiempo* (War of Time) (1976). The story fits well into the manifest *Orígenes* project in its stylized difficulty and its engagement of the pageantry of Catholicism, but it also corresponds with the latent antiblackness of the magazine in the condescending gaze it enacts upon the protagonist, "el negro Panchón" (Black Panchón). Carpentier continues to incubate in this text his fascination, both aesthetic and historical, with the role of foreboding in relation to impending and massive death, one that takes on a sociopolitical force of epic proportions in the first chapter of *Reino*. In "Oficio" the foreboding of impending death from the earthquake and the cholera outbreak in Santiago is introduced in the first paragraph with "las sombras tenían una evidente propensión a quererse desprender de las cosas, como si las cosas tuvieran mala sombra" (the shadows had a clear propensity to wish to detach themselves from things, as if the things augured badly) (32). Which "things" are those which seem to wish to separate from their shadow? It is not entirely clear from the text. However, this moment opens up to a Marxist reading of the things as fetishized commodities that seem to "wish," along with the capitalists who profit from their sale, to extricate themselves from the "shadow" of their material production (Marx, "Capital" 319–329). The shadow of materiality in the context of nineteenth-century Santiago in which the story takes place, notably, is the material context of slavery. This is the context in which, toward the end of the same paragraph, Carpentier would offer ambiguously "Nada que fuera blanco prosperaba" (Nothing that was white would prosper). Carpentier makes sure to render white the substances that would be doomed to destruction, as if to announce the fall of white power aided by the natural disaster that would ensue. In "Wax Heads," the first chapter of *El reino*, Carpentier would reprise a similar ominous tone for the setting of the destruction of white power that the Haitian Revolution would effect.

The difference between the ominous tone threatening white power in "Oficio" and that of *El reino* is the perspective of each text's Black and enslaved protagonist. In "Oficio" Panchón is disparagingly portrayed as "una especie de gigante tonto" (a kind of dumb giant), and his perspective is disconnected from the ominous setting in which the foreboding foreshadowing that would threaten white power belongs to the narrator, not to Panchón as the oppressed subject of white power. It would be difficult to imagine this portrayal, which traffics in a buffoonish and condescending image of a Black person, as admissible in *Gaceta del Caribe*, but in *Orígenes* one wonders to what extent this disparaging portrait would be a requisite accompaniment to the threat to white power otherwise personified in the "things" of this story. While Ti Noël would be much more respected by the narrator of *El reino* than Panchón is in "Oficio," racist condescension also pervades his portrayal through comparisons to animals. For example, when Ti Noël wishes to return to "the old lands of Lenormand de Mézy," the narrator suggests he acts "como regresa la anguila al limo que la vio nacer" (like an eel returning to the mud where it was born) (*El reino* 107; *The Kingdom* 86). Although the text also includes the possibility of magically transforming into animals, this moment is less about magic and more about a banal racism that objectifies Ti Noël. At the same time, Ti Noël's character is much more complex and well-developed than Panchón, and in *El reino* his perspective contributes to the threat to white power characterizing the novel's tone. The second paragraph of the novel relates Ti Noël's experience of waiting for his enslaver Monsieur Lenormand de Mézy to be shaved by a barber while imagining that the white wax heads used for adornment in the barbershop transform into a banquet meal:

> Mientras el amo se hacía rasurar, Ti Noel pudo contemplar a su gusto las cuatro cabezas de cera que adornaban el estante de la entrada. Los rizos de las pelucas enmarcaban semblantes inmóviles, antes de abrirse, en un remanso de bucles, sobre el tapete encarnado. . . . Por una graciosa casualidad, la tripería contigua exhibía cabezas de terneros, desolladas, que tenían la misma calidad cerosa. . . . Sólo un tabique de madera separaba ambos mostradores, y Ti Noel se divertía pensando que, al lado de las cabezas descoloridas de los terneros, se servían cabezas de blancos señores en el mantel de la misma mesa. (*El reino* 18)

> While his master was being shaved, Ti Noël was able to study carefully the four wax heads propped on the shelf by the entrance. The wigs' curls framed the fixed faces before spreading into a pool of ringlets on the red runner. . . . By charming coincidence, the butcher shop next door displayed the skinned heads of calves, which had the same waxy quality. . . . Only a wooden partition separated the counters, and Ti Noël distracted himself by thinking that the heads of white gentlemen were being served at the same table as the discolored veal heads). (*The Kingdom* 4)

From the very beginning of this text, then, we are served the wish for the fall of white power in a fantasy of foreboding in which narrator and protagonist conspire to transform the wax heads into the heads of animals served for a meal and implicitly into the dead heads of white men instead of the inanimate objects they are. We thus witness the enslaved protagonist lie in wait for the overturning of his own objectified position into one in which objectification for the white class of enslavers would mean death. The force of this scene rehearsed in "Oficio" would read quite differently if it followed the draft version of the novel's preface that appears in *Gaceta del Caribe*, which suggests a located aesthetic would be akin to forsaking white gods. It would, however, require an author and a readership prepared for such a decolonial blasphemy.

In addition to publishing these two distinct texts by Carpentier in 1944, *Gaceta del Caribe* and *Orígenes* also published very different reviews of his novella "Viaje a la semilla" (Journey to the Source) from the same year. The difference between their takes on the same work of fiction is indicative of the differences that polarized the two periodicals. The work itself is difficult to follow, as it proceeds against chronology, in the direction, as announced by the title, of "la semilla," or the seed. Thematically, a work so concerned with moving in the direction of birth fits well into the *Orígenes* project that seems to be almost obsessively oriented in the same direction. At the same time, Carpentier's work is a historical fiction set in the colonial period and juxtaposing a Black and white character, such that its historicity and engagement in the particular history of race relations in Cuba embeds it simultaneously in the *Gaceta del Caribe* project.

Angel Augier's review for *Gaceta del Caribe* 6 (August 1944) pays tribute to its quality and suggests its relationship to cinema in its style: "La técnica narrativa novisima y original se desenvuelve en cortes cinematográficos, las imágenes se suceden a la inversa, porque los sucesos crecen en el minuto último para regresar a sus raíces. Es como un árbol que se recorre a si mismo desde la copa hasta la semilla matriz" (The original and brand new narrative technique is elaborated in cinematic cuts, with the images moving in reverse, because the events grow at the last minute only to return to their roots. It is like a tree that returns to itself from the crown toward the original seed) (28). Augier's final flourish is key, for it insists on keeping intact the tree grown from the past to the present in the story's inverse flow toward the "original seed." Augier also situates Carpentier's work in the trajectory of his recuperation of "lo cubano en sus relieves menos palpados" (Cubanness in its least felt zones), suggesting the underrepresentation of Black Cubans that Carpentier recuperates. As Augier continues to describe what versions of Cubanness he refers to, he briefly reviews Carpentier's first novel, *¡Ecué-Yamba-O!* (1933) suggesting that it "penetró agudamente en la vida del negro cubano, para decir su angustia y su esperanza" (penetrated acutely into the life of the Black Cuban, to express his anguish and his hope), in a move that echoes the way he describes Césaire's work in an earlier review, thus connecting Carpentier's thematic centering of Black experience with Césaire's.

Luis Antonio Ladra, in his review for *Orígenes* 3 (October 1944), would also pay tribute to Carpentier's story, also drawing attention to the quality of the regression performed by the story: "Ha comenzado (esencialmente) donde todos comienzan: la muerte o un anticipo de ella, sin excepción posible, y ha tenido el coraje de terminar donde los demás huirían espantados: en ese instante, en que al hombre el 'Universo le entraba por todos los poros' para hundirse, definitivamente en sus raíces" (He begins (essentially) where we all begin: death or the anticipation of it, without any exceptions, and he has had the courage to end in the place the rest flee from in fear: in that instant, in which the man 'absorbs the Universe through all of his pores' to drown definitively, in its roots) (46). Ladra suggests that Carpentier has had a rare courage in his fictional quest for the moment of birth and the grounding beyond of ancestral roots. Ladra's review is less concerned with the historical quality of the text than in its formal work on time. Furthermore, instead of drawing attention to the racial concerns implied by such a journey in Carpentier's work, he includes a bizarre footnote: "he ignorado ex profeso los pases del negro viejo que no es otro que Melchor con más años . . ." (I have ex profeso ignored the path of the old Black man who is none other than Melchor years later). In his brief close reading, Ladra seems aware of leaving out the Black character Melchor's progressions in the story and, instead of simply ignoring the presence of racial difference in the story, he notes his "express" exclusion of the Black character. Whereas in *Gaceta del Caribe* Carpentier's commitment to Black Cuban representation is expressly included, in *Orígenes* Black Cuban representation would be expressly minimized. The two reviews are exemplary of the differences in approaches to race between the two magazines and Carpentier's location as a meeting point of their distinct projects.

Conclusion: The Arrows of the Battle's Wake

The Cuban Partido Socialista Popular, which covertly funded *Gaceta del Caribe*, held a meeting at the end of 1944 to set its political strategy after losing the presidential election. At this meeting, Nicolás Guillén presented a talk that would be crucial to the stakes of the literary battle waged between *Gaceta del Caribe* and *Orígenes*. The editors' note introducing the book of documents and talks from the meeting signals their choice to include Guillén's talk in the book with the explanation that even though it was not ratified by the assembly, they included it because it stimulated debate on the problem of racial discrimination in Cuba ("De los editores" 8). The thesis of Guillén's talk would far exceed the terms of the editors' explanation, for Guillén's analysis would be much more nuanced. He avers the centrality of Black Cubans to the Cuban polity at large by forwarding the claim that the cultural unity of Cuba was based on the foundational location of Black popular culture in the composition of national Cuban culture. As Guillén would explain, Black and white people had been present together in Cuba since colonization, and given the vast presence of enslaved Africans combined with the violently imposed decline of the Indigenous population, Black Cubans became "el germen popular en nuestra composición social" (the popular root of our social composition) ("El problema del negro" 44). This statement should not be glossed over, for it indicates that what comprises Cubanness, or *cubanía*, practiced and shared among Cubans of various racial configurations, is largely rooted in Black popular culture.

The argument is radical, for it does not stake a claim to equality in difference but instead suggests unity through a shared culture of predominantly African origin. It is the argument that had implicitly pervaded the *afrocubanismo* movement: Cuban culture is predominantly composed of Black culture, and Black Cubans are therefore not only *also* Cuban but *superlatively* so and should therefore not only *not* be derided and discriminated against, but rather they should be paid the tribute that is their due. Guillén goes on to stipulate that the equality of Black Cubans should not be sought sentimentally or out of a mechanical idea of equality but instead "como un fenómeno de retribución histórica" (as a phenomenon of historical retribution) ("El problema del negro" 44). The payment implied in "paid tribute" takes on the added weight of retribution here that also recalls Suzanne Césaire's language of "dispossession" for Antilleans of African descent. Establishing racial equality in Cuba would not only *not* be a gift bestowed on Cubans of African descent but rather the restitution of a debt, or the achievement of historical retribution. Guillén's speech, occurring after the Partido Socialista Popular candidate lost the presidential election in the context of a party meeting that opted to negotiate as much as possible with the more centrist government of Ramón Grau San Martín, elucidates the stakes of *Gaceta del Caribe*'s implicit work to forward Black aesthetics as a strategy with both literary-critical and sociopolitical ramifications.

Perhaps without the Guillén-led *Gaceta* group's push for Black aesthetic centrality, Lezama's group would not even have adopted its policy of minority Black aesthetic inclusion. Carpentier's short story "Oficio de Tinieblas" featuring a Black protagonist would appear in the final issue of 1944, Lam's first cover would appear in the following spring 1945 issue, and Aimé Césaire's poem "Batuc" would appear in the next. *Orígenes* would far outlast *Gaceta del Caribe* and succeed in reformulating Cuba's literary image significantly in its vast circulation. Its aversion to Caribbean identification would go on to geopolitically overpower the Caribbeanist tendencies exhibited by Guillén, Piñera, Carpentier, and Lam, becoming central to the Latin Americanist project of the Cuban state projected as a revolution *even as* many of its authors would go on to be condemned by this very state that would include the editorial team of *Gaceta del Caribe* in its ranks.[51]

CHAPTER 4

Bim Becomes West Indian

By December 1945, World War II had officially ended.[1] Germany surrendered to Soviet and Polish forces in July 1945, and Japan surrendered in August 1945 after the Soviet army invaded Japanese-occupied Manchuria. The Indian independence movement was fully under way and would lead to a partitioned independence in 1947. The British economy had been decimated by the war. In July 1944, the United States brokered the Breton Woods agreement inaugurating the World Bank and the International Monetary Fund. The agreement ended British trade monopoly over its empire and set up the U.S. dollar as a normative global currency.[2] As the world order transformed, so too did the Caribbean. In 1945 the British Colonial Office moved to form the West Indies Federation, a centralized governing body from which to continue colonial rule over its Caribbean territories in a new form. The Caribbean Labour Congress supported the move, considering it an avenue toward Caribbean self-government and socialist planning for the region (Lewis 365–367). The British Colonial Office would walk the tightrope between this decolonizing conception of federation and its own strategy, which was to facilitate continued colonial administration in the region.[3]

In Bridgetown, Barbados, *Bim* magazine went through a contiguous metamorphosis. Having begun as a tiny parochial venture, it would grow into a veritably West Indian literary periodical. After just three years of circulation, it boasted authorial coverage across the Anglophone Caribbean and readership on the metropolitan side of the Atlantic. *Bim* debuted in 1942 while the war raged on, just one year after Martinique's *Tropiques* and two years before Cuba's *Gaceta del Caribe* and *Orígenes*. By the end of the 1940s *Bim* had already established itself as a foundational organ for the development of West Indian or Anglophone Caribbean literature.

This highly influential periodical did not aspire to much when it began to circulate, however. It was started by a group of Bridgetown men who were members of a social and sports club for white Creoles called the Young Men's Progressive Club (YMPC). For editorial support, they brought in Frank Collymore, a teacher at the prestigious Combermere School and an actor who was also well known for his literary talents.[4] Writer, journalist, and initial editor E. L. Cozier coined the name "Bim," which referred to a person from Barbados. After the first two issues Collymore went on to edit the magazine with writer W. Therold Barnes (Baugh, "Introduction" 9–10). *Bim* was printed at the Advocate Press, which also published the local eponymously named newspaper. Unlike *Tropiques*, *Gaceta del Caribe*, and *Orígenes*, *Bim* ran with advertisements for funding.[5] Like *Tropiques*, *Bim* was small in size, 4.5 by 7 inches. Whereas *Orígenes*'s cover regularly featured the title in color and visual artwork in black and white, *Bim*'s cover included a title in color and each issue's table of contents. The magazine would feature visual art in black and white on the subsequent page of each issue. During the 1940s *Bim*'s literary contents primarily consisted of narrative texts, both fictional and autobiographical; lyric verse also appeared frequently, and as the magazine matured and expanded in size and scope, the literary texts it featured became more diverse, including drama and literary criticism as well. Also like *Tropiques* and *Orígenes* but unlike *Gaceta del Caribe*, *Bim*'s size, scope of circulation, and inclusion of experimental forms associated with literary modernism would classify it as a "little magazine." Run by Collymore and various coeditors until 1973 and continued thereafter, *Bim* is by far the longest-surviving literary and arts periodical in the Caribbean.[6]

Bim was programmatically unpolitical. Its only stated goal was to encourage the writing of West Indian writers. The editors vehemently kept out explicitly politicized content. In a 1966 letter to Edward Baugh, Collymore wrote: "I'd like you to know that BIM has been strictly non-political, non-racial, non-religious. . . . Personally, I detest propaganda in any form" (Baugh, *Frank Collymore* 178). Although racial hierarchies permeated the colonial West Indian societies fictionalized by many *Bim* contributors, there is in fact no identifiably collective racial discourse or clearly formulated anticolonial discourse in *Bim*.[7] As Raphael Dalleo surmises, *Bim* carved out a space for literature "apart from the everyday concerns of politics" and still managed to publish so many writers who would go on to be known for their anticolonialism (*Caribbean Literature* 108). Although *Bim*'s influence has received some attention, the history of its peculiar narrative evolution that is the subject of this chapter remains to be told. The obscurity of its history results largely from what Alison Donnell has demonstrated to be, until very recently, a narrow critical focus in studies of Anglophone Caribbean literature on made-in-London novels authored primarily by men in the 1950s and 1960s (*Twentieth-Century Caribbean Literature* 11). For this chapter, I suspend the presumed obviousness of a regional West Indian literature of anticolonial dimensions and inquire into the mechanisms that would render possible such a conformation in works by women and men in a purposively unpolitical magazine such as *Bim*.

Bim was not alone in the enterprise of making Anglophone Caribbean literature possible. It was preceded by a number of magazines including the Trinidad-based magazines *Trinidad* (1929–1930), edited by C.L.R. James and Alfred H. Mendes; *Beacon* (1931–1933), also edited by C.L.R. James with Albert Gomes;[8] and the Jamaica-based *West Indian Review* (1934–1970s), edited by Esther Chapman and others. Among the most well-known collective publications that were *Bim*'s contemporaries are the Jamaica-based literary anthology *Focus* (1944 and 1948), edited by Edna Manley, the sculptor who was married to Jamaican independence leader Norman Manley, and the Guyana-based *Kyk-over-Al* (1945–1961), edited by poet A. J. Seymour. This 1940s network of literary publications was itself bolstered by the connection to the BBC radio show *Caribbean Voices* (founded in 1943), which was produced in London. The show was inaugurated and edited by Jamaican poet Una Marson until 1946, when the Irish literary critic Henry Swanzy took over until 1958. Glyne Griffith has demonstrated how influential the radio show has been to both West Indian regionalism and territorial nationalism, as it helped gestate and circulate literature from the region.[9] Griffith describes the relationship between the radio show and *Bim* in particular as a "mutually beneficial" one, as *Bim* provided works for the program, "and the program, in turn, significantly increased the regional exposure" of its works (*The BBC* 21). Indeed, the short fiction works I examine in this chapter that were crucial to the development of what I call "local-regional" narrative in *Bim* were amplified by their broadcast on *Caribbean Voices*. The homegrown work of *Bim* that dovetailed with the radio show during this period demonstrates a foundational intertextual narrative evolution toward the regional and anticolonial discourse that would become typical of West Indian literature in decades to come.

A letter to Frank Collymore from George Lamming illustrates the importance of the magazine as homegrown infrastructure for incubating regional literature. Lamming served as an unofficial scout for *Bim* when he moved to Trinidad from Barbados in 1946, regularly sending Collymore recommendations of writers to publish. Because Trinidad had become by this time something of a literary hub for writers from various parts of the region, he shuttled a regional breadth of writerly representation into *Bim*. On June 1, 1949, in a letter to Frank Collymore, Lamming exclaimed that West Indian literature was "REALLY TAKING SHAPE!" His letter continued: "And I was dreaming of the day when BIM, by another name, would become a West Indian monthly with a paid editor, and whether you could attempt it after your resignation which, let us hope, isn't too far. Somehow I have such confidence and expectations where this magazine is concerned. One would think that I had something to do with its origin. But whatever happens, you must keep thinking of plans for the future. It seems to me that the editor of such a magazine through the organ itself does more for this community than all of the politicians put together" (Letters to Frank Collymore). Lamming's letter demonstrates his prescient understanding that West Indian literary production and literary culture were becoming observable realities and that *Bim* was integral to their prior, present, and future evolution. The letter also curiously indicates that the development of West Indian literature had a political significance, one that is observable beyond Collymore's own eschewing of politics.

What exactly did Collymore do with *Bim*, as an organ, for "this community" that all of the politicians had not been able to do? I asked Lamming a similar question, and he responded that the political significance of *Bim* had been its work to build community by featuring it (personal interview, June 2013). In other words, it is literary representation that may be of political consequence. Stuart Hall, whose early poetry was also published in *Bim*, has also argued for the sociopolitical function of aesthetic representation. According to Hall, "how things are represented and the 'machineries' and regimes of representation in a culture do play a *constitutive*, and not merely a reflexive, after-the-event, role" ("New Ethnicities" 443). In the margins of directly political discourse, I argue that *Bim* disseminated forms of local-regional representation that would constitute a West Indian imaginary.

Federating *Bim*

In 1945 the British Colonial Office first gathered newly elected representatives of their colonies in the Caribbean to solicit and gauge political interest in the West Indies Federation. Based on the interest garnered by this meeting, they went on to organize a foundational conference in 1947 at Montego Bay. This conference brought together the British secretary of state for the colonies and political representatives from all of the British Caribbean colonies to establish the future West Indies Federation as a colonial governing body with loose jurisdiction. It was not until 1958 that the plan would go into effect.[10] The changes precipitated by these early plans for federation nonetheless put structures into place that facilitated a "regionalist" imaginary, by which I mean that "West Indian" became a regional lens through which to perceive the location of self and community in relation to the world.

Bim dramatizes the tensions of a region in the making during this period of transition. Sonji Phillips has claimed about regionalism in *Bim* that it may "be considered a precipitating factor towards the federation of the region," for *Bim*'s own transition from a local to a regional publication indicated "that there was recognition at the non-political level of the need to come together, to blur the lines of narrowly nationalist concepts" (107–108). Even as I interrogate just how integral *Bim*'s pages were to fomenting a transnational regional vision toward sovereignty, I heed Gordon Lewis's cautionary suggestion that while it may be tempting to "see any regional body as *ipso facto*, proof" of West Indian consolidation, the primary concern expressed in the political discourse of this period was with the autonomy and singularity of each of the specific island and non-island territories implicated in the federation (368).

The tension embedded in the shift to regionalism becomes palpable in the introductory "Editors' Blarney" in *Bim* from December 1945.[11] The "blarney" begins by restating a question about the magazine's name recently received from a correspondent, referred to as "an Englishman": "Why Bim?" The editorial response to this question combines the insular, parochial perspective that initiated the magazine with a show of dismay over the obscurity of the Caribbean to English readers: "We mean . . . well, after all . . . we are aware that most Englishmen have very hazy ideas about the West Indies; but not to know that Bim is an inhabitant of Barbados, Little England, Bimshire!" (n.p.). This is the first moment that an editorial refers to *Bim*'s readership in England, and its ambivalence is striking. Instead of gushing over the fact of English readership—given that crossing the Atlantic to acquire such an audience is quite a feat for a little magazine—and instead of critiquing metropolitan ignorance of the West Indies, Collymore and Barnes submit that "the question was, we admit, a blow to our pride." They both register and poke fun at the kind of insular imaginary so attached to its place in the British Empire that it would denominate the island of Barbados as "Little England" or "Bimshire." The blarney thus suggests a colonial form of "double consciousness," to invoke W.E.B. Du Bois's concept for the doubling of the racialized self that results from internalizing the pejorative gaze of the other (2).[12] The emphasis on Barbados's invisibility to *Bim*'s readers in England deflates—at the same time that it announces—a form of imperial-insular identification, one that may not properly be considered nationalist, since its attachment to empire suggests relinquishing the national categories of sovereignty and independence. The editors' retort nonetheless implicitly disabuses *Bim*'s readers of the notion that Barbados might be located on the map of Englishness as it evinces their invisibility in the "deep, horizontal comradeship" comprising the imagined national community (Anderson, *Imagined Communities* 7).[13] Although residents of Barbados may imagine themselves as a distant part of England, the national gaze is unreturned to them.

As if to acknowledge that what ties Barbados to the rest of the West Indies is this very marginality from the British Empire's internal construction of itself as a nation, Collymore and Barnes continue by introducing the prospect of federation and juxtaposing it with a call for strengthening insular identity: "And so, to-day, when West Indian Federation looms hazily on the shifting background of world politics, we should like to take this opportunity to state our conviction that the preservation of our individuality must always be of paramount importance, and it is only by developing our inherent bimness to the utmost that we can hope to do our bit in the formation of a successful and vital commonwealth" ("Editors' Blarney" n.p.). Their ironic call for the "preservation" of "inherent bimness" is certainly evocative of nationalist discourse, but it remains tied to the imperial attachment the editors feign. It is also pitted against the rise of West Indian regionalism. *Bim*'s first note of editorial regionalism thereby arises in tension with a kind of imperial, insular identification close to but distinct from nationalism. At this time, what "West Indian" would go on to mean was in question. Regionalism was fraught between the colonial construction of the British territories in the Caribbean as the West Indies and the possibility of uniting the region for sovereignty through a renovation of these terms.

Indeed, the regional turn that took center stage in 1945 in the Anglophone Caribbean context indicates a transformation in geopolitical perspective toward a sense of the West Indies as existing in the world as a collective region, united if not by politics by the shared experiences of British colonialism and the legacy of the plantation. At this time, what "West Indian" meant was in question. Because what "West Indian" meant and would become in both political and aesthetic terms was undecided during this period, it emerges in *Bim* as a problematic rather than a resolution. By "problematic" I mean that "West Indian" is locatable in a set of "actual or potential position-takings" regarding the transition to regional unity in the British-colonized Caribbean (Bourdieu 30). Anticolonial critique is only one evolving modality of this regional turn, but *Bim*'s narrative corpus would progressively offer an intertextual pathway of regional feeling and anticolonial critique through which the transnational field of West Indian literature would proliferate in the decades that followed.

Bim before 1945: Evolving "West Indian Local" Genres

Because of the English domination of infrastructure for literary production, the promotion of the English literary canon through colonial education, and the tendency of the upper and middle classes to both dominate literary production and attach to Englishness, literature in the Caribbean colonies was institutionally tied to Englishness. As Ramchand elucidates what has become a guiding tenet of postcolonial literary studies, "For the [West Indian] student, literature has generally meant English Literature, which is set in a foreign country, which contains English characters and English situations and which, in many ways, is rooted in English life and manners" ("Introduction" 1). This aesthetic paradigm rendered the imagined English community as an elsewhere to which the colonies could attach themselves but never embody. The exportation of literary Englishness, combined with the imperial underdevelopment of infrastructures for cultural production in its Caribbean colonies, fueled what Mignolo would call "the narrative of modernity," interchangeably rendering the colonies invisible as sites from which to locate subjects and hypervisible as objects to be studied (*The Idea* 13–18).

Narrative location writing in *Bim* that I call "West Indian Local" writing thus evolved into a form that forged an epistemological break in the literary tradition of aesthetically naturalizing empire. Instead, narrative location writing in *Bim* potentiated the production of a West Indian imaginary. This form for short fiction that became a dominant tendency in *Bim* during the 1940s may be considered both "local" and "West Indian" because it emerges as explicitly local—responding to particular landscapes and social dynamics—and also resonates regionally beyond local contexts, throughout the British-colonial islands and territories in and around the Caribbean.[14] The settings for West Indian Local stories during the 1940s range from unnamed but recognizably West Indian locations to explicit references to several different West Indian locales beyond the shores of Barbados, including Dominica, Guyana, and Trinidad. Local writing would be encouraged by Collymore and Barnes in a *Bim* 4 (1944) editorial: "Above all, in writing, regard things from your own viewpoint and experience. Why worry to write about the rigours of the Alaskan winter when you can spend the month of February in St. Joseph's parish?" ("Editors' Comeback" n.p.). In this call for writers to bring their writing home, references to the United States may stand in for England as the improper and yet overdetermined site for the literary imagination of *Bim*'s early contributors. But the editors may also warn against rising U.S. influence in the region achieved between Hollywood and the military encroachment of the 1940 destroyers-for-bases deal, which authorized the United States to occupy military bases in the British colonized Caribbean.[15] The editors' stated aim is nonetheless to summon home those northern-bound literary imaginations. The editorial seems to have been effective, as stories set in Barbados and other parts of the West Indies would soon become the majority of those published in *Bim*.

As this mode of location writing evolved, what begins as a decidedly colonial literary corpus gives way to an increasingly anticolonial one. West Indian Local short fiction would develop intertextually in *Bim* primarily through three evolving genres. First, the "day in local life" story varies between distant and exoticist representations of Black characters using local dialect to social realist attempts to approximate the experiences of poor Afro-Caribbean and Indo-Caribbean characters. This strain of story takes for granted the way that colonial subjects of African and South Asian descent in the British-colonized Caribbean became classified as "native," ideologically cloaking their histories and class positions in colonial society and obfuscating Indigenous communities. Second, the "Creole colonial" story primarily features the experiences of the white Creole upper and middle class. In some instances, this variation featured references to Black characters either in nearby villages or as servants. Third, the "inter-Caribbean travel narrative" consists of residents of one part of the Caribbean relating experiences of travel to other parts of the region.[16] These narrative tendencies gradually evolve toward deeper engagements with local settings and landscape, increasingly including critiques of colonial society and ideologies.

At first, the majority of short fiction produced in *Bim* was poised to contribute to the objectification of the colonized so-called native class and women at large. Although a men's club published *Bim* in the early years, by its second issue women authors were also included in the magazine and would continue to contribute to it regularly; the most objectifying narratives were those penned by a small cadre of white Creole men. Several early instances of the "day in local life" stories feature hyperbolic forms of violence between Black women, for example. W. Therold Barnes's story "Do Fuh Do" (*Bim* 2) is prototypical of the most colonial-cum-sexist persuasion of this narrative genre. The story features local dialect and Black working-class life. Although the conflict staged in the story is between two Black male carpenters, one significantly younger than the other, the climax of the story occurs when their wives erupt into an unexpected physical fight. The "do fuh do" kind of narrative replete with derogatory portrayals of Black people would fall out of *Bim* as both the aesthetic quality and the politics of the genre evolved. By *Bim* 3 (1943) Ursula Walcott's story "The Theatre Tickets," stands out for using humor and dialect in its depiction of an older Black couple without actually making fun of them or exoticizing them. The Creole colonial genre also features condescending portrayals and views of women from the Creole colonial classes, as suggested by the title of a story from *Bim* 1, "Women Never Listen."[17] This West Indian Local genre tended to present the white Creole subjects as distant from the local working class. In one of the most developed scenarios of interracial interaction of this narrative genre—in Collymore's story "The Snag" (*Bim* 2)—the young white protagonist befriends the Black servant at his aunts' home. One of the most intriguing variants of the early Creole colonial genre was the ghost story. These early ghost stories open up to reading the Creole elite's haunting by colonial guilt.

Jan Williams's powerful lead story for *Bim* 3 (1943) "The Shilling" effects a powerful transformation in *Bim*'s West Indian Local narrative trajectory. It seems to have hushed the literary violence against the local working class and women of all classes in *Bim*. After *Bim* 3, the stories that appear in the magazine do not include the racist and sexist condescension present in the first three issues, and I offer the hypothesis that Williams's story demands precisely the shift that ensued and may have significantly influenced the future flow of narrative written and chosen for the magazine. Her story effects a fusion of the Creole colonial genre with the day-in-local-life genre and a critical encounter between the privileged Creole class and the local working class. In spite of how influential her early stories appear to have been for the narrative contours of *Bim*, Jan Williams has received scant attention in West Indian literary history. Collymore refers to her as an Englishwoman living in Barbados "who gave unstinted help to the magazine" (Baugh, "Introduction" 11). No record exists of her having published any books or larger bodies of work, and her short stories remain largely unknown with the exception of the story "Arise My Love," which can be found in Andrew Salkey's anthology *West Indian Stories* and in Campbell and Frickey's *The Whistling Bird*. As a woman—and an English-identified one—in a literary record that has primarily privileged works by men and writing that constructs local identity from the authority of "local" experience, Jan Williams has remained overlooked.[18]

Williams's first story for *Bim*, "The Shilling," inaugurates the critique of colonial society for *Bim*'s narrative corpus. The story features a serious—and finally tragic—series of encounters between a white middle-class woman with a Black poor woman. Narrated from the middle-class white woman's perspective, it begins by setting up a distant yet somehow attached gaze on an elderly Black woman whom the narrator passes regularly on her way to work: "And I always made myself 'see' her and grew to look for her . . . even loved her a little, in a secret, dispassionate kind of way, that had nothing to do with my life" (1). The story shifts upon an encounter between the two women. The elderly Black woman approaches her—for the first time—and unexpectedly asks for spare change. The request opens up for the narrator a self-reflexive critique of the colonial status quo: "Why don't we do something? We rant and rave, sermonise and theorise all the time. 'These things should not be. They should be thus and thus.' We say, yet we do nothing, nothing at all. We talk yet give up nothing" (2). Although this self-reflexive moment is nowhere near a full-fledged critique of the colonial situation or postslavery society, it is by far the most colonial-critical moment to appear in *Bim* in its first three issues. Williams's narrator has not yet become the "colonizer who refuses," whom Albert Memmi considered a constitutive contradiction in the colonies (19–34). In Memmi's terms she would, however, be renouncing a part of herself and what she has become in accepting life in a colony as one who "participates in and benefits from those privileges" that she also "half-heartedly denounces" (20). As Williams's narrator puts it herself, "We talk yet give up nothing." For Memmi, in order to truly refuse to colonize is to leave the colony by "ceasing to be a colonizer" (44). Importantly, however, Williams's story defies the masculinism of Memmi's work that presumes that the colonizer-colonized relationship was lived between men.[19]

After giving the elderly woman the one shilling in her possession, Williams's narrator departs immediately, unable to bear a thank-you, and offers to the reader her approximation of the other woman's perspective: "She couldn't really like me and my kind. We stood for something antipathetic" (2). The narrator thus internalizes the Black woman's gaze and maledicts the revolting status quo that would elevate her own life as stable and independent and relegate her interlocutor's life to economic instability and dependence. Roberto Schwarz, in the context of Brazil, has demonstrated how the postslavery economy hides the coercive relations of production through an economy of the favor in which the "free" poor depend on favors from the wealthy for their survival (22). In Jan Williams's narrative when the elderly Black woman asks for money, the violence of her dependence on favors from the "antipathetic" white colonial class becomes visible to the narrator—and to a certain extent to the reader—as endemic to the entire system of (imperial) racial capitalism.

The story is short and stands alone in its social realist seriousness in *Bim* 3 but nonetheless provides a crucial rupture in the casual joviality and occasional fright that marked most of the stories that preceded or accompanied it. Not only does it deeply indict members of the white colonial class appearing carefree in prior stories for their antipathy toward the Black working class, it also offers a serious portrait of a politically engaged white woman and a serious portrayal of a Black woman seeking survival. This hybrid narrative, read in dialogue with previous Creole colonial and day-in-local-life stories unhinges the frivolity and absurdly violent portrayals of white and Black women in previous stories.

"The Shilling" seems to serves as a conscience of sorts for *Bim*, for violence against women, rhetorical or otherwise, along with brutal depictions of Black women fighting each other would fall out of its subsequent pages. Although Collymore did not—and likely could not, given his position as editor and schoolteacher in a colony—call for his contributors to write like Williams or even to write critically about colonial life, "The Shilling" was an influential example of what West Indian Local narrative could—and indeed would—become. As *Bim* progressed, all three narrative genres of West Indian Local narrative became richer and increasingly pushed at the seams of colonial ideology.

1945: Landscape Writing and the West Indian Local

Bim 5 (February 1945) presented yet another shift in the writing of the West Indian Local. Several narratives it carried confront colonial ideology and the material circumstances of racially hierarchized colonial society in deeply engaging ways. Two of these in particular inaugurate a way of narrating local-regional landscapes that extended the social and political capacity of West Indian Local narrative. These texts are the first two of *Bim* 5: "The White Dress," a short story by Jan Williams, and "Of Casuarinas and Cliffs," a personal essay by Edgar Mittelholzer. Each piece further develops the West Indian Local through problem-posing narratives that critically interrogate colonial society in Barbados. Central to the sociopolitical and anticolonial critique embedded in these texts is the way they narrate the relationship between landscape and subjectivity.

As sovereignty over land is precisely what is withheld from the subjects of a colony, figurative forms of investigating the relationship between a colonial subject and the land make for recurrent motifs in anticolonial literature. These motifs are difficult to extract from the colonial tradition of reducing conquered territories to the beauty of their landscapes, as discussed in chapter 2 in light of Suzanne Césaire's interrogation of the terms of Caribbean visibility in "The Great Camouflage." Donnell has also observed in the context of Anglophone writers of the Caribbean that "the project of literary decolonisation has been very much involved with developing a language through which to name, affirm and cherish the beauty and sustenance that is found in a Caribbean landscape," a task that is "quite hard to achieve without seeming to accrue those rhetorical structures that romanticise or sentimentalise the Caribbean within a eurocentric frame" (*Twentieth-Century Caribbean Literature* 58). Even the practice of reclaiming territory from Europe in language has been burdened by European modes of rhetorically capturing the Caribbean's beauty. What is particularly exciting about the ways that both Jan Williams and Edgar Mittelholzer *landscaped* their texts is that they went so far as to problematize the very possibility of subjectively relating to land, or, in other words, the very possibility of landscape.

Landscape—as a possibility—requires a subjective experience of and intervention in land. The word "landscape" has both noun and verb forms, and even as an object of observation, a landscape is already the result of an action upon land—representing it, modifying it, even observing it. Landscape is thus either produced or the product of action, requiring an agent in order to exist. In the history of its usage in English, "landscape," as an aesthetic representation of land, predates the use of "landscape" as a scene or in nature. In other words, in the English history of the landscape, the art of landscaping precedes the fact of a landscape ("Landscape"). Even this later form of "landscape," however, does not exist on its own—it must be called into being by an observer, by a subject that modifies and is modified by observing a particular "scape" of land.

The constructive agency involved in the landscape is appropriately akin to the constructive literary locating that landscaping texts participate in. As I argue throughout this book, to literarily locate a text is not the work of affiliating a text to an extant setting but rather that of offering how that setting will continue to be imagined by readers as well as negotiating the terms through which that setting, and by extension the literature it locates, will be valued. The landscaping narratives Williams and Mittelholzer contributed to *Bim* in 1945 did much more than infuse their stories with landscape as "local color." Like Suzanne Césaire's anticolonial landscaping work published the very same year in *Tropiques*, they offer a critical view of an embattled landscape imbued with both beauty and struggle.

Jan Williams, whose anticolonial bent is already present in "The Shilling," becomes a literary landscaper in her 1945 story "The White Dress." This story, along with Karl Sealy's "Money to Burn," published in the same issue, transformed the day-in-local-life variation of West Indian Local narrative into social realist portrayals of the effects of local poverty. Like previous stories in that vein, these two utilize local dialect but not in order to tell light, humorous tales; instead, they tell tragic stories that demand an emotional encounter with the difficulty of poverty. In this sense their works, along with those by Mittelholzer, Sam Selvon, Ursula Walcott, and Collymore published in the first decade of *Bim*'s run, innovate in the social realist mode that by 1970 were considered to predominate in the West Indian novel (Ramchand, *The West Indian Novel* 43).[20] "The White Dress" in particular portrays a subjective experience of landscape, which I seek to draw attention to as a formative practice of anticolonial narrative in the Caribbean also exercised by the second piece of *Bim* 5, the essay "Of Casuarinas and Cliffs" by Edgar Mittelholzer. The essay narrates in the third person the perspective of a young, poor, Black girl in Barbados, Nicey. Nicey wishes to own a pretty—and white—dress, and her wish is only fulfilled tragically upon her accidental death while working instead of attending school. Throughout Williams's story, she emphasizes class-racial difference by contrasting Black / poor and white / wealthy ways of relating to landscape. The relationship the story establishes between local landscape and the socioracial divide of colonial society resists both exoticizing Caribbean landscape and naturalizing socioracial divisions present in earlier Creole colonial and day-in-local-life narratives.

The problematic of the story is set up by establishing a poignant relationship between the emblematic trees of Barbados that Mittelholzer also explores in "Of Casuarinas and Cliffs," the casuarinas. Nicey, the story's protagonist, watches the wealthy, white schoolgirls walk home from high school and envies their pretty dresses. As they recede into the distance, her vision transforms while she observes them and the casuarinas past which they walk: "Her eyes took on an old, hard look as she watched them disappear around the bend in the road where the casuarinas stood, tall and impassive, their green hair swinging in the wind" (3). The casuarinas, "tall and impassive," function in this image like a border between the two classes of girls. Nicey's gaze transforms and ages as she takes stock of the distance that separates her from these girls who, unlike her, have the privilege to "go home from school to a nice, clean house, with no work to do and no water to carry, and have a servant bring your food and go to the sea for a bathe and listen to the radio and change into a pretty dress instead of an old one at the end of the day" (2). In this image, the casuarinas, as synecdoche, naturalize the divide between these two classes of girls, between those who go to school and have servants and those who, like Nicey, do their own housework and also work in the fields. The casuarinas are adornments for one class, but for the other they function as a border. In fact, the casuarina tree is not, like racially divided colonial postslavery society, endemic to Barbados. As a transplanted or "invasion" species in the area, brought there as part of British colonial administration, it is a particularly appropriate symbol for the production of landscape for the enjoyment of the ruling class.

After her first day of work tilling fields, Nicey has a dream that paints a vivid picture of her relationship to land: "she dreamed she was in the field working, chopping out the weeds with the heavy hoe but as fast as she hacked them out they grew again. She woke up stiff and weary" (49). The dream evokes Nicey's nightmarish relationship to the land as a laborer. She does not have a sublimely enriching experience of the island's landscape. To the contrary, as the cutter of weeds that interminably return, she dreams herself a Sisyphus figure whose absurd experience of both poverty and labor is to fight a never-ending battle *against* nature—as tiller and not observer of the fields.[21] Williams's focus on Nicey's subjective experience of land thus complicates the idea of the island as paradise, one that excludes the poor and Black colonial subjects who till the land. Those who, like Nicey, toil endlessly to keep the landscape free of weeds so that rich and white colonials may profit from it and relate to it as adornment do not have the time or leisure to become those who enjoy it.

Mittelholzer's "Of Casuarinas and Cliffs" further extends the significance of landscape in the narrative production of the West Indies. *Bim* 5 inaugurated what would become his regular contributions to the magazine with two pieces, the essay "Of Casuarinas and Cliffs" and the short story "Miss Clarke Is Dying." From then on until his death in 1965, he was to contribute at least one piece to every issue of *Bim*. As such, along with Collymore, Mittelholzer was the author whose works were most circulated among *Bim*'s readership. He is associated in literary history with the group of novelists of the post-1948 Caribbean literary boom—also including Naipaul, Lamming, and Selvon—since most of his novels were published after that date. Mittelholzer was, however, the forerunner of this group, the first of them to have a novel published in London well before 1948. Many years before he ever set foot in London, Mittelholzer's novel *Corentyne Thunder* was published there in 1941 by Eyre and Spottiswoode Press. Before this date, as Juanita Cox mentions in her introduction to a later edition of the novel, only three novels written by West Indians had previously been published in London: *Jane's Career* by H. G. De Lisser (1914), *Pitch Lake* by Alfred Mendes (1934), and *Minty Alley* by C.L.R. James (1936) (5). Mittelholzer was also a trailblazer in the region for becoming, among the writers of the period, the first professional writer, which is to say the first writer to dedicate himself entirely to the craft of literature. As Lamming gushed in *The Pleasures of Exile*, Mittelholzer "refused to take any permanent employment" while he lived in Trinidad; his wife held a job while he did the housework and shopping, "leaving himself some seven or eight hours a day for writing" (40). It seems that neither Mittelholzer nor his wife were afraid to break with gendered conventions for the sake of literature.

In the same way that both of Williams's stories discussed above transformed the Creole colonial and day-in-local-life genres of West Indian Local narrative in *Bim*, Mittelholzer's essay "Of Casuarinas and Cliffs" transformed the inter-Caribbean travel genre. As an essay, it is generically different from the two travel narratives published in prior numbers: "Dominica Trek" by Dick Stokes (*Bim* 2, April 1943) describes a hike taken by the narrator and his wife on the island of Dominica, and "Pages from a Diary" by E. Gomier (*Bim* 4, April 1944) consists of diary entries from a voyage by ship taken through and around several islands including Martinique, Dominica, and St. Lucia. These prior travel pieces mainly consist of descriptions of travel activities, with very limited portrayals of human or landscape encounters. They are also not grounded in any kind of an argument, nor do they defend any position. A similarly descriptive travel narrative would appear two years after "Of Casuarinas and Cliffs," Jim Green's "Barbados Holiday" (*Bim* 7, 1946), which relates the experience of leisure travel to Barbados from Trinidad.

In contradistinction, Mittelholzer's text, while primarily narrative in its structure, is a personal essay that delivers an argument while relating personal experience. It is further unique as a narrative of inter-Caribbean travel for *Bim* in this period, as it advances an anticolonial position. An account of Mittelholzer's travels from Guyana (then British Guiana) to Barbados, the essay constructs the landscape of the island as worthy of aesthetic representation—against the colonial view of its unsuitability for art—and interrogates the writer's own subjective experience of engaging with that landscape.

Landscaping has been a central activity of Mittelholzer's writing career. J. Dillon Brown notes about Mittelholzer's novels that they display a "fascination with place and landscape" (44). Guyanese poet and editor of *Kyk-over-al* A. J. Seymour also depicts Mittelholzer's literary legacy in terms of landscaping, describing his work as containing "a literary landscape map of Guyana that we can speak of" (20). Mittelholzer's project of fictional landscaping was crucial to his first novel, *Corentyne Thunder*, set on the personified Corentyne Coast of Guyana. Juanita Cox argues that Mittelholzer's landscaping of the Corentyne Coast in this novel is in dialogue with Beethoven's *Pastoral Symphony*. Her argument dovetails well with Mittelholzer's aim in "Of Casuarinas and Cliffs," for she claims that in his dialogue with Beethoven "Mittelholzer aimed to demonstrate that British Guiana was a legitimate territory for sophisticated fiction" (15). Similarly, in "Of Casuarinas and Cliffs," what is most important about the Barbados-set landscape it produces is its aesthetic worthiness.

Mittelholzer's text in question explicitly sets out to disprove the thesis that "there's just nothing in Barbados to paint" (6). He both disputes this view and constructs a defiant structure of feeling to counter the colonialist air of desolation negating the aesthetic worthiness of the island. In his rebuttal, Mittelholzer first turns to the already-canonical impressionist painter Edgar Degas. As he narrates his personal experience as a traveler to Barbados from Guyana, he remarks about seeing the island from the plane, "I said to myself that this might have been a pattern done in pastel by Degas." He does not turn to a painter of "exotic" landscapes or scenes to authorize the paintable beauty of Barbados's landscape—such as Gauguin, the impressionist painter of Tahiti. Instead Mittelholzer brings up Degas, who is most associated with paintings of dancers but also painted rural landscapes set in France from a distance comparable to that of the small plane in which Mittelholzer would have traveled. In my reading, rather than indicate that Barbados would be painted so well by a European such as Degas, Mittelholzer suggests that Barbados could have its own landscape painter like Degas. Mittelholzer thus reflects, "I thought that the difficulty of a painter would be not to find something to paint but to wonder what to paint first" (6). This view dialogues directly with Collymore's plea in the previous issue of *Bim* for writers to narrate their own experiences and perspectives. Framing his travel narrative with this polemical reflection renders Mittelholzer's piece an example of Collymore's vision for works that feature local settings and experiences.

"Of Casuarinas and Cliffs" highlights and combats one of the greatest obstacles taken on by *Bim*: the ideological foreclosure of the region from the realm of art. As Lamming articulates this problem, the colonial middle class in the West Indies seemed to have been educated "for the specific purpose of sneering at anything which grew or was made on native soil" (*The Pleasures* 40).[22] In Lamming's view, the problem of presumed colonial inferiority would drive Anglophone writers out of the West Indies to London.

Mittelholzer constructs quite the landscape as a rebuttal to this view in "Of Casuarinas and Cliffs." For his model literary landscape, he narrates the experience of phenomena specific to Barbados's northwest coast around the town of Bathsheba: casuarina trees, cliffs against the ocean, and large rocks that line the coast. His descriptions do not fix any of the landscape images he sees into one singular—authoritative—perspective; instead, he provides many ways of perceiving (and thereby bringing into being) literary landscapes. The multiplicity of angles he provides de-authorizes his own view so that the account becomes less about a way of defining or representing the land and more about the possibility of subjectively relating to and aestheticizing the landscape. In one landscape in particular, Mittelholzer explores the subjective experience of relating to the rocks that border the coastline, significantly shifting the "blasé desperation" the piece begins with into a complex, affective proposition for relating to a beautiful *and* colonized zone. As he describes the rocks, "You cannot help admiring them. Watching them sometimes, you feel a little belligerent, a little heroic. 'I', you tell yourself, 'might be a general, and out there—ranged all along out there—are my invincible forts defying the enemy. Perhaps losing by inches—crumbling imperceptibly. But fighting. Grimly. Giving back crashing blow for crashing blow. Stopping them'" (53). Although this is a travel essay set up to illustrate the artistic potential of Barbados's landscape, in this image Mittelholzer infuses his observations of the landscape with a fantasy of warfare—in a catachresis that turns the ocean into the stronger, overwhelming, and persistent enemy.[23] Importantly, the self-reflexivity of the image brings the reader in as a possible version of the "I," a possible participant in this fantasy of commanding the rocks as the general of a defiant army against a more powerful enemy. There is a defiant subject offered in this image, a subject of insurgent warfare who is also deeply engaged with a landscape that has been marginalized from not only landscape painting but also the realm of literature. As Brathwaite would describe the context in which such a literary intervention occurred in *History of the Voice*, "And in terms of what we write, our perpetual models, we are more conscious . . . of the falling snow . . . than of the force of the hurricanes which take place each year" (8). Foreign landscapes were the subject of the extant literary models on which the writers of this period primarily depended. Mittelholzer's piece is a bold intervention in those models, one that uses them in order to establish a literary vernacular we might call "local-regional" for literarily landscaping the Caribbean.

Mittelholzer's landscape indexes colonial history only indirectly, as it is the missing link between the landscape he constructs and the battle into which he literarily transforms that landscape.[24] His self-doubting, vanquished-and-defiant subject-in-relation to an embattled landscape seems to affectively interrogate the devastating consequences of history on the colonized individual.[25] Later writers of the future West Indian canon who would continue to develop the genre of the anticolonial travel essay exemplified by "Of Casuarinas and Cliffs" would more explicitly interrogate the historical dimensions of embattled landscape.[26]

The end of Mittelholzer's piece returns to the frame thesis that there is nothing in Barbados to paint and takes it on another way, relating it to the character of Barbados vis-à-vis England and the West Indies. He repeats the painter's claim "There's just nothing in Barbados to paint" and responds to it a new way: "Perhaps not. So much depends on what we are looking for to paint" (55). As if the regional character of Barbados were somehow associated with whether or not it is paintable, he continues: "There are some people who say that Barbados is too much like England and too little like Barbados to be typically West Indian." Although Mittelholzer does not indicate what it is that relates Barbados' paintability to its national or regional character, the statement implies a link between aesthetic engagement and cultural and political identity. The statement also evokes a Barbados that somehow barely exists, as if it had to become "itself" somehow, as if aesthetic engagement played a role in this becoming. Mittelholzer does not resolve the tension he raises about Barbados's national or regional identity but instead concludes by pointing out, "For me, however, I have no argument to brew. I'm content that, paintable or not, English or truly West Indian in spirit, the island (as you might have observed) did give me a little to write about" (55). With this ending, Mittelholzer preserves to some extent an ambiguity about what kind of battle his imagined general leads the rocks that border the island into with the ocean: for or against England? The ambiguity offers precisely the tension Barbados lived at this time, of an island torn between an exceptionalist territorial identification-cum-loyalty to its colonizing country and a fomenting West Indian regionalism. In suggesting, however ironically, that those who deny Barbados's West Indian spirit deny its very selfhood, Mittelholzer implies on the one hand the facticity of West Indian regional identity and on the other Barbados's need to become itself, presumably through the locating aesthetic work of landscape fictions such as these.

In both Mittelholzer's and Williams's West Indian Local narratives, the subjective experience of relating to a landscape each writer constructs as troubled hovers around an affective disposition to that landscape—belligerence in Mittelholzer and weariness in Williams. In Mittelholzer's personal essay, he performs his belligerence as a tragic but heroic persistence. Williams's Nicey displays no such belligerence, only a dream's awareness of the persistent struggle for survival that leaves no lasting product—the endless struggle of alienated labor. The images of landscape produced in each narrative are strikingly similar—waves crashing ceaselessly and weeds growing endlessly—but the affects associated with the images differ on the basis of the social position of the subjects involved in them. In both cases, the subjective experience of landscape has social implications that bear on the anticolonial critiques of both texts and inflect the development of West Indian Local narrative practice. Both Williams and Mittelholzer extend the depth and complexity of West Indian Local narrative by employing strategies that are at once highly literary and acutely sociopolitical in character. As regional thinking entered the political imagination of the period, their narrative practices expanded the scope and depth of an evolving literature, turning local-regional narrative practice toward the task of critically examining the problems posed by the socioracial division of colonial society as well as the phantom of colonial ideology looming over local aesthetic production in the region.

West Indian Local narrative would continue to evolve in *Bim*, even though its editorials would not take stock of the changes for the next three issues. Stories published between 1946 and 1948 take place in Barbados, Trinidad, Guyana, Dominica, and Grenada. They also shift by more broadly representing the ethnic range of the region by including local characters of Indian and Chinese origins in addition to those of European and African descent. Over one year after the 1947 Montego Bay Conference establishing the West Indies Federation, the editorial of *Bim* 9 (December 1948) melancholically assumes the fact of West Indian regionalism and its imbrication in it. In the "Foreword" to that issue, the editors feign-lament the periodical's regionalizing transformation before adapting to it without comment in the issues that followed. This "Foreword" thus gives the magazine's insular identity its last word before the next issue's gesture that decisively relinquishes it: "But, alas, we are losing our insular self-sufficiency.

A glance at the contents of this volume will discover the names of many contributors who dwell beyond these shores, . . . Yet, despite this great blow to our pride, we take very great pleasure in introducing to our readers a group of five writers from Trinidad" (Collymore and Barnes, "Foreword" n.p.).

This demonstration of melancholy resistance to regionalism echoes Collymore and Barnes's earlier "Editors' Blarney" that announces a blow to insular pride due to English misrecognition of the island's own English-like identity as "Bimshire." Neither welcoming *Bim*'s own regional outlook nor lamenting it in earnest, this later editorial registers instead an ambivalent attitude toward the magazine's regional turn.[27]

West Indian at the Brink: George Lamming's First Short Story

The ambivalence embedded in the new West Indian regional feeling emerges prominently in George Lamming's first published short story featured in *Bim* 9 (December 1948). A peculiar experiment occurs in this story, one we might see as the climax of West Indian Local narrative in 1940s *Bim*. In this story, Lamming explicitly regionalizes a critical view of colonial society and presages the changes that accrue in the region from World War II and the resulting U.S. occupation of many territories of the British-colonized Caribbean.

When Lamming's first story came out, he had already published several poems in *Bim* and the British magazine *Life and Letters* and also broadcasted poems on the BBC radio show *Caribbean Voices*.[28] The story "Birds of Feather" was, however, his first published foray into narrative form.[29] In the following issue of *Bim* (June 1949) he would publish one other story, "Of Thorns and Thistles." In *Bim* 15 (December 1951) he would also contribute "Birthday Weather," an early version of the introductory episode of his first novel, *In the Castle of My Skin* (published in London in 1953 by Michael Joseph Press). After his move to London in 1950, Lamming would also go on to publish several novels and essays and become one of the most visible figures of the post-1948 West Indian literary boom.

The story "Birds of a Feather" stages a conflict that sheds light on both the colonial status quo of the West Indies and its transformation-in-progress during the postwar years. Told from the perspective of a self-declared "native," it fits the day-in-local-life story category but differs from most of these by omitting local dialect and using standard English instead. It also differs because its main conflict emerges from time spent in a typical setting for a Creole colonial story. The story therefore functions as a hybrid between these two narrative strains. Its plot is structured by a clash of perspectives that escalates into a physical fight. The main conflict of the story occurs at a party the narrator, Joe, attends that is hosted by a family called the "the Flennings." He is escorted to the party with friends of his who are U.S. soldiers, named Dalton and Hendrickson, from the local U.S. naval base where the narrator holds a job. At the party one of the soldiers fights with a man, whom the narrator calls "the West Indian." Because of the fight, the soldiers and the narrator end up locked up in a jail cell for the night, after which the soldiers are transferred from the local base back to New Jersey. Typical to Lamming's modernist narrative practice, these episodes are not relayed by the narrator in sequential order.[30] The narrative is divided into seven sections, beginning in the sequential middle, which is set, significantly, in a jail cell. It moves from the jail cell into a flashback of the confusing set of events at the party that led to Joe's imprisonment with the two soldiers, returns briefly to the jail cell, and then flashes forward to the days that proceeded from the imprisonment, culminating in a car crash.

Local setting is furthermore never mentioned directly in the story. The narrator describes "West Indian society" in it, and the presence of U.S. soldiers and a U.S. army base narrows down the story's location to anywhere in the British-ruled Caribbean where U.S. army bases were located during and in the aftermath of World War II, but the story's critique of the British colonial experience extends beyond the sites of the U.S. bases, binding together the British-colonized region even beyond the U.S.-occupied sites.[31] Lamming includes references to Port of Spain, where he resided at the time, such as the Balalaika bar, famous in the city for hosting soldiers and locals during this period, but only readers already familiar with references such as these would catch them. The overwhelming location-effect of this piece, then, is to evoke an experience that is at once local and regional.

Throughout the story the narrator juxtaposes his own perspective, that of his soldier friends from the base, and that of "the West Indian" from the fight who functions as an archetype of the ruling colonial order. In this juxtaposition of perspectives / subject positions, I argue that "the West Indian," as a category or impersonal subject position, becomes readable as what Lamming would later call the "colonial structure of awareness" of the West Indies (*The Pleasures* 36).

Lamming's use of the term "the West Indian" is curious. In the previous issue of *Bim*, W. Therold Barnes's short story "War Memorial" critiques an aspect of what Lamming would have called "the West Indian way of seeing" when Barnes hones in on an elite local woman's repudiation of a sculptor chosen for a war memorial simply on the basis of his being "West Indian." In lieu of a West Indian sculptor, the woman wanted "someone who is someone" to make the memorial (3–4). In this story, Barnes distills the social climate that Mittelholzer had also critiqued to a basic point: the a priori disqualification of people in the region from the realm of art and, by extension, of noteworthy personhood. Lamming's own use of "the West Indian" in "Birds of a Feather" intertextually pushes Barnes's critique, for it is not the disqualified artist he modifies with the regional signifier but rather the elite subject who would disqualify such an artist. In this sense, it is the colonially produced repudiation of West Indianness that Lamming names regionally.

In his study of Lamming's early novels, Gikandi poses a question that is particularly pertinent to this earlier story: "But how does a condition of estrangement engender narrative as the form that liberates the subject from the prison-house of colonialism?" (*Writing* 71). This particular story seems to address that question directly as it begins in a prison house, where the narrator ends up because of a breach of colonial social norms, a prison house that may very well signify the colonial subject's imprisonment by colonial society. In Gikandi's reading of Lamming's narrative practice, he accounts for the ways that Lamming's later location in London, estranged from the West Indies, becomes a particularly useful vantage point for this kind of narration, characterizing his displacement as "a strategic narrative possibility that allows the writer to deconstruct the colonial vision" (72). The narrative voice of "Birds of a Feather," although it was produced before Lamming's relocation to London, is also an estranged voice that critically dismantles what Gikandi calls colonial vision. The narrator is both at "home" in the setting of the story, deeply understanding the colonial social structures in place there and estranged by the circumstances of conflict and imprisonment that fuel the narrative. The story's critique of colonial vision also relies on the further estranged vantage point of the soldiers. Physical distance from the West Indies does not seem to be a requirement for Lamming's narrative estrangement; instead, estrangement is a narrative strategy he employs for unhoming, or rendering strange, the otherwise familiar structures of colonial power. It is important, however, that this story that circulated throughout the English-speaking Caribbean was produced by a writer from Barbados living in Trinidad; Lamming's ability to make the leap from a local view of colonial social dynamics to a regionalizing one may very well depend on his own inter-Caribbean travel, which permits him the comparative appraisal of colonial dynamics in both Barbados and Trinidad. In a central passage of "Birds of a Feather," the narrator reflects on the divide between his own access to colonial vision and the U.S. soldiers' ignorance of it:

> There were people whom I had always been taught to regard as different from the sweltering mass of my countrymen. Either by heritage or some other device of nature they were marked as symbols of a certain way of living; and they set the standards by which those in lower layers of society were judged. Such were the Flennings. It wasn't unnatural therefore that I should feel uneasy in accompanying Dalton and Hendrickson to their party. Moreover it must have been the cry on every lip . . . that I had found my way into company to which my calling and station of life could not grant me access. I knew it and I felt it very keenly. Dalton and Hendrickson didn't. And Americans were quite unman-

ageable when they were caught in a situation which, no matter how serious in its impact, made no impression on their minds. (33)

Joe sees those at the party seeing him as a disruption to the social order, and he sees the U.S. soldiers not seeing the impact of his presence on the rest of the party. Joe is disturbed as he notes his presence shifting the mood of the party and the disdain the partygoers emit toward him and his companions. The tension he senses escapes Dalton and Hendrickson, as it is only perceptible to those trained to see it by the colonial structure that disciplines their lives. The soldiers' disregard for the rules of this colonial society foils the colonial way of seeing in which these unspoken rules are observed. In Lamming's narration, the social order disrupted by Joe's presence becomes destabilized for the reader by both the soldiers' oblivion and the elision of distinct racial categories to differentiate the colonial elite represented by the Flennings and the mass of countrymen in the "lower layers of society" to which Joe belongs.

The violence of the colonial social order is presented in the story as a problem of class—and not racial—division. In Lamming's 1983 introduction to his first novel *In the Castle of My Skin*, he critiques this very kind of attention to social status that elides the racialization of colonial power, asserting "a false preoccupation with social status seduces the Black West Indian into wishing the racial component away" (xliii). In the same introduction to the later novel, Lamming offers what may be considered a rewrite of his first narrator's critique of West Indian colonial society. In this rendition he accounts for the effects of plantation slavery and the persisting racial structure of power on the Black majority in the West Indies: "The result was a fractured consciousness, a deep split in its sensibility which now raised difficult problems of language and values; the whole issue of cultural allegiance between the imposed norms of White Power, represented by a small numerical minority, and the fragmented memory of the African masses: between White instruction and Black imagination. The totalitarian demands of White supremacy, in a British colony, the psychological injury inflicted by the sacred rule that all forms of social status would be determined by the degrees of skin complexion" ("Introduction" xxxvii). The reflection from "Birds of a Feather" neglects to mention the way that skin color divides the elite from the "sweltering mass" of the narrator's "countrymen" and ignores the fact of African heritage. Lamming's later reflection, by comparison, seems to translate Joe's education into the terms of "White Power," "White instruction," and "White supremacy" of a British colony. The only self-aware element of the first passage that is metadiscursively clarified by the second is "the psychological injury inflicted by the sacred rule." Even the content of "sacred" colonial rule, "that all forms of social status would be determined by the degrees of skin complexion," remains obscure, or beyond the line of sight of Lamming's first narrator.

The narrator of "Birds of a Feather" does not even pretend to have a clear sense of the context or the fight that ensues, and his uncertainty drives the story. The fight occurs between the soldier named Dalton and the "West Indian," who is later revealed to have a name, Dickson. Interestingly, Dalton is an Irish surname and Dickson a Scottish one, though the origin of their names is not mentioned in the story. In the context of their fight, Dalton is the "American" and Dickson the "West Indian"; these are the impersonal positions they occupy in conflict even if there is an irony implied in the colonial histories indexed by their personal names. Dalton wins the fight with the aid of an empty bottle, but Dickson makes the final move, colonial power on his side, landing Dalton—along with Hendrickson and Joe—in prison. As the narrative jumps from the fight scene back to the jail, the narrator attests to the psychic fragmentation the events of the party inspired, concluding that he suffered "a vague feeling of dehumanisation" (34). The narrative, which begins in the disorientation of the prison house, returns to that disorientation after relaying the fight scene, settling there into the narrator's disconnected memories of the fight and the "vague dehumanisation" of imprisonment. In this second moment of narrating imprisonment, the narrator contemplates the U.S. Americans, their privilege over him, and their danger to him as well as the threat they seemed to pose to the colonial elite.

The soldiers, in their unwitting challenge of colonial social norms, function in this story as a narrative device disrupting the colonial gaze. This function may seem odd from a macropolitical perspective, since this is the period in which U.S. imperial hegemony transitioned into the place that was previously occupied by the British. But the story marks the ambivalence with which the U.S. army was received in the British-colonized region and the reality of its transformative impact on the colonial social order. Michael Anthony has suggested that in the town of Port of Spain where the story is implicitly suggested to be set, the presence of the United States forces in Trinidad caused "the social climate" that existed in the town to pass "away for all times" (73). The social shifts caused by the soldiers, in his analysis, resulted primarily from the higher wages offered by the U.S. army on its bases, which drew many Trinidadians, like the story's own "Joe," to seek work on the base (74–75). The market opened up by the presence of the soldiers also changed the economy. As suggested by the Calypsonian Lord Invader's famous song "Rum and Coca-Cola," the soldier market for prostitution also contributed to social changes.[32]

In Lamming's story, the soldiers from the United States are no heroes, but their presence and outsider perspective, by comparison, renders the arbitrariness of the British colonial order more visible. In the voice of Lamming's narrator, the threat the soldiers embody reveals the weakness and decadence of the order itself. In his words, "Their gaiety and exuberance of spirit seemed to contain an element of revolt to that delicate organism which is West Indian society" ("Birds of a Feather" 33). The narrator's portrait of this society, regionalized by the use of "West Indian" to name it, as a "delicate organism" seems threatened by the very presence of the U.S. Americans. In a more complex image that is even more critical of colonial West Indian society, the narrator critically elaborates on the antipathy the soldiers elicited in the colonial elite: "The Americans came and moved about our community like new brooms around a dust-laden room. And not a few were suffocated and choked and poisoned against them" (34). This passage sets up the colonial community as a "dust-laden room" and "the Americans" as the cleaning tools that sweep up that dust. Although it remains unstated, what the rest of the story elucidates is that those West Indians are members of the colonial elite whose position is endangered by the U.S. military's agitation of the colonial order. As Lamming's narrator indicates in the final sentence of the passage, these colonials saw the U.S. Americans as disruptive, but they did not understand that the "dust which had obscured the lives of the neglected natives," the social border that obstructed their view of the dispossessed majority of colonial society, was the object they now experienced as "blinding" (34). In other words, the narrator indicates that the U.S. occupation made the ruling Creole colonials see and experience—beyond their own awareness—the malaise of their own decadent system.

It is fitting that vision and blindness would be central to this image, for Lamming would go on to define colonialism as a field of vision. "Colonialism," as he argues, "is the very base and structure of the West Indian's cultural awareness." And as he indicates, "In order to change this way of seeing, the West Indian must change the very structure, the very basis of his values" (*The Pleasures* 36).[33] "Birds of a Feather" serves as an early aperture for this later conceptual elaboration.

Emphasizing the outsider view of the U.S. soldiers in "Birds of a Feather," the narrative perspective shifts to Hendrickson's perspective late in the story: "This world of men and women seemed so small and delicate for him. It was dangerous to join too freely in the trifles which diverted those around him" (36). Henderson's position as a U.S. soldier is contiguous to the imperial relation between Britain and the West Indies that has historically produced "this world of men and women" that seems so small and delicate to him. His distanced view, however, is in direct dialogue with the narrator's view of the fragility of "West Indian" society. In this moment of the story, Henderson perceives that even as he sees those around him, he does not understand what he sees. He had interacted with them "too freely," as if between his perception and theirs there had not existed a feeble social structure that was both all too easy and all too dangerous to disrupt. Hendrickson's perspective further alienates the reader from the narrator's insider view and as such completes the story's denaturalization of the colonial social structure.

The bar scene that develops after Henderson's perspective distances and denaturalizes colonial society is the most utopian episode in the story: the soldiers reunite with Joe the narrator, and the three of them encounter the "West

Indian" from the fight at a bar. The four men drink together, and the "West Indian" introduces himself by name to the three men. As "the West Indian," the narrator later explains that he is "the prototype of an army, a symbol of the age in which he lived" (38). As prototype and symbol, this man, depersonalized as "the West Indian," embodies ruling colonial ideology. However, in the same passage, the narrator reveals that "under the cloak of hypocrisy in which he was vested by those to whom he had sworn social allegiance there was yet some fundamental goodness" (38). Even as he stands in for an entire structure of colonial power, he contains the potential for goodness. When he is named—as Dickson—he becomes personalized and indefinite. Beneath the ideological allegiance that vests him as "the West Indian" lies "the indetermination of the person" immanent in him (Deleuze 30). Gilles Deleuze distinguishes between the transcendent definite article (the) and the immanent indefinite article (a), indicating how "the" operates to index a fixed exemplary as opposed to the way that "a" allows for the immanence of an indeterminate singularity. Lamming's alternating use of "the West Indian" and naming "a man" distinguishes this character's presence in the narrative as both symbol of colonial power (the "West Indian") and a man with the immanent potential for being something else, as Dickson.

When Dickson fights with Dalton to defend the exclusivity of the party scene and, by extension, the social boundary of the colonial elite, he becomes "the West Indian," the impersonal prototype of colonial power. But later, after the narrative has deconstructed colonial society, he is a man at a bar having drinks with three other men, all named, temporarily existing beyond their geopolitical and social determinants. During this bar scene the story's title "Birds of a Feather," from the adage "birds of a feather flock together," has the potential to mean something like "men who drink together stick together." This fraternal possibility is momentary, however; it is broken down by the introduction of the only explicitly racialized character in the entire story, whose presence enters the narrative just as Dickson once again becomes "the West Indian." "The waiter, a clean, fierce-looking Negro, looked at us out of eyes which held no meaning" (37). This man, importantly, is called "a" and not "the" Negro, and of course his gaze held meaning, a meaning begged by the very assertion of its absence. Accounting for his gaze brings attention back to the colonial structure that had been paused by the conversation among the four men and also evokes the reminder that there are people left out of the momentary bonding between the narrator, the soldiers, and "the West Indian."

In the final episode of the story, Joe reflects about the impending departure of the U.S. Americans as World War II drew to a close, "As had been the case with their arrival, it was going to strike the very foundations of my society. It was probably in the nature of our destiny that we, born in these parts, should know and feel the violence of these changes" (37). He thus suggests that the incidents that drive the story's narrative have a greater collective significance. How did both the arrival and departure of the soldiers disrupt West Indian society? It is not, of course, the narrative's job—in generic terms—to provide a specific answer to that question; instead, the narrative provides several angles from which to view the tensions and conflicts precipitated by the presence of U.S. American outsiders, tensions and conflicts through which the narrative develops a critical perspective on the injustices of the colonial hierarchies of West Indian society. In Brown's reading of Lamming's characterization as a "difficult" writer, he furthers Gikandi's view that Lamming's "desire to valorize the disruptive and diachronic functions of narrative" operates in opposition to the limited field of visibility of colonial power that renders most of West Indian society, or what the narrator calls the "native population," invisible (Gikandi, *Writing* 72).[34] As Brown would have it, "It is against these stubborn, ingrained, and effectively naturalized patterns of colonial perception that Lamming positions his literary difficulty, hoping to oblige his audience to pay more attention" (78). The story certainly falls in line with both Gikandi's and Brown's readings of Lamming's later novels, as its nonlinear construction and confluence of perspectives provide the building blocks for a dismantling critique of colonial power.

"Birds of a Feather" is a particularly good example of how "ways of seeing," to build on Lamming's term, may be constructed—and critiqued—in narrative form. The West Indian way of seeing that Lamming's story critically constructs with the foil of U.S. American obliviousness serves to indicate *a transformation of perspective*, as if to announce West Indianness as a colonially produced vantage point may shift that very vantage point toward a different kind of future: a decolonized one? At the very least, the story offers a transformation in consciousness that also implies a shift in the very meaning of West Indian regional identity.

"Birds of a Feather" interrogates, for both the narrator and the reader, what becoming regionally identified or located would mean. The story was written and published precisely during the political development of the West Indies Federation and has since circulated minimally. Its readability, along with that of the rest of the narrative works examined in this chapter, is thus subjected to the pressure of periodical time. This pressure indicates a historically specific reading of West Indian ways of seeing as colonial vision under critique and therefore as a site of transformation opening up onto a new, transnational affiliation. Jessica Berman pertinently theorizes the stakes of transnationalism in modernist narrative practice: "In narrative we open the reciprocal process of accounting for ourselves to others by asking and answering the question 'who are you?' which unite teller and listener in a mutual relationship of responsibility, though not necessarily in similarity, normativity or consensus" (18). The ethico-political relationship that narrative elicits in Berman's terms is precisely at issue in Lamming's answer to the question "who is the West Indian?" It is precisely because the West Indian is both no one and everyone who sees through what we might call "colonial eyes" that the answer binds writer and reader in a relationship of responsibility, in a commitment to address and even redress the problem of colonial vision, or the problem that to be West Indian means to have your awareness structured by colonialism. Importantly, what Lamming names "West Indian" is far from utopian; instead, it is a historically produced problem, one that the West Indies Federation, still a colonial form of administration proposed by the British government, was unlikely to solve. The story does not take a stance in favor or against West Indian unity; instead, it explicitly regionalizes the problem of colonialism and defines the region on its brink.

Conclusion: Regional Turn Accompli

By 1949, *Bim* had become West Indian. The cover of *Bim* 10 (1949) consecrated its crossing over the regional threshold. For the first time, instead of listing authors by the literary genre of their contribution, they appear listed by territory as if each island or territory were a genre of West Indian belonging.[35] The majority of contributors continue to be from Barbados in this issue, but Guyana (then British Guiana), Jamaica, St. Lucia, and Trinidad are also represented. The entire future federation had not yet made it to the list of *Bim*'s contributors, but half of its territories did for this unique edition of *Bim*. West Indianness had transformed from a looming threat of territorial identification into an accomplished fact, even though its political direction continued to remain uncertain. From 1948 onward, literary criticism would become a regular component of *Bim*'s issues, and in the literary critical pages it featured, West Indian regional identity would be stated as a fact. West Indian literature had become by then an object of inquiry discussed alongside West Indianness as a category of regional belonging and the West Indies Federation, its raison d'être. In Crichlow Matthews's review of the 1948 edition of the Jamaican literary anthology *Focus*, edited by Edna Manley, the federation overdetermined his writing: "Now that plans for West Indian Federation are being studied and discussed by government officials and parliamentary representatives throughout the British Caribbean area, it is especially urgent that there should be a continuous exchange of ideas between those men and women of these scattered colonies" united by their work in literature and the arts (175). Although he provides no political analysis of the gestating federation, Matthews refers to it as if it made regional literary circulation somehow imperative. He goes on to stipulate about *Focus* that it is "more than a West Indian magazine." *Focus* was a Jamaica-oriented territorial publication, but here its characterization includes (and exceeds) West Indianness because, as it would seem, the "time" of the West Indies had arrived. In his characterization, Matthews also seems unable to describe the political import of *Focus* and its pedagogical mission; he only suggests that it is "more than" West Indian, its politics seemingly exceeding what had indeed become a vogue category of regional pertinence.

Frank Collymore's essay in the same issue, "An Introduction to the Poetry of Derek Walcott," also asserts West Indian identity—in this case, Walcott's—as a depoliticized fait accompli. The essay is the transcript of a talk that excerpts several poems by Walcott from his first self-published collection, *25 Poems* (printed in 1948 in both Barbados and Trinidad).[36] "Let us listen to Derek Walcott, the West Indian," says Collymore, whose essay is primarily about the English influences in Walcott and his originality as a poet (127). The excerpt of one of Walcott's poems that proceeds from Collymore's assertion that he is West Indian seems, however, to encapsulate the literary evolution toward regionalism of this period as it circulated in *Bim*. The poem's title, "Travelogue," indicates a travel narrative, but the text that follows actively undermines the genre evoked by its title. The poem's excerpt is an irony-laden invitation to would-be travelers to an unnamed West Indian island. The irony of the invitation to travel to the speaker's island is immediately apparent in the description of those killed in battle that follows from it (17). The landscape transformed into a defiantly fighting battalion in Mittelholzer's "Of Casuarinas and Cliffs" becomes in this later poem a defeated—and slain—battalion upon which the pride of the island rests. As the poem continues, it seems to illustrate the view the would-be traveler would have of the island's people, echoing the perspective of the U.S. American soldier in Lamming's first story in its reference to people who are "small" and build their futures "in small rooms." The landscapes of this poem are neither adorned nor alienated. Instead, Walcott's landscapes, though politicized, refuse to engage with their observer; they are "aloof" with cause, as he spells out the imperial and racialized structures of dispossession implied in both Williams's and Mittelholzer's landscapes. The poem's speaker suggests that the land belongs not to those "conquering teeth" that control it but to "lost red and black tribes," admonishing the traveler to "keep looks of their gods" (17). Walcott thus asserts, in anticolonial dismay, the land's illegitimate conquest and warns of spiritual retribution in the reference to "their gods." At the end of the poem, he captures the idealism of federation with an ironic ambivalence. As he personifies the voice of "History":

> . . . Let all on islands of the heart construct the day
> Of the federated archipelago, black
> and white live apart, if so, but dream the same dreams. (18)

History's favoring of federation falsely resolves the racial divide of colonial society by suggesting that both Black and white dream the same dream. Neither dream enters the poem, however; instead, "history" speaks for empire in its aim to render with federation "such peace as traveller expects of islands." In these terms, Walcott's poem presages the insufficiency of federation for undoing the havoc wrought by colonialism—of racial segregation and usurped land.[37]

Becoming West Indian, as this poem by Walcott as well as Lamming's first short story suggest, was no antidote to empire for the British-colonized Caribbean. Becoming West Indian operates in their works, however, as an avenue to critique the British-colonial experience across all the islands and territories included in the regional design of federation. West Indian literary location made it possible to diagnose local-regional social and political maladies and to circulate them beyond the region onto the world literary stage, thereby contributing to independence from British rule, at least in perspective. Literature thereby became West Indian as it evolved toward practicing what Lamming has called "sovereignty of the imagination" (Lamming and Scott).

Throughout the 1940s, *Bim* was by no means an explicitly anticolonial or socially engaged magazine; it was not driven by the programmatic commitments to transforming literature or society that characterized both *Tropiques* and *Gaceta del Caribe*. Even when West Indian Local narrative reached its anticolonial height in Lamming's "Birds of a Feather," the critique of colonialism offered remains subtle, much more understated even than that of *Tropiques* under Vichy censorship. The story does, however, establish a foundational narrative genealogy of critically interrogating local-regional landscapes and colonial social settings that set the tone for the future of West Indian literature as *Bim*'s publishing aperture engulfed the region, consolidating the very possibility of an Anglophone regional literature.

CHAPTER 5

Polycentric Maps of Literary Worldmaking

Before, during, and after World War II, Caribbean literary magazines mapped cross-sections of world literature and contributed to literary worldmaking through social, political, and aesthetic networks. They recorded these in reprints from literary magazines or other literary institutions, in reviews of other magazines, and in reports of publications abroad. For example, *Tropiques* would reprint from *Cahiers d'Haïti* Cuban author Alejo Carpentier's essay, "L'evolution culturelle de L'Amerique Latine" (The cultural evolution of Latin America). *Bim* would regularly reprint poems and short stories featured on the radio show *Caribbean Voices*. *Orígenes* would run advertisements for the Argentinian literary magazine *Sur*, and *Gaceta del Caribe* would also reprint news and work from *Cahiers d'Haïti*. The set of magazines whose genealogies I examine in the preceding three chapters do not, alas, make up a cohesively connected literary network during this period. They were, however, part of multiple networks, some of which overlapped. Literary magazines and the international networks they coordinated participated foundationally in the histories that shaped the ways Caribbean writers have gotten on the *map* of world literature, or achieved international recognition. They have been the "vehicles," to use Lino Novás Calvo's terminology, that have shuttled writers to geographic visibility in the world literary marketplace and to their writing contracts abroad ("11 Síntomas" 3).[1]

Location writing combined with what I understand as the map function of Caribbean literary magazines have fueled their struggles for visibility and cultural capital in world literary space. In *The World Republic of Letters*, Pascale Casanova elucidates how the unequal conditions writers from the peripheries face are obscured by the fiction of literary universality and equality: "The creative liberty of writers from peripheral countries is not given to them straight away: they earn it as a result of struggles whose reality is denied in the name of literary universality and the equality of all writers as creative artists, by inventing complex strategies that profoundly alter the universe of literary possibilities" (177). Such writers struggle, she argues, "to create the conditions under which they can be seen." In other words, from the perspective of the false claim of literary universality, the work that peripheral writers do to become visible and negotiate the inequalities of the literary marketplace becomes obscured. Casanova's work, as I have argued elsewhere, fails to represent the extent of the literary marketplace's inequalities, but she renders overwhelmingly apparent that the burden of becoming visible and valuable to the imperial centers where capital investments fuel literary production, is overwhelmingly incumbent on the writers from the outposts of empire.[2] Although Casanova regularly uses literary magazines as sources, she does not consider how responsible they are for putting writers from the outposts of empire on the map, so to speak, of world literature.[3] As I argue throughout this book, literary magazines are primary venues and agents of these struggles, and the protomapping technologies they practice are their primary methods for setting the terms of their visibility and accruing geopolitical and aesthetic cultural capital in the world literary system, or in my terms, the empire of literary value.

As I argue in this chapter, the protomapping technologies of Caribbean literary magazines set the terms of visibility for the particular locations they offer through practices of literary worldmaking.[4] In addition to the location writing strategies I argue for in the preceding chapters, literary magazines also provide coordinates for maps of their literary networks or worlds that indicate the relational forms of dialogue and exchange that shaped their perspectives and interventions in world literary space. Anjali Nerlekar offers the term "cartographic impulse" for literary works that have a mapping function, and Monxo López Santiago indicates that the maps we find in literary works "allow us to re-imagine geographies" (Nerlekar 621; López Santiago 153). In this chapter, I trace the "cartographic impulse" of literary magazines in order to reimagine the geographies of world literatures. Franco Moretti suggests that "for geography, locations as such *are* significant; geography is not just 'extension' . . . but 'intension' too: the *quality* of a given space" (55). Whereas my study of location writing throughout most of this book pertains primarily to geographical *intension*, or the writing of locations *as such*, in this chapter I am concerned with their geographical *extensions*, or the mapping of literary networks. I trace maps of Caribbean magazine authorship, circulation, and influence in order to demonstrate that while Caribbean magazines have been unable to compete infrastructurally with metropolitan magazines produced in Europe and the United States, they participate in polycentric forms of literary worldmaking that reconfigure the world literary system.[5]

Cartographies of Magazine Worldmaking

> Et mon original géographie aussi; la carte du monde faite
> à mon usage, non pas teinte aux arbitraires couleurs des
> savants, mais à la géometrie de mon sang répandu
>
> —Aimé Césaire, *Cahier d'un retour au pays natal* (1939)[6]

In Césaire's formulation, "the world map made" critically refashions the world map configured by European empires. We may read the bloody warfare of empire and transatlantic slavery through Césaire as imprinted on and made invisible by the map. The map, as both a tool of empire and a medium that exceeds empire, is also, in this very instance, repurposed by Césaire and thereby disposed to *his* "own use." Whereas the map of empire and transatlantic slavery set the terms of geographic (in)visibility, Césaire's poetic use of the map resets the terms and thus uncovers what the map both facilitated and visually concealed (people treated like objects) and recovers what the work of the map suppressed (the agency, power, and resistance of conquered and enslaved peoples and their descendants).[7] As Jessica Marie Johnson describes the dilemma that confronts the viewer of maps that both do and do not record the history of slavery, "the viewer contends with the use of white space that has been emptied of life, even as it was epistemologically called in to do the work of outlining the New World. Obliterated are the bound and blackened bodies that occupy, produce, and reproduce in the wake of colonial intervention" (6).[8] Césaire's poetic invocation of cartography disturbs the epistemological work of the map of slavery and empire that is also the historical and economic base of the world literary marketplace.

Césaire's double-take on cartography does not *exactly* map onto the literary magazine medium, but like Césaire's repurposing of the map, the magazine has been as much disposed to reinforcing the power of imperial cultural centers as it has been to subverting and circumventing that power by literary actors positioned against the empire, or those who, without necessarily opposing the empire, find themselves up against the literary power added to its geopolitical might. A medium itself is not politically oriented. To invoke Stuart Hall's theory of encoding and decoding, a medium is not the code but rather the interface between encoding and decoding ("Encoding / Decoding"). As W.J.T. Mitchell similarly puts it, "A medium is just a 'middle,' an in-between or go-between" (4). The trick of the medium happens in the work inscribed into it through its composition and circulation. Like the map, the *work* of the magazine—and not the medium *in* itself—its formal construction, the locatedness of its orientation, and the audiences addressed (and composed) by its pieces—determine its *use*, or function. For the magazine, the institutional network, both mapped and mappable by its enunciated routes of circulation and its curated selection of authors, determine the scope of its intervention in the empire of literary value.

Although the proximity between the medium of the map and the medium of the magazine may not be self-evident, theoretical approaches to periodicals approximate the map in several ways. First of all, theoretical models of the magazine are very close to J. B. Harley's poststructuralist critique of cartography. Harley suggests that cartography is embedded in two forms of power: an external exercise of power with which the map is employed and an internal exercise of power that directs the map as a representation in itself (12). Richard Ohmann's work on the field of power exercised by consumer magazines suggests that magazines shape their readers even more than they may be shaped *by* their readers. In Ohmann's terms, magazines cannot be viewed as cultural commodities to be used by readers. He makes the compelling case that instead magazines have shaped their readers and commodified their resulting subjectivities, as they "presented their attention, their needs, their aspirations, their anxieties, as use values to unseen third parties [advertisers, product-makers]" (8). The readers thus shaped by magazine projects would in turn become the commodities sold to advertisers. If we extend Ohmann's conception of the work magazines do to shape their readers to the sphere of literary magazines, what comes into view is the literary magazine's power to shape the disposition of readers for the literary marketplace and for social movements, geopolitical imaginaries, and political projects. Margaret Beetham in turn has addressed the interior and exterior field of the periodical as united in the medium. In her theory of the periodical as a publishing genre, she sums up a periodical as a form that is at once open and closed: open because of the fluidity of genres, authorial voices, and dialogue with texts outside of its boundaries and closed insofar as it constructs for its readers "a recognisable self" (29).

I consider the infrastructural capacity of a magazine to generate literature to be shaped by the set of possible relations it may establish to other forms of literary infrastructure. I thus seek to extend Beetham's idea of the periodical as an open system to the relations of production and circulation that make possible the acquisition and accumulation of literary capital. This system may be mappable with the coordinates provided in a magazine's pages and contribute to the way it projects itself and, by extension, its readers as a part of a broader network, or literary world. The power of periodicals thus exists both *in* them as they shape the desires, tastes, and other sensibilities of their readers and *outside of them* through their ability to extend their visibility and cultural capital by circulating through a literary world of magazines and other literary institutions.

In addition to the theoretical proximity between the map and the magazine's interior and exterior forms of power, recent theoretical contributions to understanding African, Caribbean, and Latin American magazines productively build on cartographic metaphors. Eric Bulson both explicitly and implicitly assimilates the magazine to the map. He draws attention to the coordinates present in African magazines that highlight the geography of their networks of circulation and relation to the world, and he describes modernist magazines broadly, as "forward-looking, eager to map out new directions of an experimental literary culture" ("Little Magazine" 269). Here, mapping pertains to the directive aesthetic work of the magazine, as if it were a cartographic endeavor. Whereas Bulson explicitly employs mapping as a future-reoriented practice that would direct literary futures, I am specifically interested in how Caribbean magazines sought to cartographically orient themselves or, in other words, how they mapped themselves as integral to the literatures they fomented and in relation to other magazines and other literatures.[9]

Other scholars utilize cartographic imagery in order to highlight the value of the magazine as an archive for literary, social, and political history. For example, Chelsea Stieber suggests that the Haitian magazine *Revue Indigène* "allows us to map Haiti's evolving attitudes toward the literary and cultural production of the former metropole and toward the emerging global literary field of the early twentieth century" (22). In her reading, the magazine exists internally as a social map of the literary and cultural field, opening up to the external power of the scholar as cartographer. Claudia Gilman's work on Latin American cultural magazines of the 1960s and 1970s in turn suggests that magazines both contain maps and fulfill a cartographic function: "El mapa de la época que las revistas permiten constituir también se caracteriza por su propia vocación cartográfica: en esos años, los discursos de las revistas inventaron sistemáticamente un objeto, al hablar de él: Latinoamérica, la Patria Grande y su literatura" (The map of the period that magazines may compose is also characterized by its own cartographic vocation: in those years, magazine discourses systematically invented an object, in voicing it: Latin America, the Great Patrimony and its literature) (78). Gilman goes so far as to suggest that these magazines constructed Latin America and Latin American literature by invoking their existence. Similarly, Beatriz Sarlo has forwarded the notion of "cultural geography" for understanding the work of literary and cultural magazines: "Las revistas tienen sus geografías culturales, que son dobles: el espacio intelectual concreto donde circulan y el espacio bricolage imaginario donde se ubican idealmente" (Magazines have their cultural geographies, which are doubled: the concrete intellectual space where they circulate and the imaginary bricolage space where they ideally situate themselves) (qtd. in Kanzepolsky 151). Sarlo's sense that the cultural geographies of magazines may be doubled pertains to both the ways they map their own locus of enunciation and the map implied by their field of circulation.

Indeed literary magazines in the region have also projected the literary worlds they contributed to making through protocartographic literary practices that set the terms of Caribbean visibility. Bulson explains about African literary magazines that they did not have a "center" and instead created "a decentered literary universe" ("Little Magazine" 270). I draw on this conception to suggest further that Caribbean literary magazines contain polycentric maps of world literature.

They offer the cartographic coordinates for these maps: in their authorial distribution; in the routes of circulation they publish; in their reviews, in news of other magazines; and in the debates they proliferated. These coordinates yield maps that evince literary worldmaking strategically positioned to intervene in the empire shaping the world literary market.

Mapping Authorship: *Bim* and *Orígenes*

The maps of authorship immanent in the Barbados-based magazine *Bim* and the Cuba-based magazine *Orígenes* demonstrate how central authorial representation was to the work of each magazine. Perhaps more than any other Caribbean magazine, *Bim* presented itself most like a map when, for its tenth issue in 1949, its editors rearranged the table of contents on the magazine cover and replaced the lists of authors divided by literary genre into lists of authors divided by West Indian territory. The editorial intervention signaled that by *Bim* 10 this literary magazine had completely transformed from a local publication for writers in Bridgetown to a veritably regional West Indian literary periodical.[10] *Orígenes* did not approximate a map of authorial coverage as closely as *Bim*, but mapping its authorial coverage demonstrates the repeated persistence of Cuban authors alongside authors from other parts of Latin America, the United States, and Spain. While this magazine occasionally covered authors from other countries, it is clear that the primary routes of coverage *Orígenes* was committed to traversing connect Cuba's literature to its Latin American neighbors and to the imperial centers that structure its political economy. Mapping magazine authorship in both cases permits a view of both the internal geography of each periodical's publication record and the external geography of its range of circulation. In *Bim*'s case, the progressively regional work of literary location writing in its corpus is reinforced by its regional coverage. In *Orígenes*'s case, the magazine's projection of itself-in-the-world-of-literature takes on a more precise image of literature constructed through a postcolonial reactivation of routes of literary influence that recenter Latin America in relation to the United States and Spain.

Authorial distribution in *Bim* 10, the final issue of the decade, extends across the West Indies more than any other issue of *Bim* during the 1940s (Map 1). This issue represents a culmination of West Indian representation for the magazine and operates as a literary precursor to political participation in the West Indies Federation (Map 2). Alison Donnell suggests that the federation appears to have taken a stronger hold in literature than in politics ("West Indian Literature" 84–86). *Bim* 10's federated authorial distribution flaunted by its cover supports that argument, as it outlines the conformation of a federated literary body that would far outlive the political body.

The map of *Bim* 10's authorial distribution and the map of the later West Indies Federation overlap significantly. The West Indies Federation would be inaugurated

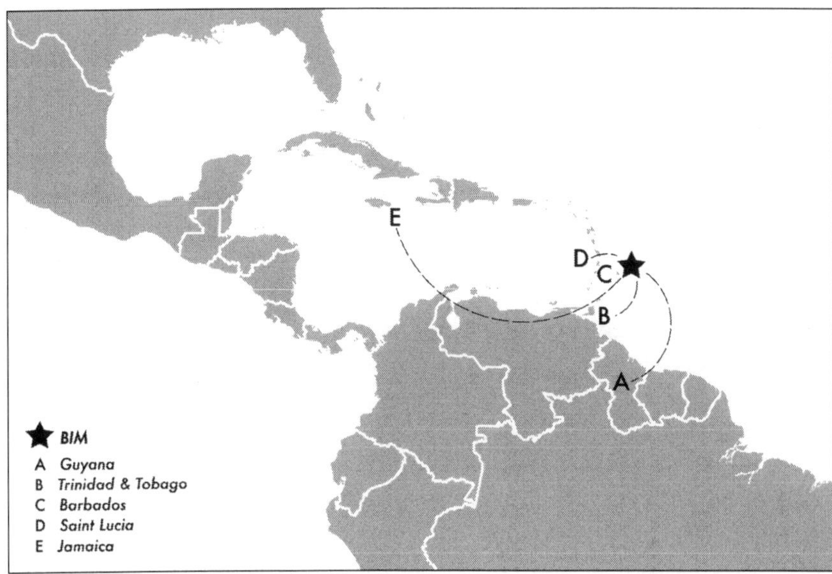

Map 1. *Bim* 10

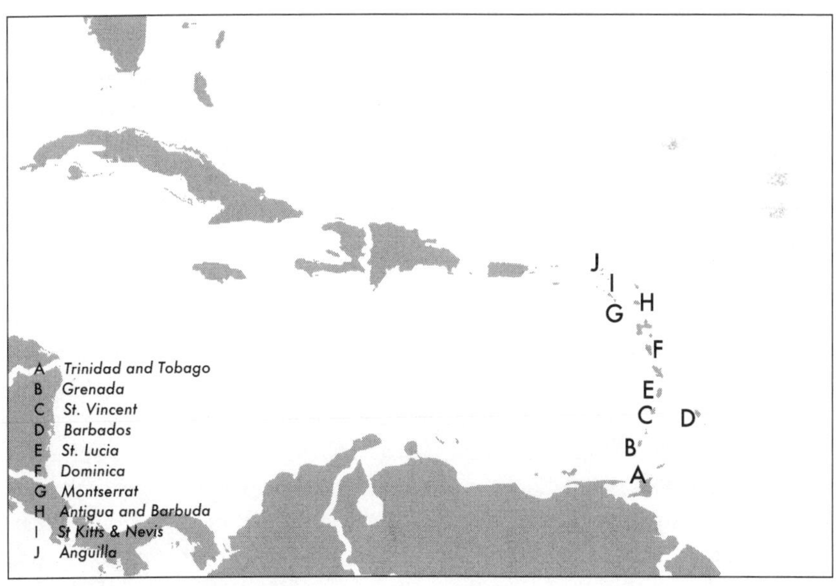

Map 2. The West Indies Federation

in 1956 and be in effect for only four years, from 1958 to 1962.[11] The plan to convene a federation of British colonies had already been established by the 1947 Conference at Montego Bay, however. Although representation from the British colonies in the Caribbean was comprehensive at Montego Bay, not all territories represented there would go on to become part of the federation (*Conference*, Part 1 12–13). The structure of the regional governing body would be debated between 1947 and 1956, but only the following territories would sign on: Antigua and Barbuda, Barbados, Dominica, Grenada, Jamaica, Montserrat, St. Kitts-Nevis-Anguilla, St. Lucia, St. Vincent, and Trinidad and Tobago. As the map of the federation above indicates, all the representative territories except Jamaica were part of the Winward and Leeward Islands chains. The map of *Bim* 10 represents only half the number of territories: Guyana, Jamaica, St. Lucia, Trinidad, and of course, the magazine's capital of Barbados.

Although the territories on *Bim* 10's authorial distribution map are less in number than those that would be part of the federation, the map's geographic extension reaches farther than the geographic extension of the federation. This extension is based on the longstanding participation of Guyanese authors, beginning with Edgar Mittelholzer, in *Bim*. Representing authors form Jamaica to Guyana means that *Bim*'s authorial reach would exceed that of the federation. Indeed, Guyana's opting out was tragic for the proponents of this political body as an avenue toward collective independence. C.L.R. James would lament the move and seek to change it by delivering a lecture there in 1956 exhorting his Guyanese public to join the federation. James conceived of the West Indies Federation as an avenue for a new West Indian nation and argued that "*federation is the means and the only means whereby the West Indies and British Guiana can accomplish the transition from colonialism to national independence, can create the basis of a new nation; and by reorganising the economic system and the national life, give us our place in the modern community of nations*" ("Lecture" 90). This national vision would not materialize, but West Indian literature as a regional phenomenon would become an observable and even marketable reality by the next decade. The West Indian literary world *Bim* contributed to constructing and projecting would be a principal contributor to this phenomenon.

Orígenes did not explicitly offer the geographic coordinates of its authorial distribution as *Bim* 10 did, but we can still use the table of contents in each of its issues to map the geography of its own literary worldmaking (Map 3). Between 1944 and 1945 Cuban authors predominate in its pages, but the magazine also includes at least one author from the United States in each issue and beginning with the second issue at least one author from Spain. In these years, other Latin American authors as well as other European authors and artists are also regularly featured in *Orígenes*, but Spain and the United States stand out as regular locations of authorial provenance for the magazine. The resulting map of its

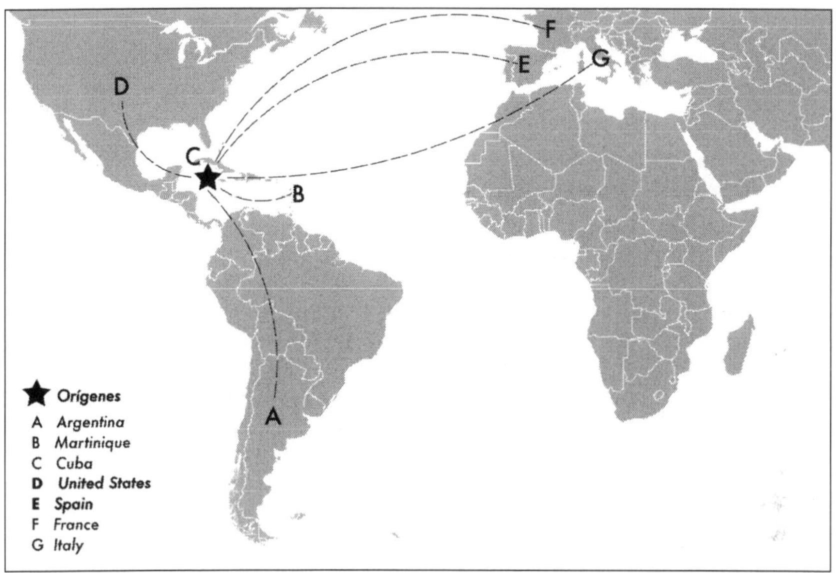

Map 3. *Orígenes*'s authorial distribution, 1944–1945

authorial representation suggests the strong affiliation forged by *Orígenes*'s editors to U.S. American literature and Spanish literature.

To some extent, the geography of *Orígenes*'s authorial distribution may be regarded to have eroded the imperial hierarchy that would subordinate Cuban literature to Spanish and U.S. American literature. To be sure, *Gaceta del Caribe*'s authorial distribution achieved a similar erosion, but in *Orígenes* writers and critics from the neoimperial metropole of the United States and from the former Spanish metropole proliferate even more than in *Gaceta del Caribe*. Adriana Kanzepolsky argues that *Orígenes* disrupted the imperial notion that U.S. American authors would serve as models for Cuban literatures by suggesting instead a more horizontal dialogue with these literatures: "El otro, al que *Orígenes* traduce, no es vislumbrado como un modelo sino como alguien con quien dialogar, como alguien que pertenece a la misma comunidad, un ciudadano, que a pesar de hablar otra lengua, habita con ellos la ciudad de las letras" (The other, who *Origenes* translates, is not revealed as a model but rather as someone with whom to dialogue, as someone who belongs to the same community, a citizen, who in spite of speaking another language, lives with them in the city of letters) (150). Kanzepolsky's argument is based on the notion that authors such as Eliot, Bishop, and others published in *Orígenes* had not yet become literary institutions when they were published there, which lends simultaneity to their publication with Cuban writers on the rise and deauthorizes them in relation to their publications. I would amend this view, however, for by 1944 at least T. S. Eliot had reached a significant and widely recognized stature as both poet and critic. Eliot's theory of a literary review elaborated two decades before may indeed serve as a model for *Orígenes*. However, the editors theoretically expand the reach of Eliot's prescription for a literary review so much that much like the *Tropiques* group's renovation of the Bretonian terms of surrealism, it transforms and indeed becomes a new form altogether.[12] In this sense, *Orígenes* may be understood to approximate Lezama Lima's earlier elaborated theory of the "undertow" for insular influence by foreign sources, in which the foreign influence is absorbed and transformed.[13]

In my reading, the effect rendered by *Orígenes*'s regular inclusion of authors from Spain and the United States is less an image of the three countries as neighbors in the international city of letters than a scene of carefully selected Spanish and U.S. American visitors in an habanero literary salon, sharing their work from contexts that are decidedly and powerfully other. I read their role in *Orígenes* as ambivalent: they both function as authorized others from infrastructurally replete literary worlds of great cultural capital and as foreigners whose authority to intervene in this context is limited by lacking contextual knowledge and understanding. However ambivalent the move to regularly feature Spanish and U.S. American voices in *Orígenes*, it has the strategic effect of offering a literary cartography that would elevate Cuban literature through the borrowed cultural capital of the United States and Spain, garnering interest in Cuban letters abroad through exchange and augmenting the desirability of the magazine in Cuba and throughout Latin America by featuring the first translations of contemporary U.S. poets and new works by Spanish poets. Here the move is classic postcolonial hybridity: it is precisely by maneuvering the imperially funded cultural capital of Spain and the United States that *Orígenes* sought to raise the value of its literary stocks. The cost of this business, as I argue in chapter 3, however, is to unseat the centrality of Black aesthetics in Cuban literature. This maneuver was never totalizing, but it has had far-reaching effects on the future of Cuban literature.

Mapping Circulation: *Gaceta del Caribe* and *Tropiques*

Mapping the circulation routes announced by literary magazines also reveals their literary worldmaking. Both *Tropiques* and *Gaceta del Caribe* published evidence of their networks of international circulation. *Gaceta del Caribe* included letters to the editor from abroad and halfway through its run featured a note mentioning all of the places abroad where the magazine circulated. *Tropiques* sporadically included a section called "Revue des revues" (Magazines in review), which featured excerpted and sometimes translated reproductions of magazine articles produced around the hemisphere. Whereas the magic of the map in *Bim* was the achievement of regional representation for a literary magazine that had

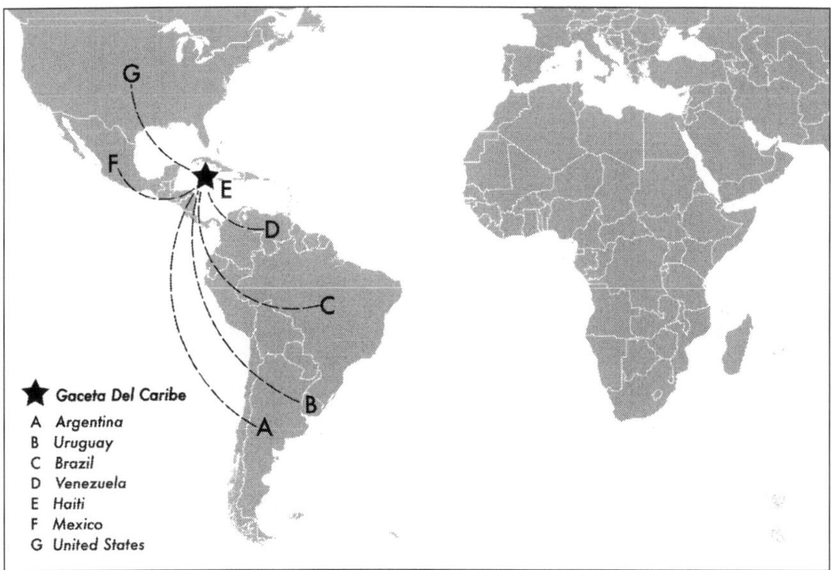

Map 4. *Gaceta del Caribe*'s circulation

begun as a local phenomenon, both *Gaceta del Caribe* and *Tropiques* demonstrated an internationalist aperture in their maps of authorship and their maps of circulation, which was likely attributable to the Marxist and antifascist political connections of their editors. Their maps of circulation particularly reinforce the Caribbean center of their international networks, however, highlighting trans-American connections in particular.

In the fourth issue (June 1944) of *Gaceta del Caribe*, an editorial note titled "Pedimos la palabra" (We request a word) both laments the paper shortage they suffer from and boasts about the extent of the magazine's circulation. They announce having reached a rate of distribution of 1,000 copies per issue to date and to be circulating in Haiti, Brazil, Venezuela, Uruguay, Argentina, Mexico, and the United States (31) (Map 4). The Caribbean-centered and trans-American locus of enunciation established in *Gaceta del Caribe*'s introductory editorial becomes reinforced by this trans-American literary geography of its reception.[14]

The networks announced by this map of circulation would also feed *Gaceta del Caribe*'s authorship and source its literary mapping of the world. News from the state-sponsored Haitian magazine *Cahiers d'Haïti* and work by Haitian authors Jacques Roumain and Roussan Camille would also feature in its pages. Mexico would be a key locus in its network, as coeditor José Antonio Portuoundo was living in Mexico City at this time. Mexican literary critic Alfonso Reyes would be featured as a contributor. News of Venezuelan politics would enter its pages. U.S. authors, including a review of work by Richard Wright, would also be included. The connections to Haiti, Venezuela, Argentina, Mexico, and the United States would also overlap in the network protomapped by *Tropiques.*

Tropiques's "Revue des revues" section featured publication news and reproductions from a set of literary magazines evincing a literary world of politicized aesthetic debates. The map of *Tropiques*'s magazine network is significant in a number of ways, but one of the functions of naming its coordinates was to demonstrate to a local audience how valued *Tropiques* was abroad (Map 5). In a 1943 "Revue des revues" article, Aristide Maugée contrasts the sympathetic readership of the magazine abroad to the unsympathetic lack of readership at home: "Puisque *Tropiques* a reçu á l'étranger une plus large audience encore qu'aux Antilles. . . . Puisque de grandes voix amies nous disent leur affection et leur sympathie, au delà de la mer Caraïbe, à Cuba, Curaçao, Mexico, New-York" (Because *Tropiques* has received an even greater audience abroad than in the Antilles. . . . Because great friends have expressed their affection and their sympathy, on the other side of the Caribbean Sea, in Cuba, Curaçao, Mexico, New York) (59). Maugée positions this hemispheric map of *Tropiques*'s readership abroad *against* neglect and even derision at home in the Francophone Antilles. The internalization of what in *Gaceta del Caribe* Lino Novás Calvo called a "colonial mentality," which he likened to an "inferiority complex," combined with and facilitated by lacking publishing infrastructure at home, has pushed up heavily against Caribbean writers, whose ideal target audiences at home, made up primarily of the educated middle and upper classes, were predisposed to undervalue them, as they implicitly and explicitly undervalued local writers and overvalued European and U.S. American writers.[15] *Bim* too would be derided by local audiences even as it facilitated the London-based publishing careers of so many writers. George Lamming would similarly critique the predominantly middle-class reading public that would disdain local writers when he described *Bim* as "a kind of oasis in that lonely desert of mass indifference, and educated middle-class treachery" (*The Pleasures* 41). If *Orígenes*'s positioning of foreign literary representation could bolster cultural capital for its writers before reading audiences who valued foreign work over local work, *Tropiques* could critique and potentially override local derision by drawing attention to its foreign readership. Announcing publications and reviews of Aimé Césaire's poetry abroad would potentially have a similar effect. They served to *deliver* what Emilio Jorge Rodríguez has called the "foreign seal of approval" (29).[16]

The "Revue des revues" section in *Tropiques* would indeed deliver foreign approval and provide a location record of its circulations by reprinting excerpts from other literary magazines in its network. *Tropiques*'s internally recorded map of circulation, like *Gaceta del Caribe*'s, would be hemispheric.[17] In addition to *Tropiques*'s reprint of Alejo Carpentier's text published in *Cahiers d'Haïti*, a reprint from the Caracas-based literary magazine *Viernes* (Friday) demonstrates a key dialogue across French and Spanish about literary theory.

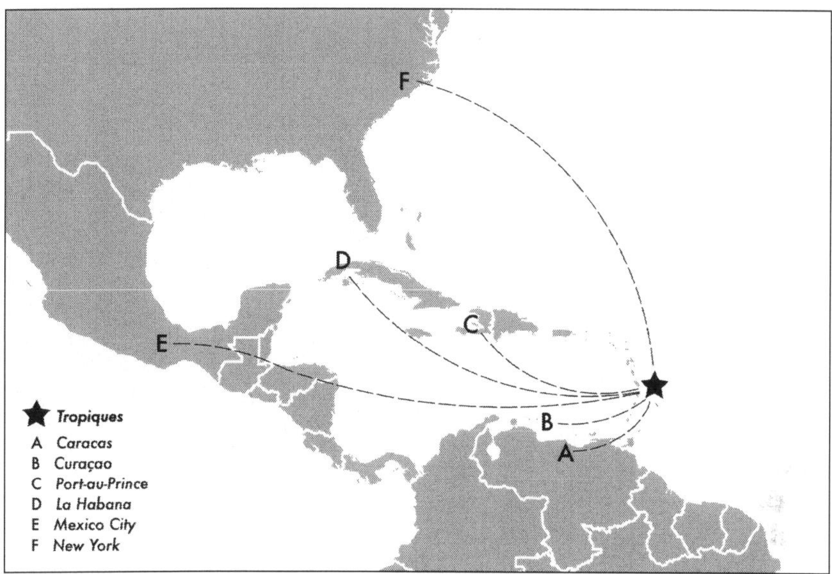

Map 5. *Tropiques*'s *Revue des revues* network

Tropiques would reprint and dialogue with a *Viernes* article that took a position on social art that resonated strongly with the *Tropiques* project. This reprint is from an essay by Venezuelan journalist, newspaper editor, and occasional literary critic Jose Ratto-Ciarlo. The essay titled "Horacio: Poeta bimilinario y el arte social" (Horace: two thousand-year-old poet and social art) was first published in the August–September 1940 issue of *Viernes* (Villasana and Amengual 34).[18] *Viernes* was a literary magazine dedicated to poetry and criticism that ran for two years in Venezuela, from May 1939 to May 1941 (9). It was founded by a literary group known as "los Viernistas" (the Fridayists), named for the day of the week in which they held literary salon meetings. Ratto-Ciarlo's text demonstrates a great intellectual proximity between the aesthetic debates that *Tropiques*, *Orígenes*, and *Gaceta del Caribe* participated in and those occurring in Venezuela during the same period.

Ratto-Ciarlo breaks down the dichotomous aesthetic theories, between abstract art and social art, that also divide *Gaceta del Caribe* and *Orígenes* in Cuba in ways that elucidate the space between this dichotomy that *Tropiques* occupies. As the translation of Ratto-Ciarlo reads:

> En effet certains intellectuels défendent avec obstination l'art le plus abstrait, un art dégagé de toute intention sociale "politique" comme on dit, adoptant en conséquence une position réactionnaire même sans le vouloir . . . Par contre il y a de [*sic*] fervents adorateurs de l'Art Social qui dans leur incompréhension manifeste de l'intérressante modalité surréaliste de nos jeunes poètes

> adoptent une attitude puérilement sectaire qui les conduit en fait à prêter leurs services gratuitement . . . à la cause du dogmatisme classique. (55)
>
> In fact certain intellectuals obstinately defend more abstract art, an art disengaged from all social "political" intentions, as they say, thereby adopting a reactionary position, even beyond their own wishes. . . . On the other hand there are fervent adorers of Social Art who in the miscomprehension manifested by the interesting surrealist modality of our young poets adopt an attitude that is childishly sectarian, that leads them, in fact, to lend their services freely . . . to the cause of classical dogmatism.

With this text Ratto-Ciarlo establishes the *Viernes* group in a way that resonates strongly with the *Tropiques* group, as neither proponents of socially disengaged art nor advocates of social engagement alone, seeking to establish a space between abstract art and social art, or a commitment to both aesthetic innovation and social engagement, at the same time. Having established the rupture of this dichotomy, Ratto-Ciarlo forwards the work of *Viernes* as an avant-garde product of modernity, one that, like *Tropiques*, is close to surrealism but is not assimilable to the European model of it: "Nous croyons nécessaire cependant de déclarer que nous ne nous sommes pas ajoutés, simplement, au surréalisme mort dans une Europe moribonde" (We think it is necessary, however, to declare that we have not simply added ourselves to the dead surrealism of a dying Europe) (57). The distinction here is key for the imagery of death associated with European surrealism that makes the critique both aesthetic and social in tenor is quite forceful.

Ratto-Ciarlo's essay predates Alejo Carpentier's famous critique of European surrealism in the preface to his novel *El reino de este mundo* (*The Kingdom of This World*) by nine years and contributes to the deviation or transformation of surrealism that *Tropiques* too contributed to forging. If the "*Viernistas*" would be associated with surrealism, they would demand, rather than be included in its terms, to be seen to work distinctly from the surrealism advocated by Europeans such as Breton. As the unsigned note that proceeds from the reprint (likely penned by René Ménil) states, "Mais ajoutons-nous: Néo-surréalisme . . . (On évitera les graves erreurs philosophiques du maître français)" (But we would add: Neo-surrealism . . . (We will avoid the serious philosophical errors of the French master)) (58). This note translates the work of the reprint into the *Tropiques* project, demonstrating the wish to resist absorption into Breton's version of surrealism. Naming the *Viernes* and *Tropiques* work neo-surrealist also reinforces the node of aesthetic solidarity established between *Tropiques* and *Viernes* by the reprint. The route of aesthetic exchange between *Viernes* and *Tropiques* ultimately shifts the presumption of exchange and influence emanating *from* Europe *to* the Americas. Instead, we see a map of surrealism transformed through travel and dialogue across the hemisphere.

Mapping Influence: Jacques Roumain's Traveling Theory of Poetry as a Weapon

Haitian poet and Marxist political activist Jacques Roumain would leave the coordinates for a map of magazines that circulated variations on his theme of "poetry as a weapon" during the first half of the 1940s. The theme would first be printed in New York. The text would then travel to Havana, and it would not make a Haitian homecoming to Port-au-Prince until after stopovers in Fort de France and in Santo Domingo (then called Ciudad Trujillo after the dictator).[19] The map of Roumain's Marxist theory of poetry adds to the theoretical dialogue between *Viernes* and *Tropiques*, contributes to understanding the importance of Marxist politics to the anti-imperial map of world literature, and suggests the centrality of Caribbean magazines to the archive of what we might call Caribbean literary theory (Map 6).

Jacques Roumain, like Nicolás Guillén from Cuba and Aimé Césaire from Martinique, is as crucial a figure for Caribbean literature as he is for Black Marxism. Roumain is perhaps most well known for the novel *Gouverneurs de la Rosée* (Masters of the Dew), published posthumously in 1944, the year of his

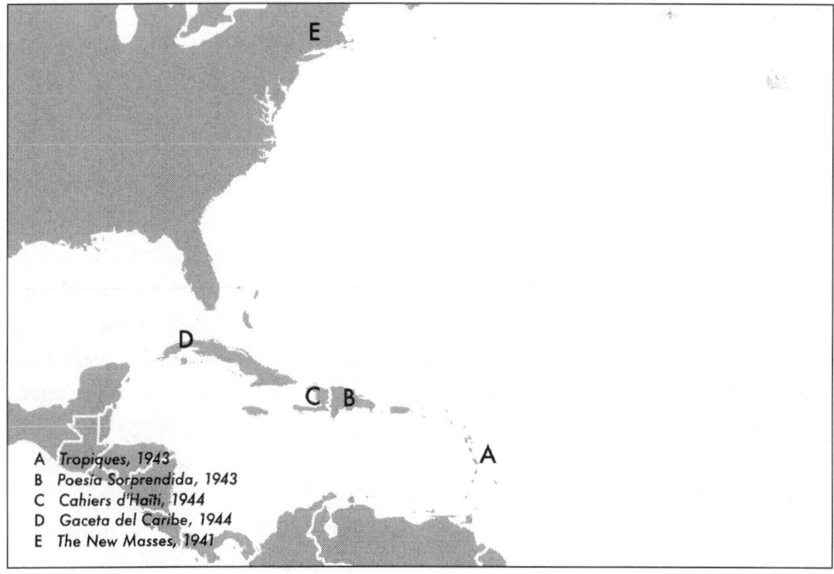

Map 6. "Poetry as a weapon"

death. He was one of the founding writers of the literary magazine *Revue Indigène* (1927–1928), which I understand as a key precursor to *Tropiques*. He was also importantly the founder of the Haitian Communist Party, in 1934. Roumain would go into exile in France in 1936 after political imprisonment, and he would befriend Nicolás Guillén in Spain in 1937, at an antifascist writers' conference (Augier, *Nicolás Guillén* 214).[20] He left France in 1939, the same year that Césaire published the first version of his famous poem *Cahier d'un retour au pays natal* (Notebook of a Return to the Native Land). Roumain would spend the summer in Fort-de-France in 1939 before traveling to New York, where he stayed until near the end of 1941 (Hoffmann 817–820). He would go on to spend almost six months in Havana in 1942, before returning to Haiti and being appointed to a diplomatic position in Mexico by President Elie Lescot (820–822). He would return to Haiti from Mexico periodically until 1944, when he died an untimely death at age thirty-seven, just three years after introducing the revolutionary conceptualization of poetry as a weapon.

The first source for Roumain's idea of poetry as a weapon is his English-language essay "Is Poetry Dead?" (1941). This essay had been delivered as a speech in a poetry forum sponsored by the American Writer's League in New York and was published in the January 7, 1941, issue of *New Masses*, a Marxist magazine closely associated with the Communist Party, that ran from 1926 to 1948. *New Masses* was the party-run revival of *The Masses*, a heterodox and independent magazine that ran from 1911 to 1917 (Morrison 171). The essay has a complicated critical reception in scholarship on Roumain's poetry, for it takes a militant position on the role of poetry, one that intensifies in the Spanish and French versions of the same essay. Michael Dash offers a reading of Roumain's poetry that suggests a disconnect between this theory of poetry and Roumain's poetic practice: "Roumain is at his least convincing in his attempts to follow an orthodox Marxist line in his public pronouncements on the writer's role in society. His prescription for literary engagement presents the writer as an activist whose craft is harnessed to an ideological position" (*Literature and Ideology* 13). Sarah Ehlers suggests that from the perspective of paradigms for reading lyric poetry, "imagining poetry as a weapon (in theory) and writing lyrics (in practice)" may appear paradoxical (147). Yves Dorestal recovers Roumain's Marxist practice and theory in dialogue with Latin American Marxist currents and suggests in turn that while Roumain was a multifaceted writer and thinker, there is no reason to presume a disconnect between theory and practice in his works (23, 129–144). While Roumain was indubitably aligned with the *Gaceta del Caribe* group that would defend social engagement in literature above all else, the conceptual itinerary of his theory of poetry as a weapon suggests that it significantly influenced the *Gaceta* group, the more aesthetically concerned *Tropiques* group, and the Dominican *Poesía Sorprendida* group.

Roumain sets up the essay as an inquiry into the fate of poetry in light of the social and political exigencies of the time and offers a vision of poetry that integrates it into the ideological sphere of reality. "Poetry is a part of the ideological system whose manifold reflections, be they psychology, art, morals, philosophy, or any other manifestation of the human mind, express a concrete historical reality" ("Is Poetry Dead?" 22). This pronouncement would be a radical intervention in the idealist view of poetry, such as that forwarded by the New Critics and *Orígenes* magazine in Cuba, as an escape from mundane and oppressive realities, including ideology. Indeed, as Ehlers notes, the apolitical methodology (and ideology) of literature known as New Criticism in the United States was in the process of becoming institutionalized at the time of Roumain's essay (147). Just as Ratto-Ciarlo testifies that advocates of social art were embattled with advocates of abstract art in Venezuela, and just as the *Orígenes* camp was embattled with the *Gaceta del Caribe* camp in Cuba, the New Criticism school in the United States was embattled with Marxist literary criticism.[21] It is against this literary front that Roumain would refuse to poetry an extrasocial and extrapolitical status. Roumain goes on to offer that "on the eve of a fundamental historical transformation, the crumbling old society finds in idealistic construction . . . the ideological weapons of counter-revolution" ("Is Poetry Dead?" 22). He reads here the trend to value poetic abstraction à la Mallarmé as a weapon of the writer and literary critic as bourgeois capitalist. In his English words, "Thus one discovers the pitiful petty bourgeois overwhelmed by an abject anguish, seeking refuge in the cocoon of pure poetry or of what *they* call the 'freedom of the spirit'" (22). In this context, Roumain proclaims about the poet as a historical actor that "his art must be a first-line weapon at the service of the struggle of the masses." Here, the aesthetic function of poetic form is most certainly subject to the sociopolitical function of the work. The idea both approximates and differs from the methodological theory of poetry as freedom we see in *Tropiques*, aligns almost completely with the sociopolitical primacy of aesthetics in *Gaceta del Caribe*, deviates completely from the argument of the anterior role of aesthetics for politics in *Orígenes*, and is too politically oriented to coincide with *Bim*'s explicitly apolitical posture that also neglected during this period to elaborate or promote a theory of literature.

The idea that literature should be a revolutionary practice, as Claudia Gilman has indicated, would become commonplace in Latin American letters during the 1960s and 1970s (19–29). But Roumain's is a crucial yet often missing reference for *that* genealogy too, for by the 1960s the boom of Latin American letters would leave Haitian literature out of its narrative. In the essay's conclusion, Roumain elaborates further the suggestion that poetry may be a weapon, in the terms that would become its traveling signature: "Poetry today must be a weapon *as effective* as a leaflet, a pamphlet, a poster" ("Is Poetry Dead?" 23, my emphasis). In this comparison between poetry and political communication Roumain hails poetry as a revolutionary device in the ideological warfare of racial and imperial capitalism.

The essay appears with a new title, "La poesía como arma" (Poetry as a weapon) in the inaugural issue of *Gaceta del Caribe* in 1944. The placement of Roumain's essay in the first issue of *Gaceta del Caribe* would serve its battle with *Orígenes* perfectly, as it indirectly portrays the *Orígenes* camp as antirevolutionary and bourgeois.[22] The translation of the essay is unsigned, and the editors of Roumain's complete works suggest that he might have translated it himself (Hoffman 725). The mystery of the text's translator takes on greater significance when we consider that it is very close to the English text except for one key difference: Roumain's conclusion to the essay appears in Spanish as "El arte del poeta de hoy debe ser un arma *semejante* a un volante, un panfleto o un cartel" ("La poesia" 15, my emphasis). The English translation of this would be "The art of today's poet must be a weapon *similar to* a leaflet, a pamphlet, or a poster." To recall, the English version of the essay renders this sentence as "Poetry today must be a weapon *as effective* as a leaflet, a pamphlet, a poster" (23, my emphasis). The difference is important, for instead of comparing the effectiveness of a political communiqué to a poem, it suggests more broadly that poetry should be similar to, or *like*, these other forms. This shift appears to turn up the volume on Roumain's politicization of poetry to such an extent that one might argue that the latter version distills poetry *completely*, and not just its political effectiveness, to political communication.

In November 1944, months after Roumain's death, the essay would appear yet again, this time in Haiti, in *Cahiers d'Haïti* (1943–1945), an official organ of the Haitian state that included literature and essays alongside reports of President Elie Lescot's political activities. *Cahiers d'Haïti* would notably establish a Latin American–located discourse rather than a Caribbean-located one, serving as a counterpoint, along with *Poesía Sorprendida*, to the tendency of Caribbean location observable throughout this book. Unlike *Orígenes*, however, its claim to Latin Americanism did *not* result in the minimization of Afrocentric work. In the particular case of this Haitian periodical, there may be no necessary correlation between disavowing the Caribbean and disavowing blackness. Instead, its Latin American positionality serves as a potent reminder of how egregious the *longue durée* distancing of Latin America from Haiti has been.

The French version of Roumain's text for *Cahiers d'Haïti* was translated from the Spanish by Jacques Léger. It employs the same title as the Spanish, "La poésie comme arme" (Poetry as a weapon). This essay would of course more closely approximate the Spanish than the English in the same sentence: "L'art du poète d'aujourd'hui doit être une arme *semblable* à un tract, un pamphlet ou à un placard" (The art of today's poet must be a weapon *similar to* a leaflet, a pamphlet, or a poster) ("La poésie" 22, my emphasis). In this version, "*semblable*" is the word for "likeness" or "similarity" that suggests the French version's direct correlation to the Spanish. How capacious might Roumain's theory of poetry be between both of these options and across either one of such distances?

Roumain's idea of poetry as a weapon also travels notably in the Caribbean before both the *Gaceta del Caribe* or *Cahiers d'Haïti* versions of the essay, however, likely as a result of his travels to Martinique and Cuba and / or the circulation of his essay in Caribbean networks. In October 1943 this idea appears in a transformed state, and without any reference to Roumain, in the opening editorial of the Dominican literary magazine *La Poesía Sorprendida* (Surprised Poetry), published between 1943 and 1947 in the capital of the Dominican Republic. Its editorial committee included Alberto Baeza Flores, Franklin Mieses Burgos, Mariano Lebrón Saviñon, and Freddy Gatón Arce. Although she would not be on the editorial committee, one of *Poesía Sorprendida*'s greatest claims to the Dominican literary canon would be its frequent publications of the highly influential poet Aida Cartagena Portalatín. In part because the editors, like those of *Tropiques* in Martinique, received homages for their work from André Breton, the magazine is often associated with surrealism, but like *Tropiques*, *Viernes*, and other magazines at this time in dialogue with surrealist currents, *Poesía Sorprendida* elaborated a sui generis, capacious poetic platform that cannot be reduced to Breton's conceptions of surrealism.

The poetic element of surprise would be the primary emphasis of the poetic platform established in *Poesía Sorprendida*'s opening editorial, penned by Alberto Baeza Flores, the antifascist Chilean poet who spent most of his life away from Chile and a large portion of it in Cuba, where he also published poetry and literary magazines and had connections to the *Orígenes* group. The editorial, titled "Apasionado destino" (Passionate destiny), offers poetry as a weapon.[23] After establishing poetry as magical, quiet, and total in its radiance, Baeza Flores proclaims about poetry: "Necesitamos de ella en un planeta sordo, para que ella sea la estrella de la sorpresa y lo inesperado de su luz. La poesía, es entonces un arma, menos evidente, gráfica o corporea, pero con una fuerza capaz de desbaratar esas mismas armas reales." (We need poetry on this deaf planet, so that it may be the star of surprise and the unexpected element of its light. Poetry is then, a weapon, subtly so, a graphic or corporeal weapon that has the power to break down those very same real weapons) (n.p.). Baeza Flores writes from Trujillo's dictatorship, so it makes sense for there to be some obscurity in the missing reference for "esas mismas armas reales" to subtly suggest without proclaiming the idea that poetry could defeat the real weaponry of the dictatorship. The rationale he goes on to provide, however, appears to turn Roumain's idea of poetry as a weapon on its head. Rather than articulating poetry's power to do explicit social and political work, Baeza Flores argues that poetry's power stems from activating interior life. It would be difficult to ascribe to this editorial an explicitly antifascist or Marxist discourse, however. As Dalleo has argued, its "ideology of the literary" that connects it to *Tropiques* opposed economic and political instrumentalism (*Caribbean Literature* 97). Like the *Viernistas* in Venezuela and *Tropiques*, *Poesía Sorprendida* appears to have articulated a more aestheticized position from which to launch poetic weaponry.[24]

The very same month in *Tropiques*, after the fall of the fascist Vichy regime, Aimé Césaire also inscribed a coordinate for the map of Roumain's idea in his essay "Maintenir la poésie" (Maintaining Poetry). Although René Ménil has attested to the presence of Roumain in Martinique during the time of *Tropiques*, Césaire would not cite Roumain for this idea (Ménil, "Sous l'amiral" 152). Christiane Chaulet Achour has also noted the conspicuous absence of Roumain in Aimé Césaire's poetic references even though Césaire and Roumain overlapped in Haiti in 1944 (83–84). Césaire's poetic essay "Maintenir la poésie" establishes an idea of poetry as insurrection contiguous to Roumain's: "Ici poésie egale insurrection" (Here, poetry equals insurrection) (7). Césaire establishes a French genealogy for such poetry in this essay that includes Baudelaire, Rimbaud, Breton, and Claudel, but Haitian poets such as Roumain are missing from the list. In this text and others, Césaire would advocate for poetic practice as a radical intervention *in itself*, one as socially engaged as it is inventive, and it is likely that he found Roumain's theory of poetry too instrumental, but Roumain's absence, along with the absence of other French-language poets from the Caribbean, is nonetheless palpable on Césaire's list of citations. Césaire would nonetheless go on to continue to affirm this theoretical genealogy by naming his first collection of poems *Les armes miraculeuses* (Miraculous Weapons).

The textual history of the map of Roumain's conception of poetry as a weapon traverses a theoretical problem space for the relationship between poetry and politics in the Caribbean that was germane to a diverse set of Spanish- and French-language magazines. The moving map of this intellectual history is curious for New York operates on it as a source location for literary theory by an author from the Caribbean that moves to various parts of the Caribbean instead of as the site from which to import foreign ideas to the Caribbean.

Conclusion: Polycentric Maps of World Literature

The literary cartographies I have traced begin to suggest what world literature would look like if it were conceptualized as a series of polycentric maps that do not reify imperial systems of value by presupposing that literary value always reverberates from the imperial centers that economically and geopolitically govern the world literary marketplace. Caribbean literary magazines offer maps for reimagining literary and geopolitical community that consistently return a refracted and transformed view of the world literary system rather than reflect back to the imperial centers the ideology of their primacy as theoretical and aesthetic models to be emulated. They also regularly map South-South aesthetic and geopolitical affiliations that escape critical gazes that persistently move North-South or South-North and back and forth through lenses encoded by imperial capitalism that presume to always already know the (subordinated) Otherness of the other. The univocality of the imperial capitalist map of (literary) value is not only disposed for reclamation by Caribbean authors and literary magazine editors such as Césaire. This map has also been revised, cut up, and transformed—over and over, issue by issue.

The result is a set of polycentric maps. Chelsea Stieber indicates about the Haitian magazine *Revue Indigène* that its editors and contributors "reoriented their focus away from Paris toward Port-au-Prince, which served as their new center or 'Greenwich Meridian' of literary production" (28). In my reading, this reorientation of the literary world may broadly characterize the cartographic function of Caribbean literary magazines: to symbolically steer home the center of the literary world from faraway imperial capitals of literary infrastructure. Together, these maps thereby contribute to decolonizing the terms of literary value.[25] Beware of how victorious this conclusion might sound, however. While such magazine work may certainly be understood to intervene in the imperial parameters of the world literary system, the scope of their reach, along with the field of their power, has been limited, miniscule even in comparison to the force of imperial armies and book industries. In the words of Aimé Césaire from the opening editorial of *Tropiques*, "Et vainement sur cette terre nôtre la main sème des graines" (And in vain on our own land the hand scatters some seeds) ("Présentation" 5). The circulation of these records remains infinitesimal before the Goliath of imperial routes of production and circulation. And yet, these maps nonetheless chart the decolonizing work of literary worldmaking and invite us to reformulate the world maps of literature and literary theory toward a polycentrism that would unseat the imperial hegemony of literary criticism.

Epilogue

THE BRIDGE GOES UP / THE BRIDGE FALLS DOWN

The narrative arc of this book is attuned to a delicate and tenuous place. At times my prose might jump victoriously, as if I were to suggest a monumental achievement of decolonization. It is doubtful that I have overcome the very tendency I critique in my first chapter, that of methodological resistance. But even when my prose jumps victorious, it falls hard, repeatedly, necessarily, into critique, defeat, and that narrow place between victory and defeat, that place that is so easy to overlook, that place I seek to make seeable in all of its thinness, the interstice of thinking otherwise overexposed by the camera of empire. I do not mean an ontological reality or an epistemological arrival. I mean a vanishing point that is easy to miss because it is not for sale at your local bodega.

Tiphanie Yanique's short fiction "The Bridge Stories: A Short Collection" offers the contiguous image of a falling archipelagic bridge that we may understand as a figure for Pan-Caribbean discourse. Yanique, a contemporary rising star of Caribbean letters hailing from the U.S. Virgin Islands, fictionalizes a commissioned bridge extending across the Caribbean, from Miami to Guyana "paid for by the Yankees" (Yanique 15). The bridge maker hired for this project, an archetype of the Caribbean artist of highly politicized stakes and limited infrastructural access, was accustomed to making miniatures. "He made bridges that people put in their earlobes and around their fingers. Tiny little bridges. Decorated and beautiful and perfect" (15). This bridge maker did not have the means or the experience to build a bridge of the scale that was commissioned: "But the bridge was built like his others, the only way he knew how, delicate and pretty but not able to bear weight" (15). From the very first page of this short fiction that is also a collection of intertwined fictional fragments, the untenability of this bridge is set up quite clearly. Written in the mythological style of a folktale, Yanique's "The Bridge Stories" elucidates the historical tragedy of Pan-Caribbean discourse in the Caribbean: the ubiquity of empire in its elaboration and the imperially produced fragility of infrastructure to bear its decolonial weight. Like the limited architectural infrastructures of the Caribbean that crumble before the devastation of hurricanes and earthquakes, the bridge cannot hold. Like the Caribbean literary magazine that establishes links across and beyond the region charting alternatives to imperial routes of intellectual and aesthetic production, the Pan-Caribbean bridge in Yanique's tale is beautiful, fragile, and tenuous.

Yolanda Martínez-San Miguel has argued convincingly for the archipelago as "a geographical category, metaphor, and structing motif" in Yanique's "The Bridge Stories" ("Colonial and Mexican Archipelagoes" 166). The polyphony of characters from a range of ethnic backgrounds and Caribbean locations certainly comprises a microcosm of the archipelago. The role of rumor as a network of circulation is also central to the narrative, as each tale is spun through the indirect discourse of another character. Furthermore, Yanique's archipelago importantly extends to Miami, covering the area known as the Greater Caribbean and accounting for the city's U.S.-located Caribbean hegemony. At the same time the archipelago reaches to Guyana, rectifying in a sense the country's opting out of the West Indies Federation. Finally, the story is set in the U.S. colonies of the Virgin Islands, a set of Caribbean locations often excluded from Pan-Caribbean formulations.

The tragedy is revealed from the outset: the bridge falls. "When the picture flashed—a big, beautiful, blinding light—the bridge fell apart. And not only in that spot but in places all over the Caribbean, so that the many families who had gathered to take pictures (without express permission) also went into the ocean" (Yanique 15). The flash of representation coincides with the bridge's tragic disassembly. The light is beautiful and blinding: it overexposes the bridge as it falls. The story then proceeds in a flashback from the fundamental tragedy of the bridge's falling to reprise the fall from several perspectives. Standing in for the Caribbean archipelago, "the story is divided into insular narratives that do not seem to work together even though they are totally intertwined," but as Martínez-San Miguel rightly cautions, "this story is not about the failure of the archipelagic narrative" ("Colonial and Mexican Archipelagoes" 168).

Although I concur that Yanique's story successfully binds the archipelago in the relational network it establishes that converges on the falling bridge, I insist that beyond failure, the falling of the bridge, like the region's inability to achieve meaningful postimperial sovereignty, is a tragedy. The task is not to misread the tragedy: the work of empire and persisting forms of racialized power—and not of endemic racial, ethnic, linguistic, religious, or territorial difference—appears to be consistently embedded in the fabric that limits the decolonial dream of Caribbean unity.

The three dialogically interwoven bridge stories of Yanique's work become entangled through longing and a sense of betrayal. A "Frenchy" fisherman recently left by his wife for another man of greater economic means longs to be close to his son before his departure to college in the United States, so they arrange to go fishing near the bridge when it is complete. An elderly Muslim woman from Dominica whose children have found homes in other religious traditions inexplicably finds her way to the bridge and jumps over in pursuit of a mirage of her husband and another woman on a boat. A light-skinned Puerto Rican beauty queen runs away from the pageant she has won because she cannot bear the feeling that she won due to her light skin rather than her beauty. There is an absurdity embedded in the tragedies of these three disparate characters whose stories intersect at the point where (and when) the bridge falls. The fisherman lives to tell the tale, but his son dies in an attempt to save the elderly woman who also dies while the young woman falls from the bridge to her own demise.

The bridge collapses on Emancipation Day, symbolically enhancing the significance of the collapse. Emancipation Day, the day before U.S. Independence Day, commemorates the end of slavery in 1848 for the Danish Empire that previously held dominion over the Virgin Islands. The characters who come together for the bridge's collapse on Emancipation Day cross imperial borders in their reference to the British, French, Spanish, and U.S. empires in the Caribbean. They are united in a disparate longing that focalizes on the bridge and the commemoration of the auspicious end of slavery, a fact that is difficult to reconcile with the contemporary realities of empire that appear more continuous with slavery than with emancipation.

Pan-Caribbean discourse, embedded in the critique of imperial violence, appears as the repeated building of a bridge that cannot hold. The value of the decolonial imaginary charted by the repeated formulation of this discourse, itself a bridge constructed in its inability to hold, lies in the gift of vision beyond the borders imposed by empire that produces, if not political sovereignty, the sovereignty of the imagination. Pan-Caribbean discourse is neither the newly minted bridge nor the fallen bridge but rather the practice of building a bridge that is likely to fall, the bridge that is forged as it falls, the rumors of those who came together as the bridge fell.

Acknowledgments

This book has been guided by numerous gifts, blessings, and privileges. I could not have written this book without the extraordinary privileges afforded by the great wealth of the U.S. academy that is undergirded by the very processes of empire and racialized forms of dispossession and exploitation that I hope my work contributes to destabilizing and dismantling. My early research in Cuba, Martinique, France, and Barbados was facilitated by the Tinker Foundation and Brown University research grants for graduate students. The Goizueta Foundation also provided an early research grant at the Cuban Heritage Collection at the University of Miami. An Emerson College Faculty Advancement Fund Grant permitted me to complete late-stage research in Paris, London, New York, Miami, and Cambridge. Additional funding from Emerson College has supported my conference and research travel. Thanks to my chairs Maria Koundoura and Roy Kamada, Dean Robert Sabal, Provost Michaele Whelan, and President Lee Pelton for facilitating this support at Emerson. The Ford Foundation dissertation fellowship and the Mellon Foundation Early Career Enhancement fellowship were both essential to the research and writing of this book.

The Mellon Mays Undergraduate Fellowship has supported my growth as a scholar for many years. I am grateful to Mignon Moore, Samuel Roberts, and Hazel May for their unforgettable work leading the Columbia Mellon Mays program. As the graduate student mentor to the Mellon Mays fellows at Brown University, collaborating with mentor extraordinaire Besenia Rodriguez and working with the awe-inspiring program fellows became the raison d'être of my research when I felt overcome by the force of coloniality pervading the academy. Thanks to Callie Waite for her great leadership of the Social Science Research Council program for Mellon Mays fellows in doctoral programs. These programs led to many important relationships of support, collaboration, and accountability for my work. I am especially grateful to Trimiko Melancon and Shana

Benjamin for programs they led and to my accountability partners, Mamyrah Prosper, Donovan Ramón, Diego Millán, and Isabel Porrás.

I have consulted magazines, first-edition books, correspondence, and other archival materials at several libraries and archives. I am grateful to the generous librarians and staff who have supported my research at Brown University, Columbia University, the University of Texas at Austin, Harvard University, the University of Massachusetts at Amherst, the University of Florida, Princeton University, Yale University, the New York Public Library, and the Library of Congress. I am also grateful to the librarians and staff at the Schomburg Center for Research in Black Culture, the Morgan Library and Museum, the National Library of France, the National Library of Spain, the National Archives of Barbados, the Schoelcher Library in Martinique, the archive of Éditions Gallimard, the George Padmore Institute, and the Cuban Heritage Collection at the University of Miami where I conducted key research for this book.

I presented my work at several lectures and panels in recent years. Thanks to Alejandra Bronfman for inviting me to present at the Department of Latin American, Caribbean, and U.S. Latino Studies at SUNY at Albany in 2019. Thanks to her, Glyne Griffith, Johanna Londoño, and María Alejandra Aguilar for great feedback and recommendations. I am grateful to Alejandro de la Fuente and Cary Yero García for featuring my work in a session of the Cuba Studies Seminar at Harvard in 2019 and for sharing important sources and key feedback. Thanks to Laurie Lambert for organizing the ASWAD (Association for the Study of the African Diaspora) 2019 panel "Afterlives of Caribbean Revolutions," and thanks to her and Raj Chetty for an inspiring and lively discussion around the panel. Thanks to Kaiama Glover, Kelly Baker Josephs, and Alex Gil for organizing the Caribbean Digital V conference in Trinidad in 2018, which was such a generative experience for my work on this book. I am especially grateful to Lizabel Mónica for collaborating with me for a presentation on print and digital Caribbean literary magazines. Thanks to Yolanda Martínez-San Miguel for inviting me to co-organize the two-panel series "Con-federating the Archipelago" at the West Indian Literature Conference at the University of Miami in 2018. I am grateful for the transformative exchanges with her and the rest of the panelists: Jossianna Arroyo, Alison Donnell, Kahlila Chaar-Pérez, Glyne Griffith, Raphael Dalleo, and Ángel Rivera. Thanks to Kelly Kreitz for organizing the panel at LASA (Latin American Studies Association) on media and literature for which I presented in 2016. Thanks also to Debra Rae Cohen for organizing the MLA (Modern Language Association) panel "Fiction and the Media Ecology" for which I also presented in 2016.

I am grateful to have had extraordinary mentors who have offered a rare generosity and upheld a high ethical standard as scholars that I strive to reach. The paradigms of thought and refusal I have learned from Frances Negrón-Muntaner in over two decades greatly shape my work. Esther Whitfield has provided rigorous guidance and feedback on most of my scholarly work thus far, greatly impacting my thinking, research methods, and writing. Paget Henry's feedback on my work, materialist frameworks of analysis, and timelessly long lunches have greatly influenced my work. Thangram Ravindranathan spent many hours with me studying Aimé Césaire's *Cahier d'un retour au pays natal* and *Tropiques* and pushed me to articulate the most nuanced versions of my ideas. Michelle Clayton provided invaluable feedback on my writing and thinking and taught me about the book publication process. Flora González Mandri's feedback on my chapters and guidance through my book revision both greatly improved my work and helped me stay on schedule when it was difficult. Yolanda Martínez-San Miguel helped me answer crucial research questions about the history of Pan-Caribbean discourse, provided excellent feedback on my chapters, and was an extraordinarily generous and rigorous research collaborator as I completed this book. John Trimbur's feedback on my chapters, encouragement, and formative teaching collaboration as I completed this book were also invaluable.

This book would not have been possible in its current state without a number of people I would like to thank. Since I met him in 2009, Víctor Fowler Calzada has always known before me where this book was going next, and my dialogues with him through the years, from La Habana to Cambridge, have greatly enriched this book. Kora Véron's guidance, encouragement, and disagreements have also been central to my elaboration of this book. Anthony Bogues was very generous with book recommendations and connected me to George Lamming in Barbados, who went above and beyond in his support and lively conversation with me and granted me permission to study his correspondence with Frank Collymore at the Barbados National Archives. Ellice Collymore also granted me permission to study this correspondence and Frank Collymore's papers pertaining to *Bim* magazine. Eskil Lam was very kind in facilitating my research at the Archives SDO Wifredo Lam. While I researched this book as a graduate student, I was fortunate to get to know Lorenzo García Vega, who was a renegade member of the *Orígenes* group. This book is indelibly marked by my conversations and correspondence with him.

I have also had excellent research and thought collaborators along the way. I am especially grateful to Freda Fair, my co-mentor, who has inspired and supported me regularly through the writing of this book. I would also like to extend a special thanks to Martin Tsang, Alex Gil, and Jackqueline Frost for being such generous research collaborators. I am grateful to María Pizarro Prada and to Caridad Tamayo Fernández for invaluable research support. For thinking with me, I would also like to thank Reina María Rodriguez, Lizabel Mónica, Thayse Leal Lima, Adrian López-Denis, Sharada Balachandran Orihuela, Perla Guerrero, Chana Morgenstern, Larissa Brewer-García, Kaysha Corinealdi, Tao Leigh Goffe, Fredo Rivera, and Raj Chetty. I am very grateful for supportive colleagues at Emerson College who provided feedback on my writing and supported my process in numerous ways. Thanks especially to Wendy Walters, Yu-jin Chang, Megan Marshall, John Rodzvilla, Kristin Lieb, Maria Koundoura, Roy Kamada, Jabari Asim, Douglas Ishii, Adele Lee, and Adam Spry.

I cannot thank my students at Emerson College enough for how much they have taught and sustained me in my research. Many thanks to my research assistants at Emerson, Zoë Gadegbeku, Winelle Felix, Oscar Mancinas, Christine Chen, and Regina Tavani. Your work and dialogue with me have made my book better. I am also grateful to Catherine Lazerwitz for translating Aimé Césaire's "En guise de manifeste littéraire" poem with me. A special thanks to those students who have taken numerous courses with me and engaged directly with my work, especially Massiel Torres Ulloa, Katytarika Bartel, Al Reitz, Evan Cutts, Richie Wheelock, and Luis Ernesto Prieto. An extra special thanks to Massiel Torres Ulloa for securing sources when quarantine and library closures made access more challenging and to Oscar Mancinas for crafting this book's index.

Many others have provided support in the process of writing this book. Thanks to Kim Guinta and Jasper Chang for excellent editorial support. Thanks to Raphael Dalleo and my other anonymous reviewer for excellent feedback that helped me finalize this book. Thanks also to David Scott and my anonymous reviewers at *Small Axe* who helped me improve work that also appears in this book. Thanks also to Gregson Davis and Michaeline Chritchlow for great feedback on my article on *Tropiques* for *South Atlantic Quarterly* that I draw on for this book. Thanks to everyone who supported my work in meetings and correspondence, including Jennifer Wilks, Odette Casamayor Cisneros, Rachel Price, Jacqueline Loss, Lillian Manzor, Ana Cairo Ballester, Maggie Mateo, Enrique Saínz, César Salgado, Lanie Millar, Jacqueline Couti, Jessica Berman, Alexis Pauline Gumbs, Michael Hardt, Walter Mignolo, Bruce Robbins, Kaiama Glover, Franklin Knight, Takkara Brunson, Elda María Román, Pearl Brilmyer, Lorgia García Peña, Leticia Alvarado, Dixa Ramírez, Clement White, Julio Ortega, Laura Bass, Suzanne Stewart-Steinberg, Stephanie Merrim, Timothy Bewes, Madhumita Lahiri, Gavin Arnall, Lanny Thompson, Michelle Stephens, and Rosemary Feal. Thanks to everyone who helped house and keep me company on research trips, especially Petra Costa, Lian Andrade, Maggie de la Cuesta, Adrian López Denis, Fredo Rivera, Fari Nzinga, Mitsy Chanel-Blot, Annie Gibson, Carolina Caballero, Vitalina Alfonso, Juan Carlos Flores, Mayra López Gutiérrez, Legna Rodríguez Iglesias, Oscar Cruz, Jose Ramón Sánchez, Mamyrah Prosper, Alex Fernández, Laura Loth, Maria Ali-Adib, Tom Pravda, Raquel Otheguy, and Gabriel Wuebben. Thanks to those friends who have made academic life more fun and meaningful, including Anjana Sharma, Rebecca Jacobs, Joyce Kim, Melissa Adeyemo, Ellen Reid, Nate Treadwell, Sophia Beal, Ana Marin, Emily Bloom, Simone Sessolo, Cristina Serverius, Karina Mascorro, Moustapha Diop, Marguerite Deloney, Ezio Neyra, Adler Prioly, Priya Lal, Somy

Kim, Alexandra Chreiteh, Nitsan Shakked, Lily Mengesha, Katrice Williams, Michael Broadman, and Cara Moyer-Duncan.

The differences of race, ethnicity, and class that shape the history of my family have been primary sources of curiosity that have driven my learning from my childhood to the present. I am grateful to all of my family for everything you have taught me. Thanks to the González, Hernández, Seligmann, and Pace crews in Miami; the Gils in the United States and the Dominican Republic; the Engstroms, the Monroys, and the Williamses in the United States; the Almeidas in Miami and Cuba; the Carcanos in Italy and Colombia; the Echeverris and the Jordans in Colombia; and the Levys in France. A spiritual connection to my great-grandparents and a wish to reach my young grandparents fueled the best and worst times of writing this book. Gracias a Esther, Julieta, Kurt, y Raúl por haberme proveído una fundación en desarraigo desde la cual ubico el pensamiento. Thanks to my father Paul Seligmann Jordan for making sure that I know the histories of my family and for surpassing all limitations in your example. Thanks to my mother Maria del Carmen González-Gil for learning with me, completing research with and for me, editing my translations from French and Spanish for this book, and believing in me against all odds. Thanks to my stepfather José Gil for the epic debates on Caribbean history. My brother Kyle Engstrom was my favorite person to show Caribbean graphic art to, and I have him to thank for the cover image of this book and for bringing my magazine maps to life. Thanks to Kyle and to my sister-in-law Graciela Monroy for also being the most supportive sibs. Thanks to Nelson Eduardo for teaching me to smile like I never had before. Finally, so many thanks to Erika Renée Williams, my comrade and my muse, for every writing retreat, for every lesson, for every song, and much more.

Notes

CHAPTER 1 — LOCATION WRITING IN MAGAZINE TIME

1. For more on how pervasively influential the framework of development has been and the continuities of imperial geopolitics in this framework, see Saldaña-Portillo; Hardt and Negri.

2. I examine this publication at length elsewhere. See Seligmann, "Cabrera's Césaire."

3. I am grateful to Marc Césaire and the Césaire Estate for granting me permission to cite from this unpublished letter. Kora Véron's work first drew my attention to this letter ("Césaire at the Crossroads in Haiti" 439). Jackqueline Frost and Jorge Lefevre Tavárez also draw on this letter in relation to Aimé Césaire's first trip to Cuba in 1968 ("Tragedy" 30).

4. Aimé Césaire would, for example, refer to his identification with Guadeloupe and Haiti in addition to Martinique as "identification with such countries of my heart's geography" ("La poésie" 12). For Véron's detailed research on Aimé Césaire's life and work, see her biography *Aimé Césaire, configurations*. For more on the Césaires in Haiti, see also Chaulet Achour and Joseph-Gabriel.

5. I use "articulation" in a double sense here. I mean both the more common usage of the term in English that is a synonym of "expression" and the more common usage of the term in Spanish that is a synonym of "joint." Brent Hayes Edwards has theorized this latter usage in his work on the active process of "articulating" Black internationalism through the disjunctures in racial ideologies across languages (10–12).

6. Whereas Antonio Benítez-Rojo has forwarded the thesis of a "repeating island" as both a creative trope of Caribbean literature and an ontological understanding of the region's commonalities, I would like to suggest that the repeating trope is not "the island" but the positioning of a Pan-Caribbean vision that is necessarily partial (*The Repeating Island*).

7. In my offering of "methodological resistance" I draw on the idea of "methodological nationalism" elaborated by Andreas Wimmer and Nina Glick Schiller in "Methodological Nationalism and Beyond" (301–334) and expanded on by Yarimar Bonilla (45) and Gary Wilder (3). In my use of "capture" here, I am thinking of Freda Fair's work on

the surveillance of Black women in the Midwest. See their "Surveilling Social Difference." See also Fair's forthcoming book, *The Black Midwest.*

8. In my conception of colonialism, its social and economic residues, and contemporary imperialism as a state of war, I draw on a number of sources including Nelson Maldonado-Torres's *Against War*, Achille Mbembe's *The Postcolony*, and Simone de Beauvoir's *The Second Sex*. My conception of a "structure of desire" is adapted from Raymond Williams's concept of "structures of feeling" (129–135).

9. The sense of being-in-relation I evoke here draws both on Emmanuel Levinas's *Entre Nous: Thinking-of-the-Other* and Édouard Glissant's *Poetics of Relation* without being reducible to either of these works.

10. The literary magazine form in the Caribbean dates back at least to the nineteenth century. In 1824 Havana, the periodical *El Habanero* was released. Located in Barbados but printed in London, *West India Magazine* was a colonial literary publication initiated in 1840. In Port-au-Prince, the influential *La Ronde* would come to light in 1898. As the modernist form of the magazine proliferated throughout Europe, Latin America, and the United States, it also saw an expanded presence in the Caribbean. In 1913 *Revista de las antillas* would emerge in San Juan. The 1920s would bring about *Pancho Ibero* in San Juan, *Revue Indigène* in Port-au-Prince, *Lucioles* in Fort-de-France, and *Revista de Avance* in Havana. The 1930s would see *West Indian Review* in Kingston, *The Beacon* in Port of Spain, and *Espuela de Plata* in Havana. I do not attempt a comprehensive history here and instead offer a brief and partial genealogy of the magazines that precede the 1940s in the region.

11. A thorough Pan-Caribbean history of literary magazines would have to account for how to define the genre as it develops in the Caribbean region, for the literary magazine was regularly interdisciplinary here, and many magazines categorized as literary may not appear literary to all observers. The African American literary magazines produced during the Harlem Renaissance, especially *The Crisis*, edited by W.E.B. Du Bois, are perhaps generically closest to those magazines produced in the Caribbean.

12. Gaztambide-Géigel suggests that more English-language maps referred to the West Indies than the Caribbean in the eighteenth century, and my research on the historical antecedents to the West Indies Federation so far corroborates this view ("The Invention" 132).

13. As Donna Haraway clarifies, such knowledge is situated and partial (581–586).

14. As Simon Gikandi cautions, "literary discourses do not simply produce change" because they too are inscribed in history (*Maps of Englishness* 4).

15. A number of recent works also offer Pan-Caribbean paradigms of analysis including Martínez-San Miguel, *Coloniality of Diasporas*; Rodríguez Navas, *Idle Talk, Deadly Talk*; Murray-Román, *Performance and Personhood in Caribbean Literature*; Torres-Saillant, *An Intellectual History of the Caribbean*; Quintero-Herencia, *Caribe Abierto*; Dalleo, *American Imperialism's Undead*.

16. See also Shona Jackson, *Creole Indigeneity*.

17. For this insight, I am indebted to Frances Negrón-Muntaner's teachings. See *Boricua Pop*.

18. See, for example, Bosch, *De Cristobal Colón a Fidel Castro*; Williams, *From Columbus to Castro*.

19. See Martínez-San Miguel and Seligmann, "Con-Federating the Archipelago"; Gaztambide-Géigel, "The Rise and Geopolitics of Antilleanism."

20. See Naranjo Orovio and Buscaglia.

21. See Robinson; Quijano; Quijano and Wallerstein; Wynter, "Unsettling the Coloniality of Being / Power / Truth / Freedom"; Hall, "Race, Articulation, and Societies Structured in Dominance."

22. I hope this statement will be a provocation to future scholars who will be able to relate the history of the book in the Caribbean with greater specificity.

23. According to Bruce King, Walcott sent the book to Port of Spain to be printed by the printery at the *Trinidad Guardian* (the newspaper that "took outside jobs") because "there was not a local printer used to producing works of literature" in St. Lucia (56). The book would also go on to be printed in Barbados at the *Advocate* (also newspaper) printery.

24. Frank Collymore, the editor of *Bim*, would send a manuscript of his to BBC *Caribbean Voices* editor Henry Swanzy in London, and Swanzy in turn would correspond with Walcott and connect him to a London-based publisher.

25. I have also defined literary infrastructure this way in Seligmann, "The Void, the Distance, Elsewhere" (2).

26. Aimé Césaire also used the language of the "void" to describe the "lack" of cultural production in the Antilles, which I address in chapter 2.

27. Jennifer Wilks dates the play *Aurore de la liberté* to 1952 based on evidence that it was performed that year by the Martinican theater troupe Scènes et Culture (108, 217).

28. Throughout this book, all translations are mine unless stated otherwise. While I provide source quotations and translations of primary source materials, some secondary sources are provided in translation only.

29. See Haigh; Nesbitt "Caribbean Literature in French."

30. I suspect that an even greater number of Haitian literary works have been published in France than at home, but I have not conducted enough research on this point to go that far. I am grateful to Kaiama Glover for talking to me about the circumstances of Haitian literary publishing at home. As she explains about the Spiralist Haitian writers, their "adamant refusal of displacement" came at a real cost ("Haitian Literature," n.p.). Chelsea Stieber also notes that in "the entirety of the nineteenth century and into the twentieth, the majority of Haitian monographs and anthologies were published in France" (21).

31. I am grateful to Yolanda Martínez-San Miguel for pointing out this fact.

32. I develop this argument at length elsewhere. See Seligmann, "The Void, the Distance, Elsewhere."

33. For example, Casanova suggests that "if Latin America was an altogether marginal and remote literary space in the 1930s, lacking any international recognition, thirty years later virtually the opposite was true" (184–185).

CHAPTER 2 — LOCATING A POETICS OF FREEDOM IN *TROPIQUES*

1. Parts of this chapter are reprinted with permission from Duke University Press and *South Atlantic Quarterly* editor Michael Hardt from my article: "Poetic Productions of Cultural Combat in *Tropiques*," *South Atlantic Quarterly*, vol. 115, no. 3, 2016, pp. 495–512.

2. See Paxton, *Vichy France*, preface and chap. 1.

3. As I argue in chapter 1, I am concerned throughout this book with the function of constructing a Caribbean locus of enunciation, or the location where discourse is situated.

4. In 1944, another small magazine dedicated primarily to poetry emerged in Fort-de-France by the name of *Caravelle*. Only two numbers remain at the Archives Départementales de Martinique. In 1927, Gilbert Gratiant had also edited the literary magazine *Lucioles*.

5. The newspaper *Courrier des Antilles* started in Fort-de-France in 1933 with a weekly run that covered local and international political affairs, occasionally reporting on cultural events such as performances, films, and reviews by books published in metropolitan France that had reached the island. In 1938, a cultural section was added to the newspaper.

6. Although some accounts mention only Aimé Césaire and René Ménil as editors while others include Suzanne Césaire as well as Aristide Maugée and Lucie Thésée on the editorial committee, the three editors / primary contributors whose work I focus on are by far the most regular contributors to the magazine, and their texts, as my analysis will demonstrate, are in such close dialogue with each other that the literary-cultural project of the magazine seems to belong primarily to this triumvirate.

7. Aimé Césaire was elected president of the Martinican students' association in Paris in 1935 and instigated the title change of the organization's magazine to *L'Etudiant noir* to include African students and students from other parts of the African diaspora studying in Paris (Véron and Hale 15).

8. As has been well documented, the magazine was indeed shut down by censors temporarily, in May 1943. The censure letter accused the group of "sectarianism" and "racism" in a rejection of antiracist Black race-pride as if it were oppositional to other races, the kind of move that white supremacists throughout the Americas have turned to repeatedly from well before this moment and at least until the present. The *Tropiques* group famously responded by allying themselves with the so-called racism of Toussaint Louverture. For more on the censorship letter and response, see Ménil, "Sous l'amiral," 151–153.

9. Many of these were double issues (6–7, 8–9, 13–14).

10. Cuban reception was implied by the mentions of Afro-Chinese-Cuban painter Wifredo Lam's stopover in Martinique on his way home from France. Haitian reception was indicated by the republication of two articles from *Cahiers d'Haïti*, by Ménil's discussion of Jacques Roumain's stay with them during the war ("Sous l'amiral"), and by Aimé Césaire and Suzanne Césaire's months-long Haitian sojourn in 1944. Curaçao received mention as one site of reception in Aristide Maugée's "Revue des revues" (Review of magazines) article in *Tropiques* 6–7.

11. As Kora Véron sums up Césaire's poetic travels at this time, "Poems from *Tropiques*, as well as others not published in the journal, now began to appear in New York in the journals *VVV* and *Hémisphères;* in Havana, with the Spanish translation of *Cahier d'un retour au pays natal*; in Santiago in *Leitmotiv*; in Buenos Aires in *Lettres françaises*; and in Algiers in *Fontaine*, before the collection *Les armes miraculeuses* was published by Gallimard in Paris in 1946" ("Césaire at the Crossroads in Haiti" 430). For a discussion of Césaire's migrant poetry, see also Alex Gil's chapter "Adaptation" in his dissertation "Migrant Textualities."

12. See Arnold, "Beyond Postcolonial Césaire"; Richardson.

13. I use "black internationalism" following Edwards's work in *The Practice of Diaspora* on the earlier establishment of a transnational network of Black intellectuals in Paris, from Africa and the diaspora. I employ this term for *Tropiques* because beyond

affiliating to the Black diaspora, *Tropiques* also sought to affiliate the Antillean Black diaspora to a present, colonized Africa.

14. Another way Quijano defines this epistemological work is the "Eurocentrist perspective on knowledge production" (qtd. in Buscaglia-Salgado xiii).

15. For a discussion of how Pétain's "return to the soil" ideology fomented nationalist discourses against French colonialism under Vichy, see Jennings, *Vichy in the Tropics* 20–22.

16. For a detailed account and analysis of this period for Aimé Césaire, see Véron, *Aimé Césaire, configurations.*

17. In his essay "Poésie et connaissance," Aimé Césaire discusses his view of poetry's capacity to signify multiply, even meanings in constitutive contradiction, as well as the importance of context in accruing meaning to the word of the poem (166–170). In my reading of his poetry that I develop in this chapter, the theory and practice match up.

18. For Vichy's imperial policy that favored Nazi economic interests, see Jennings, *Vichy in the Tropics* 14–15.

19. For the history of this escape route, see Jennings, "Last Exit from Vichy France."

20. I first consulted this source in the form of a typescript housed in Damas's papers at the Schomburg Center for Research in Black Culture. See also Damas, "Négritude in Retrospect" (undated).

21. Because it has been customary to render "Antillais" as either "West Indian" or "Caribbean" in English, it is not surprising that Damas's essay, produced in English, would employ "West Indian" instead of "Antillean." I continue to use "Antillean" where possible to inflect my specific reference to the French colonies in the Caribbean at this time.

22. The resonance with Friedrich Nietzsche's *Birth of Tragedy* is crucial to this text and to the Dionysian tendencies spurred on by Ménil and later by Aimé Césaire in his "Poésie et connaissance."

23. Stieber uses "dépaysment" to refer to what French magazines would have evoked in Haiti in contradistinction to the way that Haitian magazine *Revue Indigène* brought literature home to Haiti (31).

24. Although the *Tropiques* group does not focus on developing existentialist ideas, both Ménil and Suzanne Césaire employ an existentialist framework for understanding cultural authenticity and for their views on cultural alienation.

25. Although the essay is more broadly about art, Ménil refers specifically in it to the art of poetry.

26. For example, in "Situation de la poésie aux Antilles" Ménil stresses the importance of finding a way to be "universellement pris en considération" (universally taken into consideration) for those he identifies as "nous qui voulons nous reclasser dans l'humanité" (those of us who would like to be reclassified within humanity) (131).

27. The resonance with the "L'experience vecu du Noir" heading in Fanon's *Peau noire, masques blancs* is apropos (88).

28. In Brazil, Oswald de Andrade would similarly call for literature to cannibalize European traditions in his 1928 "Cannibalist Manifesto."

29. I have been convinced by Dixa Ramírez's point that the closest Anglophone Caribbean equivalent in use for the rugged elevated terrain associated with Maroon history, the difficult to translate spaces called "*el monte*" and "*le morne*" in Spanish and French, is "the hills" ("Black Horror"). In Jamaican literature, for example, there is Sylvia Wynter's

The Hills of Hebron, which would certainly translate well to "Le morne de Hebron" or "El monte de Hebron."

30. The translator of this essay has translated "*Antillais*" ("Antillean") as "West Indian."

31. This view deviates from Breton's surrealism, which proposes an internal poetic revolution.

32. In chapter 3 I discuss Carpentier's critique that is central to his preface to his 1949 novel *El reino de este mundo*.

33. For discussions of the Césaires in Haiti, see Dash, *The Other America*, chap. 3; Véron, "Césaire at the Crossroads in Haiti"; Joseph-Gabriel, "Beyond the Great Camouflage."

34. I amend here my earlier view that this passage conscribed the freedom of the reader to the coordinates of meaning-making provided by the poem in response to thoughtful feedback from Yu-jin Chang. See Seligmann, "Poetic Productions of Cultural Combat in *Tropiques*" (501).

35. According to Donna V. Jones, Césaire's view of "the poetic as a cognitively superior mode" drew from Nietzsche's "vitalist critique of language" (153).

36. Michael Richardson has also suggested that Césaire's poetry served as "a starting point for the theoretical and philosophical issues raised" in the magazine (8).

37. The next published entry of the *Cahier* would appear as a bilingual volume including an English translation by Yvan Goll and Lionel Abel. This poem-entry of Césaire's *Cahier*, which would not be published until early 1947 in New York by Brentano's, would include the text of "En guise de manifeste littéraire." Most of the antimanifesto would also appear in the next published entry, which differs significantly from the New York entry even though it was published only two months later in Paris by Bordas. The subsequent entry, which for a long time circulated as if it were "the poem" itself, would not appear until 1956 in Paris, by Présence Africaine. This poem-entry includes much less of the text of "En guise de manifeste littéraire." In both of the installments published in 1947, the text of "En guise de manifeste littéraire" appears with some interruption and few changes, but by the 1956 entry only several parts of the antimanifesto appear, scattered into the poem. See Gil, "Bridging the Middle Passage"; Véron and Hale; Arnold and Gil.

38. The latest Présence Africaine edition of *Cahier d'un retour au pays natal* includes the piece in question in the appendix (69–74). The publishers even include a reference to the pages in the poem's latest version that correspond to this piece, making it easier for scholars to compare the two versions.

39. Wynter, in turn, was certainly in dialogue with Césaire's poetics and legacy.

40. All translations of "En Guise de Manifeste Littéraire" are by Catherine Lazerwitz and myself.

41. It is rarely noted that Césaire also indicates the importance of the comical in poetry in "Poésie et connaissance." There is so much gravity in his writing that the comical and ironic elements remain oft overlooked.

42. In chapter 1 of *Black and Blur*, "Not in Between," Moten cites without attributing Césaire's *Cahier* when he asks, "What does the African bring to the 'rendezvous of victory'?" (2).

43. See Williams, "The Queer Gift of Black Folk." See also Nesbitt, "Antinomies of Double Consciousness in Aimé Césaire's *Cahier d'un retour au pays natal*."

44. The *créolité* manifesto also refers to those writers "so-called dou douist" without attributing the critique to Suzanne Césaire (78).

45. Mylène Priam also draws attention to the *créolité* manifesto's debt to Aimé Césaire that exceeds the recognition he receives by its authors (22–23).

46. Sartre's essay "Orphée Noir" (Black Orpheus), the preface to Leopold Senghor's 1948 *Anthologie de la nouvelle poésie nègre et malgache de langue française* (Anthology of New Black and Malagasy Poetry in French) would critique the poetry associated with "négritude" in ways that resonate with the Vichy censors of *Tropiques*. There would be later elaborations of "négritude" as a movement, and there would also be many critiques of what has been described as a metaphysical, transcendental, and / or essentialist view of blackness in these ideas. *Tropiques* is certainly not responsible for theoretically elaborating or even naming "négritude" *as a movement* or *philosophy* even if the magazine significantly contributed to activating revolutionary Black consciousness.

47. Although they do not cite the authors of *Tropiques* for any of the ideas they invoke, they do, curiously, cite Aimé Césaire and René Ménil's work on Creole folk tales published in *Tropiques*, demonstrating their awareness of it and the ideas expounded therein (Bernabé, Chamoiseau, and Confiant 122).

CHAPTER 3 — *GACETA DEL CARIBE* V. *ORÍGENES* IN CUBA

1. This political party was affiliated at the time with the international Communist Party.

2. The Communist Party had been legalized in Cuba in 1938. According to McGillivray, "In 1938 Batista moved further from his army power base and invited workers into the state. He legalized the Communist Party and allowed it to start a newspaper and radio station in the hope that communists could organize 'the masses' around their new democratic 'savior.' He officially stepped down as chief of the army and began campaigning for the 1940 presidential elections" (244–245).

3. For detailed analyses of these historical transformations, see Whitney; McGillivray; de la Fuente.

4. In a letter to José Antonio Portuondo during his doctoral studies in Mexico with Alfonso Reyes, Alejo Carpentier's wife describes the food shortages; see Romero and Castillo. In a 1943 book, *Falange*, the U.S. investigative journalist Allan Chase wrote about the fascist movement of the Americas. The book was translated into Spanish, published in Cuba, and reviewed in *Gaceta del Caribe* 1 in 1944.

5. The majority of magazines during the republican period in Cuba were produced from 1902 to 1930 (53%) (Esquenazi-Mayo xii).

6. As Esquenazi-Mayo notes, understanding this context requires defining a publishing company (xix). For example, José Ricardo refers to a number of "companies" that Smorkaloff in her work refers to as "presses." In my view, capital backing would make the difference, and while Smorkaloff asserts that only two short-lived "publishing projects" financed book production, Ricardo does not refer to the role of capital in the entities he calls "companies" (Smorkaloff 47–62; Ricardo 148).

7. The Manzanillo-based *Orto* (1912–1957) might not have been as influential, but it certainly deserves more attention as a long-lasting project tied to a printing press that also published numerous books on the eastern part of Cuba. For more on the *Orto* project, see Smorkaloff 33; and Ricardo 144–145. Another important precursor to *Gaceta*

del Caribe was *Revista de Estudios Afrocubanos* (est. 1937), edited by Fernando Ortiz. See Arroyo, *Travestismos culturales* 238–240.

8. I have surmised the source of *Gaceta del Caribe*'s funding from a series of letters that connect the dots.

9. Research on *Gaceta del Caribe* is on the rise in recent years, but its bibliography is slim compared to the vast list of works that address *Orígenes*.

10. I use "Afrocentric" here in a way that is related to my use of "Eurocentric," to refer to the orbit or orientation of the work independent of the racial presentation or identification of the author. It is worth clarifying that Afrocentric French-language poetry referred to with the language of *négritude* differs as a genealogy of poetry produced explicitly by Black-identified poets. Both poetic tendencies pertain to the rising popularity of Black arts in the 1920s and 1930s throughout the world and in particular in Paris, as a cultural center in both the French- and Spanish-speaking worlds and beyond. For thorough approaches to their underpinnings and significance, see Edwards, *The Practice of Diaspora*; Arroyo, *Travestismos culturales*. See also Anderson, *Carnival and National Identity in the Poetry of Afrocubanismo*.

11. I do not mean to suggest that all work that might be classified as "Black aesthetics" is of equal value. Although work by Black and white authors has often been distinguished in this vein, it is important to acknowledge the prevalence of white Cuban authors in the field. Richard L. Jackson has indicated aptly that white *negrista* poets did not see Black Cubans "*por dentro*," and the distinction between establishing Black subjectivities with developed interiorities and objectifying Black Cubans in exterior representations is a key for distinguishing between the poetry that is continuous with racism and the poetry that resists and dismantles racist gazes (Jackson 40–44; Arnedo-Gómez 43). In this chapter I employ "Black aesthetics" in more sweeping terms, however, because the literary battle I recuperate does not appear to be primarily about these distinctions but instead about securing a central place for Black representation in Cuban arts (*Gaceta del Caribe*) versus marginalizing Black representation into a minoritarian position (*Orígenes*).

12. For its first two issues, the dramatist Felix Pita Rodríguez was also part of the committee. In a letter to Portuondo, Pita Rodríguez indicated that he had been ousted from the editorial committee after the first two issues, though he does not explain why. For the series of letters written to Portuondo while he studied in Mexico during much of *Gaceta del Caribe*'s run, see Romero and Castillo.

13. Nicolás Guillén would go on to serve on the advisory board of the 1946 journal of the Instituto de Intercambio Cultural Cubano-Soviético (Cuban-Soviet Institute of Cultural Exchange), *Cuba y la USRR*.

14. Although as Leitch notes the Communist Party populist "People's Front" strategy is dated for 1935–1939, the antifascist coalitional politics it gave rise to exceeded its timeline and is clearly at work in *Gaceta del Caribe* and was also at work in other parts of the Caribbean during the 1940s. I am grateful to Jackqueline Frost for clarifying the prevalence of such antifascist politics in the Caribbean during this time based on her research on anticolonialism and antifascism. See Frost, "The Past of Future Life."

15. Senel Paz's book *El lobo, el bosque, y el hombre nuevo* and Tomás Gutiérrez Alea's film based on it, *Fresa y chocolate*, would go on to deconstruct the ideological code of deviance from normative gender and sexuality but after the fact of the Military Units to Aid Production (UMAP) labor camps.

16. This position was in accordance with the Communist Party's commitment to fight for the right of all workers in Cuba regardless of nationality. For the communist responses to the "50 percent law," see McGillivray, chap. 7.

17. He had also authored the book of short fiction *La luna nona y otros cuentos* (The ninth moon and other stories), also published in Buenos Aires in 1942. For more on Novás Calvo, see Marturano.

18. See also Seligmann, "The Void, the Distance, Elsewhere."

19. In his description of the coloniality of power, Quijano notes that although colonialism gave rise to the racialization of power, "it has proven to be more durable and stable" than the colonial matrix that inscribed it (533).

20. In chapter 5, I examine the textual itinerary of Roumain's text as it circulated through Caribbean magazines in the first half of the 1940s.

21. Paloma Duong has suggested that the importance of letters in Marxist history pertains to the way they reveal what is unsayable in public for a host of political reasons. In this case, even the letters utilize a code that marks an unsayable element beyond what is said ("'Conspiracy of Silence'"). See also Michael Hardt, "How to Write with Four Hands," for more on the history of Left collaborative and anonymous writing that also explains the anonymous and likely collectively produced works in *Gaceta del Caribe.*

22. See chapter 2 for more analysis of Césaire's *Cahier d'un retour au pays natal.*

23. See Seligmann, "Cabrera's Césaire." See also Maguire, "Two Returns to the Native Land."

24. See also Odette Casamayor-Cisneros, "Piñera, Lam, y los Origenistas."

25. Although it is unlikely that Baquero's recommending Césaire for literary tourists reached the *Tropiques* group, this kind of reception highlights the danger implicit in Suzanne Césaire's "Le grande camouflauge," discussed in chapter 2: the danger that even antiexoticist Caribbean-located poetry would be received with an exoticizing gaze.

26. Both Supervielle and Lautréamont are French-canonized poets who were born in Uruguay to French parents.

27. For more on Césaire's reception in Cuba during this period, see also Fowler (113–137).

28. The first number of *Revista Orígenes* is dated "Spring 1944," so the exact month of its release is unclear.

29. The first two issues of *Orígenes* name two other members of its editorial board, Alfredo Lozano and the painter Mariano, but Lezama Lima and Rodríguez Feo remained at the helm for much of the magazine's run with the exception of a brief period at the end when they parted ways.

30. Attesting to *Orígenes*'s connections to elite institutions in the United States, originals I have consulted from the 1940s at Harvard University and Columbia University are dated very close to the release dates.

31. In chapter 5 I examine the role of the United States and Spain in *Orígenes*'s literary geography.

32. Salah Dean Assaf Hassan also notes the magazine's dialogue with New Criticism (80).

33. As César Salgado indicates, Lezama would later go on to reposition *Orígenes* as a future-oriented project whose aesthetic creationism could guide the renovation of the

state (24). In this sense, Salgado is close to Rodríguez Matos's argument that the "formless" quality of Lezama Lima's writing was "infrapolitical" and sought to innovate in the very form of the political (80). While I find compelling and influential nodes in Lezama Lima's poetic and theoretical work, I consider the early composition of *Orígenes* I focus on and Lezama Lima's poetry during this period to be much more ideologically infused with the banalities of the social and political present it embodied than many of the magazine project's critics.

34. *Orígenes* published other work by Eliot in 1944, and George Lamming's letters to Frank Collymore also testify to both Lamming and Collymore's influence by Eliot.

35. Irlemar Chiampi has also noted about this editorial that it presents the magazine as a subject (2).

36. Chapter 2 examines the centrality of location to the theories of literature espoused by *Tropiques*.

37. For the legacy of Lezama's essay in contemporary Cuban poetics, see Whitfield.

38. Lezama omits the African location of Frobenius's work, which was also highly influential to the *Tropiques* group precisely as a record of African cultural legacies.

39. Vera Kutzinski and Arnedo-Gómez elaborate the way that Afro-Cuban culture in particular appeared "uncontaminated" by U.S. culture and therefore as representative for national manifestations of anti-imperial art (Kutzinski 141; Arnedo-Gómez 33).

40. See also Quijano and Wallerstein, "Americanity as a Concept."

41. The text would be published in January 1938 in *Revista Cubana*, but Lezama dated the text for June 1937.

42. I use "African-Cubans" to distinguish African-born members of the polity.

43. When *Tropiques* was censored for a brief period, the rationale included a similar accusation of "racism" for the racial character of the magazine's antiracist discourse.

44. Gastón Baquero would go on to sustain that *afrocubanismo* reinforced the ideological subordination of Black Cubans (Arnedo-Gómez 8).

45. Fowler notes Heller's indication that although this poem would not be published until 1954, it was penned by Lezama in 1944, the same year that gave rise to *Orígenes* (135).

46. See also Jesus Barquet, who draws attention to these inclusions in the context of a very different argument.

47. In chapter 2 I also discuss Paget Henry's concept of "communicative inequality."

48. I am adopting Gramsci's term in *Selections from the Prison Notebooks* for the kind of massive political struggle that is not military, although by no means do I mean to equate a mass movement and a literary magazine; I mean instead to suggest that *Gaceta del Caribe*'s cultural battle has similar aims of overturning a politically disengaged cultural hegemony tied to Cuba's political present and future.

49. Roberto González-Echevarría notes that Carpentier did not publish this book as a novel, as it was published with the parenthetical "*un relato*" descriptor, marking it instead as short fiction (156–157). The text is, however, divided into parts and chapters, giving it the form of a novel. Furthermore, the *Gaceta del Caribe* excerpt was published with the title "Capítulo de novela," suggesting precisely the plan for a novel.

50. My use of "prefatory threshold" is a reference to Gérard Genette's book *Seuils*, which elaborates a theory of "paratexts," or those texts that work on the thresholds of literary texts, including prefaces, called *seuils* [thresholds].

51. I discuss the official Latin Americanist position of the revolutionary Cuban state in chapter 1. See also Seligmann, "Caliban, Why?"

CHAPTER 4 — *BIM* BECOMES WEST INDIAN

1. Parts of this chapter are reprinted with permission from Duke University Press and *Small Axe* editor David Scott from my article: "Un-nationalisms of the Federated Archipelago," *Small Axe*, vol. 24, no. 1, 2020, pp. 69–77.

2. For an in-depth study of the Bretton Woods agreement and its effect on the global economic order, see Steil, *The Battle of Bretton Woods*.

3. Lewis reads the federation on the British side as a matter of administrative convenience for colonial rule, but the transitional—if minimal—concession implied in the move to federation is also evident in the official discourse promulgated at the Montego Bay conference (364–365). See also *Conference on the Closer Association of the British West Indian Colonies*, Part II, Proceedings.

4. Although, as Baugh explains, the YMPC was started with the hopes of inspiring political participation among "the young, educated class of men," by the 1940s it was exclusively a social club that also had sports teams. Before *Bim* the YMPC published the *YMPC Journal* dedicated to club news with some literary texts mostly published anonymously or with pseudonyms. As the literary section grew, the idea to have an exclusively literary publication emerged, leading to *Bim* (*Frank Collymore* 167–168). Furthermore, Frank Collymore had published two stories in the *YMPC Journal*, but he was not a member of the organization when he was solicited to edit *Bim*.

5. *The Advocate* newspaper was established in 1895, sixty-one years after the *Gleaner* (now *Daily Gleaner*) in Jamaica, which emerged in 1834. Trinidad and Tobago's *Guardian* would not be established until 1917.

6. *Bim* ran with little interruption with Frank Collymore at the helm and supported by various coeditors between 1942 and 1973. Collymore coedited the first two numbers of *Bim* with E. L. Cozier in addition to W. Therold Barnes, who would stay on to assist with editing until his death. Collymore's coeditors have also included A. N. "Freddie" Forde, E. K. Brathwaite, Harold Marshall, and John Wickham (Baugh, *Frank Collymore* 170). As Collymore himself explained, however, he edited almost entirely alone since *Bim* 3, and coeditors served to give advice when needed, to be regular contributors, and to recruit other contributors (Baugh, *Frank Collymore* 169). John Wickham edited it for twenty years after that, and in 2007 it was revived with funding from the Barbados national government under the leadership of George Lamming with the new name, *Bim: Arts for the 21st Century*. It is currently edited by Esther Phillips.

7. Collymore and Barnes were so careful to guard the unpolitical character of *Bim* that the most obviously political narrative to ever enter its pages during the 1940s appears in a note referring to a rejected story. At the end of the introductory editorial of *Bim* 10 (June 1949), they note that a rejected manuscript from Trinidad has been stolen and apologize to the author for not being able to send the story back. To identify the story, they specify that it is about a corrupt politician "who received his due desserts" (Collymore and Barnes, "Introduction" n.p.). The editors go so far as to express the hope that the thief enjoy this rejected story without naming the cause of rejection. The mention of the story is as directly political as the editors and their selected works of short fiction would be during the 1940s.

8. James coedited until his departure to England in 1932.

9. For in-depth examinations of the pivotal role played by *Caribbean Voices* in directing the future of West Indian literature, see Griffith, *The BBC and the Development of Anglophone Caribbean Literature, 1943–1958*; Kalliney, *Commonwealth of Letters*.

10. See *Conference on the Closer Association of the British West Indian Colonies*, Parts I and II. Upon the withdrawal of Jamaica in 1961 "in a referendum that triggered independence negotiations" the federation collapsed in 1962 (Martínez-San Miguel and Seligmann 41).

11. Although this piece remains unsigned, the editors of *Bim* at this time were the writers and regular contributors, Frank Collymore and W. Therold Barnes, though Collymore would go on to be considered the main editor of *Bim*, as he stayed at its helm for the majority of its shelf life.

12. Interestingly, Mignolo makes a similar point about the Latin American Creole elite in the nineteenth century: "Creole consciousness was indeed a singular case of double consciousness: the *consciousness of not being who they were supposed to be (Europeans)*" (*The Idea* 63). For a thorough analysis of the postcolonial ambivalence of absorbed, even if unrecognized forms of Englishness in the British colonies, see Gikandi, *Maps of Englishness*.

13. Naipaul uses a similar tone in his Caribbean travel memoir, *The Middle Passage*, when he points out how "anti-Jamaican" sentiment in England relates to Jamaica being the only Anglophone Caribbean location that most English people register (21–22).

14. Although geographically "West Indies," like "Antilles" in French and "Antillas" in Spanish, is an insular demarcation, it is clear that in politics and literature alike, the category of "West Indian" absorbed the noninsular territories that were also included in the West Indies Federation program of 1947, Guyana (British Guiana), and Belize (British Honduras). In later years, the category would alternate between including only British-colonized spaces around the Caribbean, such as Lamming's use of the term in *The Pleasures of Exile* (1960), and the use of "West Indian" interchangeably with "Caribbean" to absorb parts of the region that were colonized by other powers, such as C.L.R. James's use of "West Indian" in his 1962 appendix essay to the later edition of *The Black Jacobins*, "From Toussaint L'Ouverture to Fidel Castro."

15. Naipaul discusses his personal experience of admiring the true "style" of Hollywood movie stars growing up in Trinidad during the 1940s (53–56).

16. Importantly, the local was not the only setting for *Bim*-published narratives in the early years. Besides those mentioned previously by Collymore and Cozier set abroad, many stories had war-themed plotlines, mostly set abroad. Additionally, the local narratives varied significantly. Some stories are told as barroom humorous anecdotes; others are ghost or fantastic stories told in an eerie key. A disproportionate number of stories involve love interests and men attempting to decode women's behavior in matters of love and jealousy.

17. Although this is peripheral to my argument in this chapter, it should be noted that many of the stories in the colonial narrative strain may be considered neogothic or at least include gothic tendencies and in later years become ironic-humorous twists on gothic and / or crime fiction motifs.

18. Gail Low notes evidence of Jan Williams's never-to-be-published novel having been sent to BBC *Caribbean Voices* editor Henry Swanzy to be scouted for publication (105).

19. Susan Gilson Miller, in her "Afterword" to Memmi's text, points out that "women as personalities in the colonialist drama are largely absent from Memmi's account" (164).

20. Ramchand traces this mode to fiction produced in the late 1920s and early 1930s by C.L.R. James and Alfred H. Mendes in the Trinidad-based periodicals *Trinidad* and *Beacon* (43–50).

21. See Camus, "The Myth of Sisyphus."

22. This is the same problem, surveyed in chapter 3, that Lino Novás Calvo called Cuba's "colonial mentality," which in his view caused Cubans to favor foreign cultural production.

23. Mittelholzer spent 1941–1942 in the British Royal Navy. According to A. J. Seymour, Mittelholzer found a way to be dismissed from the navy by acting in ways that would make him deemed mentally ill (13).

24. In a later personal narrative by Mittelholzer published in *Bim*, "Romantic Promenade: A Divertissement in Minor Chords," Mittelholzer directly examines his relationship to romanticism, setting up his way of literarily bringing trees and buildings to life in opposition to the capitalist relation to objects for the purpose of greater accumulation (12–13).

25. As Roy Osamu Kamada argues, "Postcolonial writers lack the luxury of an ahistorical landscape. The landscapes that they write about are necessarily politicized; their own subjectivities are intimately implicated in both the natural beauty as well as the traumatic history of the place; they confront and engage to varying degrees the history of their postcolonial geographies, the history of diaspora, of slavery, of the capitalist commodification of landscape, and the devastating consequences this history has on the individual" (3).

26. One example of an obvious inheritor of this mode of writing is Kincaid's anticolonial and antitourism travel essay, *A Small Place*.

27. According to Baugh, "With regard to the sharpening of *BIM*'s West Indian perspective, No. 9 (from December 1948) marked a decisive development" (*Frank Collymore* 172). The decisive development consisted of including, in addition to the Guyanese regular Edgar Mittelholzer, four new contributions from Trinidad: poems by Harold Telemaque, Ruby M. Waithe, and C. L. Herbert and an essay by Ernest Carr.

28. From George Lamming letters to Frank Collymore dated April 23, 1947, and July 22, 1948.

29. Lamming mentions having written two short stories and having ideas for two more in his letter to Collymore dated October 2, 1946, but he does not send these stories to Collymore at this time and instead only includes poetry with that letter. Lamming would send two stories later, which presumably are "Birds of a Feather" and his next published story, "Of Thorns and Thistles," along with his letter dated April 23, 1947.

30. For examinations of the significance of modernism in Lamming's novels, see Gikandi, *Writing in Limbo*; Brown.

31. Through the 1940 destroyers-for-bases deal, the United States occupied naval bases during World War II in Trinidad, St. Lucia, the Bahamas, Antigua, Guyana, Bermuda, and Newfoundland. For accounts of how the Trinidadian capital of Port of Spain transformed through the U.S. occupation, see Michael Anthony, *Port-of-Spain in a World at War 1939–1945* and Harvey R. Neptune, *Caliban and the Yankees*. See also Jason C. Parker, *Brother's Keeper*.

32. This song was depoliticized in the stolen version that circulated in the United States by the Andrews Sisters.

33. In her "Foreword" to the book, Sandra Pouchet Paquet notes that the essays of *The Pleasures of Exile* are aimed at "dismantling" what Lamming calls "the colonial structure of awareness which has determined West Indian values" (x–xi).

34. Brown examines Lamming's novels through their critical reception in London. As Brown explains, Lamming was read to be a "self-consciously difficult" writer in the vein of Joyce, Faulkner, and Woolf (73).

35. See chapter 5 for more on the significance of this cover as a map.

36. The Advocate Press, which printed *Bim*, also reprinted Walcott's book in Barbados.

37. See Seligmann, "Un-nationalisms of the Federated Archipelago" for further analysis of this poem (73–74).

CHAPTER 5 — POLYCENTRIC MAPS OF LITERARY WORLDMAKING

1. In chapter 3 I discuss Novás Calvo's critique of limited infrastructure for literary production in Cuba in which he refers to such infrastructure as "vehicles."

2. For my reparative critique of Casanova in dialogue with Caribbean literary history, see Seligmann, "The Void, the Distance, Elsewhere."

3. In chapter 1 I set up my argument about the centrality of literary magazines as homegrown literary infrastructures that have sustained the development of Caribbean literature.

4. My interest in conceiving of magazine "worldmaking" for this chapter draws on several sources, but among those that are not clearly cited otherwise in the text are Adom Getachew's work on political forms of postimperial "worldmaking" in Africa and the Caribbean and Howard Becker's work on art "worlds."

5. In chapter 1 I develop the argument that the infrastructural minimalism of the Caribbean bears on the asynchronous temporality of Caribbean literary magazines.

6. And my original geography too; the world map made / for my own use, not inked in the arbitrary colors of / geniuses, but in the geometry of my spilled blood.

7. Although the imperial history of the map is located in it, the medium exceeds its imperial history. As Patricia Mohammed notes, although mapping has been embedded in the European project of empire, "Cartography has been used differently and developed for varied reasons in different geographical spaces and should not be viewed primarily as the invention of a Western tradition" (55). Records of Chinese cartography, for example, date back at least to 2100 BC (56). The map thus exceeds the European imperial design with which it has become associated, and through dialogue and negotiation with this very imperial history, the medium itself may be disposed to dismantle, or at least disrupt, the results of this history.

8. Yolanda Wood also alludes to the history of empire producing a distance between Caribbean islands and coastal territories not visible on maps, a distance that would facilitate magazine travel from Caribbean outpost to metropole more than across the imperial borders of the Caribbean (87).

9. Although Bulson's article does not extend the "map" to his own analysis of geographic coordinates in African magazines, I understand the work he does in cartographic terms that more closely approximate the medium of the map than his symbolic use of the "map" in this formulation.

10. I also discuss this transformative moment in chapter 4.

11. For more on the history of the West Indies Federation and literature, see Martínez-San Miguel and Seligmann, "Con-Federating the Archipelago." See also Griffith, "*Caribbean Voices* and the Communicative Failure of the West Indies Federation"; Dalleo, "Regionalism, Imperialism, and Sovereignty."

12. See chapter 2 for my argument about *Tropiques* and Breton and chapter 3 for my argument about *Orígenes*'s editorial that engages and bypasses Eliot.

13. I discuss this theory in chapter 3.

14. In chapter 3 I examine *Gaceta del Caribe*'s editorial location writing that constructs a trans-American and Caribbean locus of enunciation.

15. For more on Novás Calvo's critique, see chapter 3.

16. Griffith makes a similar argument about the effect of the London-produced radio show Caribbean Voices on Caribbean-based audiences (*The BBC*).

17. As I note in chapter 3, Gil also argues for Aimé Césaire's hemispheric positioning during this period ("Aimé Césaire and the Broken Record" n.p.).

18. A collection of *Viernes* is housed at the Spanish National Library in Madrid, but sadly, the issue including Ratto-Ciarlo's essay is missing from the collection.

19. Although I was not able to locate this copy and it is also not reproduced in his complete works, this text was sent for publication to Argentina before going to Cuba.

20. For Roumain's antifascist political activity in France, see Frost.

21. In chapter 3 I discuss this history in dialogue with Vincent Leitch's history of American literary criticism in order to illuminate how similar the tensions between Marxist literary criticism and New Criticism in the United States were to the contemporaneous literary critical debates in Cuba.

22. In chapter 3 I examine the sociopolitical ramifications of the literary-critical battle waged between both magazines and also suggest the significance of Roumain's essay publication in this context.

23. Dalleo also examines this editorial in his analysis of *Poesía Sorprendida*, but I am adding the connection to Roumain's own text on "poetry as a weapon" in my analysis (*Caribbean Literature* 112).

24. As Dalleo also indicates, in the February 1944 issue of *Poesía Sorprendida*, they would feature Cuban authors, including *Orígenes* editor José Lezama Lima, as well as Haitian authors (*Caribbean Literature* 111). Roumain would not be included among the Haitian poets they published, but Roussan Camille (who would also go on to appear in *Gaceta del Caribe* with a report on Roumain's funeral that same year) would be.

25. I am also thinking through Nelson Maldonado-Torres's dialogue with Eduardo Mendieta's idea of "hetereo-chronotopology" in my conception of polycentric maps. As Maldonado-Torres argues, decolonizing knowledge consists of guaranteeing "the expression of different voices and ways of mapping the world" ("Toward a Critique" 72).

Works Cited

Aguirre, Mirta. "*Virgilio Piñera*: La Isla en Peso." *Gaceta del Caribe*, no. 3, May 1944, p. 30.

Aguirre, Sergio. "Hubo Conspiración de la Escalera?" *Gaceta del Caribe*, no. 1, Mar. 1944, pp.12–13.

Anderson, Benedict. *Imagined Communities: Reflections on the Origin and Spread of Nationalism*. 1983. Verso Books, 2016.

Anderson, Thomas F. *Carnival and National Identity in the Poetry of Afrocubanismo*. UP of Florida, 2011.

Andrews Sisters. "Rum and Coca-Cola." Morey Amsterdam, 1945.

Anthony, Michael. *Port-of-Spain in a World at War 1939–1945: The Making of Port-of-Spain*. Vol. 2, Paria, 1978.

Arnedo-Gómez, Miguel. *Writing Rumba: The Afrocubanista Movement in Poetry*. U of Virginia P, 2006.

Arnold, A. James. "Beyond Postcolonial Césaire: Reading *Cahier d'un retour au pays natal* Historically." *Forum for Modern Language Studies*, vol. 44, no. 3, 2008, pp. 258–275.

Arnold, A. James, and Alex Gil. "Cahier d'un retour au pays natal: Présentation." *Aimé Césaire: Poésie, Théâtre, Essais et Discurs*, edited by A. James Arnold, CNRS, 2013, pp. 65–73.

Arroyo, Jossianna. *Travestismos culturales: Literatura y etnografía en Cuba y en Brasil*. 2003. Almenara, 2020.

———. *Writing Secrecy in Caribbean Freemasonry*. Palgrave Macmillan, 2013.

Augier, Angel. *Nicolás Guillén: Estudio biográfico crítico*. Ediciones Union, 2005.

———. "*Retorno al país natal*, por Aimé Césaire." *Gaceta del Caribe*, no. 1, Mar. 1944, p. 30.

———. "Viaje a la semilla, por Alejo Carpentier." *Gaceta del Caribe*, no. 6, Aug. 1944, p. 28.

Babcock, William H. "Antillia and the Antilles." *Geographical Review*, vol. 9, no. 2, 1920, pp. 109–124.

Badiane, Mamadou. "Négritude, Antillanité et Créolité ou de l'éclatement de l'identité fixe." *The French Review*, vol. 85, no. 5, 2012, pp. 837–847.

Baeza Flores, Alberto. "Apasionado destino." *Poesía Sorprendida*, no. 1, Oct. 1943, n.p.

Bakhtin, M. M. "Forms of Time and of the Chronotope in the Novel." 1981. *The Dialogical Imagination: Four Essays*, edited by Michael Holquist. Translated by Caryl Emerson and Michael Holquist, U of Texas P, 1994, pp. 84–258.

Baquero, Gastón. *Darío, Cernuda, y otros temas poéticos*. Editora Nacional, 1969.

———. "Tendencias de nuestra literatura." *Anuario Cultural de Cuba 1943*. Ucar, García y cía., 1944, pp. 261–287.

Barnes, W. Therold. "Do Fuh Do." *Bim*, no. 2, 1943, pp. 17–19.

———. "War Memorial." *Bim*, no. 8, 1947, pp. 2–6.

Barquet, Jesus. "El grupo Orígenes ante el negrismo." *Afro-Hispanic Review*, vol. 15, no. 2, 1996, pp. 20–31.

Baugh, Edward. *Frank Collymore: A Biography*. Ian Randle, 2009.

———. "Introduction." *An Index to Bim: 1942–1972*, edited by Reinhard W. Sander, U of the West Indies, Trinidad & Tobago, 1973, pp. 7–17.

Becker, Howard S. *Art Worlds*. 1982. U of California P, 2008.

Beetham, Margaret. "Towards a Theory of the Periodical as a Publishing Genre." *Investigating Victorian Journalism*. Palgrave Macmillan, 1990, pp. 19–32.

Benítez-Rojo, Antonio. *The Repeating Island: The Caribbean and the Postmodern Perspective*. Translated by James E. Maraniss, Duke UP, 1997.

Bennet, David. "Periodical Fragments and Organic Culture: Modernism, the Avant Garde, and the Little Magazine." *Contemporary Literature*, vol. 30, no. 4, 1989, pp. 480–502.

Berman, Jessica. *Modernist Commitments: Ethics, Politics and Transnational Modernism*. Columbia UP, 2011.

Bernabé, Jean, Patrick Chamoiseau, and Raphaël Confiant. *Eloge de la Créolité/In Praise of Creoleness*. Translated by M. B. Taleb-Khyar, 1989. Gallimard, 2010.

Birkenmaier, Anke. *Alejo Carpentier y la cultura del surrealismo en América Latina*. Iberoamericana Vervuert, 2006.

Bonilla, Yarimar. *Non-Sovereign Futures: French Caribbean Politics in the Wake of Disenchantment*. U of Chicago P, 2015.

Borges. "The Argentine Writer and Tradition." *Labyrinths*, edited by Donald A. Yates and James E. Irby. Translated by James E. Irby, New Directions, 2007, pp. 177–185.

Bosch, Juan. "Cien Años." *Gaceta del Caribe*, no. 1, Mar. 1944, pp. 19–20.

———. *De Cristobal Colón a Fidel Castro: El Caribe frontera imperial*. 1971. Miguel Ángel Porrua, 2009.

Bourdieu, Pierre. *The Field of Cultural Production: Essays on Art and Literature*. Edited by Randal Johnson, Columbia UP, 1993.

Brathwaite, E. K. *History of the Voice: The Development of Nation Language in Anglophone Caribbean Poetry*. New Beacon Books, 1984.

Breton, André. "A Great Black Poet: Aimé Césaire." *Refusal of the Shadow: Surrealism and the Caribbean*, edited by Michael Richardson. Translated by Michael Richardson and Krzysztof Fijalkowski. Verso, 1996, pp. 191–198.

———. *Manifestes du surréalisme*. Éditions Gallimard, 1979.

———. "Martinique charmeuse de serpents: Un Grand poète noir." *Tropiques*, no. 11, 1944, pp. 119–126.

Bronfman, Alejandra. *Isles of Noise: Sonic Media in the Caribbean*. U of North Carolina P, 2016.

Brown, J. Dillon. *Migrant Modernism: Post-War London and the West Indian Novel.* U of Virginia, 2013.

Bulson, Eric. *Little Magazine, World Form.* Columbia UP, 2017.

———. "Little Magazine, World Form." *The Oxford Handbook of Global Modernisms,* edited by Mark A. Wollaeger and Matt Eatough, Oxford UP, 2012, pp. 267–287.

Buscaglia-Salgado, José. *Undoing Empire: Race and Nation in the Mulatto Caribbean.* U of Minnesota P, 2003.

Campbell, Elaine, and Pierette M. Frickey, editors. *The Whistling Bird: Women Writers of the Caribbean.* Lynne Reiner, 1998.

Camus, Albert. *The Myth of Sisyphus and Other Essays.* Translated by Justin O'Brien, Vintage International, 1983.

Carpentier, Alejo. "Capítulo de novela." *Gaceta del Caribe,* no. 3, May 1944, 12–13.

———. *¡Ecué-Yamba-O!.* 1933. Siglo Veintiuno, 2002.

———. *El reino de este mundo.* 1949. Seix Barral, 2004.

———. *The Kingdom of This World.* Translated by Pablo Medina, Farrar, Straus & Giroux, 2017.

———. "Oficio de Tinieblas." *Orígenes,* no. 4, Dec. 1944, 32–38.

Casamayor-Cisneros, Odette. "Piñera, Lam, y los Origenistas: Suspenso, tragedia, o comedia de enredos con fondo tropical." *Una isla llamada Virgilio,* edited by Jesús Jambrina, Stockcero, 2015, pp. 13–50.

Casanova, Pascale. *The World Republic of Letters.* Translated by M. B. Debevoise, Harvard UP, 2004.

Césaire, Aimé. *Cahier d'un retour au pays natal.* Bordas, 1947.

———. *Cahier d'un retour au pays natal.* 1956. Présence Africaine, 1983.

———. "Cahier d'un retour au pays natal." *Volontés,* no. 30, 1939, pp. 23–51.

———. *Cahier d'un retour au pays natal / Memorandum on My Martinique.* Translated by Lionel Abel and Ivan Goll, Brentanos, 1947.

———. "Conquista del alba." Translated by Virgilio Piñera, *Poeta,* no. 2, 1943, n.p.

———. "En guise de manifeste littéraire." *Tropiques,* no. 5, 1942, pp. 7–12.

———. "La poésie, parole essentielle." Interview by Daniel Maximin. *Présence Africaine,* no. 126, 1983, pp. 7–23.

———. *Les armes miraculeuses.* Gallimard, 1946.

———. "Maintenir la poésie." *Tropiques,* no. 8–9, 1943, pp. 7–8.

———. "Poésie et connaissance." *Tropiques,* no. 12, 1945, pp. 157–170.

———. "Présentation." *Tropiques,* no. 1, 1941, pp. 5–6.

———. *Retorno al país natal.* Translated by Lydia Cabrera, Ucar, García y cía., 1943.

Césaire, Suzanne. "1943: Le surréalisme et nous." *Tropiques,* no. 8–9, 1943, pp. 14–18.

———. "1943: Surrealism and Us." *Refusal of the Shadow: Surrealism and the Caribbean,* edited by Michael Richardson. Translated by Michael Richardson and Krzysztof Fijalkowski. Verso, 1996, pp. 123–126.

———. "The Great Camouflage." *Refusal of the Shadow: Surrealism and the Caribbean,* edited by Michael Richardson. Translated by Michael Richardson and Krzysztof Fijalkowski. Verso, 1996, pp. 156–161.

———. "Le grande camouflage." *Tropiques,* no. 13–14, 1945, pp. 267–273.

———. "Leo Frobenius et le problème des civilisations." *Tropiques,* no. 1, Apr. 1941, pp. 27–36.

———. "Malaise d'une civilisation." *Tropiques,* no. 5, Apr. 1942, pp. 43–49.

———. "Misère d'une poésie." *Tropiques*, no. 4, 1942, pp. 48–50.

Chaulet Achour, Christiane. "Aimé Césaire et Haïti-1944." *dEmanbrE*, no. 3, 2014, pp. 82–89.

Chiampi, Irlemar. "La revista Orígenes ante la crisis de la modernidad." *Brazilian Journal of Latin American Studies*, vol. 12, no. 1, 2002, pp. 1–16.

Clifford, James. *The Predicament of Culture: Twentieth Century Ethnography, Literature, and Art*. Harvard UP, 1988.

Collymore, Frank. "An Introduction to the Poetry of Derek Walcott." *Bim*, no. 10, 1949, pp. 125–132.

———. "The Snag." *Bim*, no. 2, 1943, pp. 13–15, 77, 79, 81, 83, 85, 87, 89.

Collymore, Frank, and W. Therold Barnes. "Editors' Blarney." *Bim*, no. 6, 1945, n.p.

———. "Editors' Comeback." *Bim*, no. 4, 1944, n.p.

———. "Foreword." *Bim*, no. 9, 1948, n.p.

———. "Introduction." *Bim*, no. 10, 1949, n.p.

Conference on the Closer Association of the British West Indian Colonies, Montego Bay, Jamaica, 11th–19th September, 1947. Part I: Report. His Majesty's Stationery Office, 1948.

Conference on the Closer Association of the British West Indian Colonies, Montego Bay, Jamaica, 11th–19th September, 1947. Part II: Proceedings. His Majesty's Stationery Office, 1948.

Cox, Juanita. "Introduction: 'A Quiet Revolution.'" *Corentyne Thunder*, by Edgar Mittelholzer. Peepal Tree, 2009, pp. 5–20.

Cruz-Malavé, Arnaldo. *El primitivo implorante: El "sistema poético del mundo" de José Lezama Lima*. Rodopi, 1994.

Dalleo, Raphael. *American Imperialism's Undead: The Occupation of Haiti and the Rise of Caribbean Anticolonialism*. U of Virginia P, 2016.

———. *Caribbean Literature and the Public Sphere: From the Plantation to the Postcolonial*. U of Virginia P, 2011.

———. "Regionalism, Imperialism, and Sovereignty: West Indies Federation and the Occupation of Haiti." *Small Axe*, no. 61, 2020, pp. 61–68.

Damas, Léon-Gontran. "Negritude in Retrospect." *Léon-Gontran Damas, 1912–1978: Founder of Negritude; A Memorial Casebook*, edited by Daniel Racine, UP of America, 1979, pp. 255–263.

———. "Negritude in Retrospect." Undated. Léon-Gontran Damas Papers, 1949–1978. Box 2, Folder 2. Schomburg Center for Research in Black Culture, New York Public Library

Dash, J. Michael. *Literature and Ideology in Haiti, 1915–1961*. Barnes & Noble, 1981.

———. *The Other America: Caribbean Literature in a New World Context*. U of Virginia P, 1998.

Davis, Gregson. *Aimé Césaire*. Cambridge UP, 1997.

de Andrade, Oswald. "Cannibalist Manifesto." Translated by Leslie Bary. *Latin American Literary Review*, vol. 19, no. 38, 1991, pp. 38–47.

de Beauvoir, Simone. *The Second Sex*. Translated by Constance Borde and Sheila Molavany-Chevallier. 1949. Vintage Books, 2011.

de la Fuente, Alejandro. *A Nation for All: Race, Inequality, and Politics in Twentieth-Century Cuba*. U of North Carolina P, 2001.

Deleuze, Gilles. "Immanence: A Life." *Pure Immanence: Essays on a Life*. Translated by Anne Boyman, Zone Books, 2005, pp. 25–33.

"De los editores." *Los socialistas y la realidad cubana: Informes, resoluciones y discursos.* Ediciones del P.S.P, 1944, p. 8.

Díaz, Duanel. *Los límites del origenismo.* Editorial Colibrí, 2005.

Donnell, Alison. *Twentieth-Century Caribbean Literature: Critical Moments in Anglophone Literary History.* Routledge, 2006.

———. "West Indian Literature and Federation." *Small Axe*, no. 61, 2020, pp. 78–86.

Dorestal, Yves. *Jacques Roumain (1907–1944): Un communiste haïtien: le marxisme de Roumain ou le commencement du marxisme en Haïti.* C3 Editions, 2015.

Du Bois, W.E.B. *The Souls of Black Folk.* 1903. Dover, 1994.

Duong, Paloma. "'Conspiracy of Silence': The Dunayevskaya-Marcuse-Fromm Correspondence." Unpublished manuscript. Presented at the Latin American Studies Association (LASA). Washington, D.C. 29 May 2013.

Eagleton, Terry. *The Function of Criticism.* 1984. Verso, 2005.

Edwards, Brent Hayes. *The Practice of Diaspora: Literature, Translation, and the Rise of Black Internationalism.* Harvard UP, 2003.

Ehlers, Sarah. *Left of Poetry.* U of North Carolina P, 2019.

Eliot, T. S. "The Idea of a Literary Review." *New Criterion*, vol. 4, no. 1, Jan. 1926, pp. 1–6.

Esquenazi-Mayo, Roberto. *A Survey of Cuban Revistas, 1902–1958.* Library of Congress, 1993.

Fair, Freda. *The Black Midwest: Fugitivity, Visual Culture, Queer Objects.* U of Minnesota P, forthcoming.

———. "Surveilling Social Difference: Black Women's 'Alley Work' in Industrializing Minneapolis." *Surveillance and Society*, vol. 15, no. 5, 2017, pp. 655–675.

Fanon, Frantz. *Peau noire, masques blancs.* Seuil, 1952.

———. "West Indians and Africans." *Toward the African Revolution.* Translated by Haakon Chevalier. 1964. Monthly Review, 1967, pp. 17–27.

Fernández de Castro, José Antonio. *Tema negro en las letras de Cuba (1608–1935).* Mirador, 1935.

Fernández Retamar, Roberto. *La poesía contemporánea en Cuba (1927–1953).* Orígenes, 1954.

Fowler, Víctor. "Impactos de Césaire en *Orígenes.*" *Paseos corporales y de escritura.* Letras Cubanas, 2013, pp. 113–140.

Fresa y Chocolate. Dir. Tomás Gutiérrez Alea. Cuba, 1993.

Fritzinger, Jerald. *Pre-Columbian Trans-Oceanic Contact.* Lulu.com, 2016.

Frobenius, Leo. "Que signifie pour nous l'Afrique." *Tropiques*, no. 5, 1942, p. 62.

Frost, Jackqueline. "The Past of Future Life: Anticolonialism, Antifascism and the Poetics of Historical Time at the End of the French Empire." Cornell U Dissertation, 2020.

Frost, Jackqueline, and Jorge E. Lefevre Tavárez. "Tragedy of the Possible: Aimé Césaire in Cuba, 1968." *Historical Materialism*, vol. 28, no. 2, 2020, pp. 25–75.

Gandhi, Leela. *Postcolonial Theory: A Critical Introduction.* Columbia UP, 1998.

García-Peña, Lorgia. *The Borders of Dominicanidad: Race, Nation, and Archives of Contradiction.* Duke UP, 2016.

Gaztambide-Géigel, Antonio. "The Invention of the Caribbean in the 20th Century (The Definitions of the Caribbean as a Historical and Methodological Problem)." *Social and Economic Studies*, vol. 53, no. 3, 2004, pp. 127–157.

———. "The Rise and Geopolitics of Antilleanism." *General History of the Caribbean.* Vol. 4, *The Long Nineteenth Century: Nineteenth Century Transformations*, edited by K. O. Laurence and Jorge Ibarra Cuesta. UNESCO, 2011, pp. 430–452.

Genette, Gérard. *Seuils*. 1987. Seuil, 2014.

Getachew, Adom. *Worldmaking after Empire: The Rise and Fall of Self-Determination*. Princeton UP, 2019.

Gikandi, Simon. *Maps of Englishness: Writing Identity in the Culture of Colonialism*. Columbia UP, 1996.

———. *Writing in Limbo: Modernism and Caribbean Literature*. Cornell UP, 1992.

Gil, Alex. "Aimé Césaire and the Broken Record." 2018. http://record.elotroalex.com/chapters/03-assimilate/#fn:3.

———. "Bridging the Middle Passage: The Textual (R)evolution of Césaire's *Cahier d'un retour au pays natal*." *Canadian Review of Comparative Literature*, vol. 38, no. 1, 2011, pp. 40–56.

———. "Migrant Textualities: On the Fields of Aimé Césaire's *Et les chiens se taisaient*." U of Virginia Dissertation, 2012.

Gilman, Claudia. *Entre la pluma y el fusil: Debates y dilemas del escritor revolucionario en América Latina*. Siglo XXI Editores, 2003.

Glissant, Édouard. *Le discours antillais*. Editions du Seuil, 1981.

———. *Poetics of Relation*. Translated by Betsy Wing, U of Michigan P, 1997.

Glover, Kaiama L. "The Ambivalent Transnationalism of a Literature-World—in French." *Small Axe*, no. 33, 2010, pp. 99–110.

———. "Haitian Literature and the Insult of Dust." *sx salon*, no. 23, 2016, n.p.

Goffe, Tao Leigh. "'Guano in Their Destiny': Race, Geology, and a Philosophy of Indenture." *Amerasia Journal*, vol. 45, no. 1, 2019, pp. 27–49.

Gómez, Juan Gualberto. "Martí y yo." *Gaceta del Caribe*, no. 1, 1944, pp. 28–29.

Gomier, E. "Pages from a Diary." *Bim*, vol. 1, no. 4, 1944, pp. 29–30, 79–85.

González-Echevarría, Roberto. *Alejo Carpentier: The Pilgrim at Home*. 1977. U of Texas P, 1990.

Gramsci. *Selections from the Prison Notebooks*. Translated by Quentin Hoare and Geoffrey Nowell Smith, International Publishers, 1971.

Green, Jim. "Barbados Holiday." *Bim*, vol. 2, no. 7, 1946, pp. 40, 110.

Griffith, Glyne A. *The BBC and the Development of Anglophone Caribbean Literature, 1943–1958*. Palgrave Macmillan, 2016.

———. "*Caribbean Voices* and the Communicative Failure of the West Indies Federation." *Small Axe*, no. 61, 2020, pp. 87–95.

Guillén, Nicolás. "Cuba, negros, poesía." *Aquí estamos: El negro en la obra de Nicolás Guillén*, edited by Denia García Ronda, Editorial de Ciencias Sociales, 2008, pp. 70–77.

———."El problema del negro y la unidad nacional." *Los socialistas y la realidad cubana: Informes, resoluciones y discursos*. Ediciones del P.S.P, 1944, pp. 43–50.

———. "Prólogo." *Aquí estamos: El negro en la obra de Nicolás Guillén*, edited by Denia García Ronda, Editorial de Ciencias Sociales, 2008, pp. 32–33.

Guterl, Matthew Pratt. *American Mediterranean: Southern Slaveholders in the Age of Emancipation*. Harvard UP, 2008.

Gutiérrez Coto, Amauri Francisco. *Polémica literaria entre Gastón Baquero y Juan Marinello (1944)*. Espuela de Plata, 2005.

Haigh, Sam. *An Introduction to Caribbean Francophone Writing: Guadeloupe and Martinique*. Berg, 1999.

Hall, Stuart. "Encoding / Decoding." *Media and Cultural Studies: Keyworks*, edited by Meenakshi Gigi Durham and Douglas M. Kellner, Blackwell, 2006, pp. 163–173.

———. "New Ethnicities." *Stuart Hall: Critical Dialogues in Cultural Studies*, edited by David Morley and Kuan-Hsing Chen, Routledge, 1996, pp. 441–449.

———. "Race, Articulation, and Societies Structured in Dominance." *Black British Cultural Studies: A Reader*, edited by Houston A. Baker, Jr., Manthia Diawara, and Ruth H. Lindeborg, U of Chicago P, 1996, pp. 16–60.

Haraway, Donna. "Situated Knowledges: The Science Question in Feminism and the Privilege of Partial Perspective." *Feminist Studies*, vol. 14, no. 3, 1988, pp. 575–599.

Hardt, Michael. "How to Write with Four Hands." *Genre*, vol. 46, no. 2, 2013, pp. 175–182.

Hardt, Michael, and Antonio Negri. *Empire*. Harvard UP, 2000.

Harley, J. B. "Deconstructing the Map." *Cartographica*, vol. 26, no. 2, Summer 1989, pp. 1–20.

Hassan, Salah Dean Assaf. "The Politics of Cultural Journals in the Postwar Era, 1944–1962." U of Texas at Austin Dissertation, 1997.

Hausser, Michel. "Tropiques: Une tardive centrale surréaliste?" *Mélusine*, no. 2, 1981, pp. 238–259.

Heller, Ben A. "Landscape, Femininity, and Caribbean Discourse." *MLN*, vol. 111, no. 2, 1996, pp. 391–416.

Henry, Paget. *Caliban's Reason: Introducing Afro-Caribbean Philosophy*. Routledge, 2000.

Hoffman, Léon-François, editor. *Oeuvres Complètes / Jacques Roumain: édition critique*. ALLCA XX, 2003.

Hofmeyr, Isabel. *Gandhi's Printing Press: Experiments in Slow Reading*. Harvard UP, 2013.

Jackson, Richard L. *The Black Image in Latin American Literature*. U of New Mexico P, 1976.

Jackson, Shona N. *Creole Indigeneity: Between Myth and Nation in the Caribbean*. U of Minnesota P, 2012.

———. "The Re / Presentation of the Indigenous Caribbean in Literature." *The Oxford Handbook of Indigenous American Literature*, edited by James H. Cox and Daniel Heath Justice, Oxford UP, 2014, pp. 520–533.

James, C.L.R. "Appendix: From Toussaint L'Ouverture to Fidel Castro." 1963. *The Black Jacobins*, Vintage, 1989, pp. 391–418.

———. "Lecture on Federation." *At the Rendezvous of Victory: Selected Writings*. Allison and Busby, 1984, pp. 85–106.

Janney, Frank. *Alejo Carpentier and His Early Works*. Tamesis Books, 1981.

Jennings, Eric T. "Last Exit from Vichy France: The Martinique Escape Route and the Ambiguities of Emigration." *The Journal of Modern History*, vol. 74, no. 2, 2002, pp. 289–324.

———. *Vichy in the Tropics: Pétain's National Revolution in Madagascar, Guadeloupe, and Indochina, 1940–1944*. Stanford UP, 2001.

Johnson, Jessica Marie. "Xroads Praxis: Black Diasporic Technologies for Remaking the New World." *sx archipelagoes*, no. 3, 2019, pp. 1–21.

Jones, Donna V. *The Racial Discourses of Life Philosophy*. Columbia UP, 2010.

Joseph-Gabriel, Annette K. "Beyond the Great Camouflage: Haiti in Suzanne Césaire's Politics and Poetics of Liberation." *Small Axe*, no. 50, 2016, pp. 1–13.

Kalliney, Peter J. *Commonwealth of Letters: British Literary Culture and the Emergence of Postcolonial Aesthetics*. Oxford UP, 2013.

Kamada, Roy Osamu. *Postcolonial Romanticisms: Landscape and the Possibilities of Inheritance*. Peter Lang, 2010.

Kanzepolsky, Adriana. *Un dibujo del mundo: extranjeros en Orígenes*. Beatriz Viterbo, 2004.

Kincaid, Jamaica. *A Small Place*. Penguin, 1988.

King, Bruce. *Derek Walcott, a Caribbean Life*. Oxford UP, 2000.

Knight, Franklin W. *The Caribbean: The Genesis of a Fragmented Nationalism*. 1978. Oxford UP, 2012.

Kutzinski, Vera M. *Sugar's Secrets: Race and the Erotics of Cuban Nationalism*. UP of Virginia, 1993.

Ladra, Luis Antonio. "Alejo Carpentier: *Viaje a la semilla*." *Orígenes*, no. 3, 1944, pp. 45–46.

Lamming, George. "Birds of a Feather." *Bim*, no. 9, 1948, pp. 32–39.

———. "Introduction." *In the Castle of My Skin*. U of Michigan P, 2010, pp. xxxv–xlvi.

———. Letters to Frank Collymore. Frank Collymore Collection, Barbados National Archives.

———. *The Pleasures of Exile*. 1960. U of Michigan P, 1992.

———. Personal conversation with the author, Bridgetown, June 2013.

Lamming, George, and David Scott. "The Sovereignty of the Imagination: An Interview with George Lamming." *Small Axe*, vol. 6, no. 2, 2002, pp. 72–200.

"Landscape." Def. 1.3. *Oxford English Dictionary* Online, 1 Mar. 2015.

La Rose, John. 1968. Notes. Cultural Congress of Havana Papers. John La Rose Collection. George Padmore Institute, London. 2 Aug. 2018.

Latour, Bruno. *Reassembling the Social: An Introduction to Actor-Network-Theory*. 2005. Oxford UP, 2007.

Léger, Natalie M. "Faithless Sight: Haiti in the Kingdom of This World." *Research in African Literatures*, vol. 45, no. 1, Spring 2014, pp. 85–106.

Leiner, Jacqueline. "Entretien avec Aimé Césaire." *Tropiques 1941–1945: Collection Complète*. Jean-Michel Place, 1978, pp. v–xxiv.

Leitch, Vincent B. *American Literary Criticism since the 1930s*. Routledge, 2009.

Lepore, Jill. *Book of Ages: The Life and Opinions of Jane Franklin*. Vintage, 2014.

Levinas, Emmanuel. *Entre Nous: Thinking-of-the-Other*. Translated by Michael B. Smith and Barbara Harshav, Columbia UP, 1998.

Lewis, Gordon K. *The Growth of the Modern West Indies*. 1968. Ian Randle, Kingston, 2004.

Lezama Lima, José. "Coloquio con Juan Ramón Jimenez." 1938. *Obras Completas: Analecta del Reloj*. 1953. Instituto Cubano del Libro, 2010, pp. 31–46.

———. *La expresión americana*. 1957. Editorial Letras Cubanas, 2010.

Lezama Lima, José, and José Rodríguez Feo. "Orígenes." *Orígenes*, no. 1, 1944, pp. 5–7.

López Santiago, Angel "Monxo." "The Geography of Bernardo Vega's *Memoirs*." *Centro Journal*, vol. 30, no. 1, Spring 2018, pp. 152–177.

Lord Invader. "Rum and Coca-Cola." Rupert Grant, 1943.

Low, Gail. *Publishing the Postcolonial: Anglophone West African and Caribbean Writing in the UK, 1948–1968*. Routledge, 2013.

Maguire, Emily A. *Racial Experiments in Cuban Literature and Ethnography*. U of Florida P, 2011.

———. "Two Returns to the Native Land: Lydia Cabrera Translates Aimé Césaire." *Small Axe*, no. 42, 2013, pp. 125–137.

Maldonado-Torres, Nelson. *Against War: Views from the Underside of Modernity*. Duke UP, 2008.

———. "Toward a Critique of Continental Reason: Africana Studies and the Decolonization of Imperial Cartographies in the Americas." *Not Only the Master's Tools: African-American Studies in Theory and Practice*, edited by Lewis R. Gordon and Jane Anna Gordon, Paradigm, 2006, pp. 51–84.

"Manque." *CNRTL (Centre National de Ressources Textuelles et Lexicales)*. 2014. www.cnrtl.fr/lexicographie/manque.

Martínez-San Miguel, Yolanda. "Colonial and Mexican Archipelagoes: Reimagining Colonial Caribbean Studies." *Archipelagic American Studies*, edited by Brian Russell Roberts and Michelle Ann Stephens, Duke UP, 2017, pp. 155–173.

———. *Coloniality of Diasporas: Rethinking Intra-Colonial Migrations in a Pan-Caribbean Context*. Palgrave, 2014.

———. "(Neo) Barrocos de Indias: Sor Juana y los imaginarios coloniales de la crítica latinoamericana." *Revista de Estudios Hispánicos*, vol. 44, no. 2, 2010, pp. 433–463.

Martínez-San Miguel, Yolanda, and Katerina Gonzalez Seligmann. "Con-Federating the Archipelago: The *Confederación Antillana* and the West Indies Federation." *Small Axe*, no. 61, 2020, pp. 37–43.

Marturano, Jorge. "Lino Novas Calvo's 'the Other Key': The Other Insular Space in the Hispanic Caribbean." *Journal of Latin American Cultural Studies: Travesía*, vol. 19, no. 1, 2010, pp. 63–85.

Marx, Karl. "Capital: Volume I." *The Marx-Engels Reader*, edited by Robert C. Tucker, Norton, 1978, pp. 294–438.

Matthews, Crichlow. "Focus: 1948, Review." *Bim*, no. 10, 1949, pp. 175–176.

Matthiessen, Francis O. "Los cuartetos de T. S. Eliot." *Orígenes*, no. 2, Summer 1944, pp. 3–17.

Maugée, Aristide. "Revue des revues–Correspondances." *Tropiques*, no. 6–7, 1943, pp. 59–60.

Mbembe, Achille. *On the Postcolony*. U of California P, 2001.

McGillivray, Gillian. *Blazing Cane: Sugar Communities, Class, and State Formation in Cuba, 1868–1959*. Duke UP, 2009.

Melas, Natalie. "Untimeliness, or Négritude and the Poetics of Contramodernity." *South Atlantic Quarterly*, vol. 108, no. 3, 2009, pp. 563–580.

Memmi, Albert. *The Colonizer and the Colonized*. Translated by Howard Greenfield, Beacon, 1991.

Ménil, René. "Laissez passer la poésie." *Tropiques*, no. 5, 1942, pp. 21–28.

———. "Légitime défense." *Légitime défense*. Michel Place, 1979, n.p.

———. "Naissance de notre art." *Tropiques*, no. 1, 1941, pp. 53–64.

———. "Orientation de la poésie." *Tropiques*, no. 2, 1941, pp. 13–21.

———. "Pour une lecture critique de *Tropiques*." *Tropiques 1941–1945: Collection Complète*. Jean-Michel Place, 1978, pp. xxv–xxxv.

———. "Situation de la poésie aux Antilles." *Tropiques*, no. 11, 1944, pp. 127–133.

———. "The Situation of Poetry in the Caribbean." *Refusal of the Shadow: Surrealism and the Caribbean*, edited by Michael Richardson. Translated by Michael Richardson and Krzysztof Fijalkowski. Verso, 1996, pp. 127–133.

———. "Sous l'amiral Robert: 'Tropiques' temoin de la vie culturelle." *Cahiers du CERAG*, no. 36, 1979, pp. 144–153.

Mignolo, Walter. *The Idea of Latin America*. Blackwell, 2005.

———. *Local Histories/Global Designs: Coloniality, Subaltern Knowledges and Border Thinking.* Princeton UP, 2012.

———. "La razón postcolonial: Herencias coloniales y teorías postcoloniales." *Postmodernidad y postcolonialidad. Breves reflexiones sobre Latinoamérica*, edited by Alfonos del Toro, Vervuert, 1997, pp. 1–19.

Miller, Susan Gilson. "Afterword." *The Colonizer and the Colonized*, by Albert Memmi. Beacon, 1991, pp. 155–169.

Mitchell, W.J.T. "Addressing Media." *MediaTropes*, vol. 1, 2008, pp. 1–18.

Mittelholzer, Edgar. "Miss Clarke Is Dying." *Bim*, no. 5, 1945, pp. 24–27.

———. "Of Casuarinas and Cliffs." *Bim*, no. 5, 1945, pp. 6–7, 53, 55.

———. "Romantic Promenade: A Divertissement in Minor Chords." *Bim*, no. 8, 1947, pp. 12–13.

Mohammed, Patricia. *Imaging the Caribbean: Cultural and Visual Translation.* Macmillan Caribbean, 2010.

Montenegro, Carlos. "Doce Corales." *Gaceta del Caribe*, no. 2, 1944, pp. 13–15.

Moore, Robin D. *Nationalizing Blackness: Afrocubanismo and Artistic Revolution in Havana, 1920–1940.* U of Pittsburgh P, 1997.

Moretti, Franco. *Graphs, Maps Trees: Abstract Models for Literary History.* Verso, 2005.

Morrison, Mark S. *The Public Face of Modernism: Little Magazines, Audiences, and Reception 1905–1920.* U of Wisconsin P, 2001.

Moten, Fred. *Black and Blur.* Duke UP, 2017. Kindle.

Murray-Román, Jeannine. *Performance and Personhood in Caribbean Literature: From Alexis to the Digital Age.* U of Virginia P, 2016.

Naipaul, V. S. *The Middle Passage.* Vintage, 2002.

Nanton, Phillip. "Collymore: A Man of the Threshold." *Remembering the Sea: An Introduction to Frank A. Collymore*, edited by Phillip Nanton, Central Bank of Barbados, 2003, pp. 88–104.

Naranjo Orovio, Consuelo, and José F. Buscaglia. "Race as a Weapon: Defending the Colonial Plantation Order in the Name of Civilization, 1791–1850." *Culture & History Digital Journal*, vol. 4, no. 2, 2015, pp. 1–9.

Negrón-Muntaner, Frances. *Boricua Pop: Puerto Ricans and the Latinization of American Culture.* New York UP, 2004.

Neptune, Harvey R. *Caliban and the Yankees: Trinidad and the United States Occupation.* U of North Carolina P, 2007.

Nerlekar, Anjali. "The Cartography of the Local in Arun Kolatkar's Poetry." *Journal of Postcolonial Writing*, vol. 49, no. 5, 2013, pp. 609–623.

Nesbitt, Nick. "Antinomies of Double Consciousness in Aimé Césaire's *Cahier d'un retour au pays natal.*" *Mosaic*, vol. 33, no. 3, 2000, pp. 107–128.

———. "Caribbean Literature in French: Origins and Development." *The Cambridge History of African and Caribbean Literature*, edited by F. Abiola Irele and Simon Gikandi, Cambridge UP, 2008, pp. 643–699.

Novás Calvo, Lino. "11 Síntomas." *Gaceta del Caribe*, no. 1, Mar. 1944, p. 3.

Obszyński, Michal. *Manifestes et programmes littéraires aux Caraïbes francophones: En/jeux idéologiques et poétiques.* Brill, 2016.

Ohmann, Richard M. *Selling Culture: Magazines, Markets and Class at the Turn of the Century.* Verso, 1998.

Ortiz, Fernando. *Cuban Counterpoint: Tobacco and Sugar.* Translated by Harriet de Onís. 1940. Duke U, 1995.

Pach, Walter. "Problemas del arte americano." *Orígenes*, no. 4, Dec. 1944, pp. 17–20.

Paravisini-Gebert, Lizabeth. "The Haitian Revolution in Interstices and Shadows: A Re-Reading of Alejo Carpentier's *The Kingdom of This World*." *Research in African Literatures*, vol. 35, no. 2, 2004, pp. 114–127.

Parépou, Alfred. *Atipa: Român guyanais.* 1885. L'Harmattan, 2016.

Parker, Jason C. *Brother's Keeper: The United States, Race, and Empire in the British Caribbean, 1937–1962.* Oxford UP, 2008.

Paxton, Robert O. *Vichy France: Old Guard and New Order, 1940–1944.* Knopf, 1972.

Paz, Senel. *El lobo, el bosque, y el hombre nuevo.* ERA, 1991.

"Pedimos la palabra." *Gaceta del Caribe*, no. 4, June 1944, pp. 31.

Pérez Cisneros, Guy. "Presencia de ocho pintores." *Verbum*, vol. 1, no. 1, 1937, pp. 116–127.

Phillips, Sonji. "Bim and the Development of a West Indian Literature." *Remembering the Sea: An Introduction to Frank A. Collymore*, edited by Philip Nanton, Central Bank of Barbados, 2003, pp. 105–119.

Pineda Franco, Adela. *Geopolíticas de la cultura finesecular en Buenos Aires, París y México: Las revistas literarias y el modernismo.* Instituto Internacional de Literatura Iberoamericana, 2006.

Piñera, Virgilio. *La isla en peso.* Tipografía García, 1943.

Poe, Edgar Allen. "The Masque of the Red Death." *The Complete Tales and Poems of Edgar Allen Poe.* Vintage, 1975, pp. 269–273.

Portuondo, Antonio José. *El contenido social de la literatura cubana.* Fondo de Cultura Económica, 1943.

———. "Plácido, 1844." *Gaceta del Caribe*, no. 1, Mar. 1944, pp. 22–23.

Pouchet Paquet, Sandra. "Foreword." *The Pleasures of Exile*, by George Lamming. U of Michigan P, 1992, pp. ix–xxxiii.

Pratt, Mary Louise. "Linguistic Utopias." *The Linguistics of Writing: Arguments between Writing and Literature*, edited by Nigel Fabb et al., Methuen, 1987, pp. 48–66.

Priam, Mylène. "Beyond 'The Drama of Consciousness' and against the 'Drama of the Manifesto': Poetic License and the Creolist Discourse." *Research in African Literatures*, vol. 44, no. 1, 2013, pp. 19–35.

"Primeras palabras." *Gaceta del Caribe*, no. 1, Mar. 1944, p. 1.

"Propósito." *Anuario Cultural de Cuba 1943.* Ucar, García y cía., 1944, n.p.

Quijano, Aníbal. "Coloniality of Power and Eurocentrism in Latin America." *International Sociology*, vol. 15, no. 2, 2000, pp. 215–232.

Quijano, Aníbal, and Immanuel Wallerstein. "Americanity as a Concept, or the Americas in the Modern World." *International Social Science Journal*, vol. 44, no. 4, 1992, pp. 549–557.

Quintero-Herencia, Juan Carlos, editor. *Caribe abierto () Ensayos Críticos.* Instituto Internacional de Literatura Iberoamericana, 2012.

Ramchand, Kenneth. "Introduction." *West Indian Narrative: An Introductory Anthology.* Nelson Caribbean, 1980, pp. 3–6.

———. *The West Indian Novel and Its Background.* Ian Randle, 2004.

Ramírez, Dixa. "Black Horror." Unpublished manuscript. Presented at the Caribbean Philosophical Association Meeting, June 2019.

———. *Colonial Phantoms: Belonging and Refusal in the Dominican Americas, from the 19th Century to the Present*. New York UP, 2018.

Ramos, José Antonio. "Nao, esquife y tierra." *Gaceta del Caribe*, no. 2, Apr. 1944, pp. 9–11.

Ratto-Ciarlo, José. "Horace poète bimillinéaire et l'Art Social." Translated by Maurice Soïme. *Tropiques*, no. 3, Oct. 1941, pp. 54–58.

Ricardo, José G. *La imprenta en Cuba*. Letras Cubanas, 1989.

Richardson, Michael. "Introduction." *Refusal of the Shadow: Surrealism and the Caribbean*, edited by Michael Richardson. Translated by Michael Richardson and Krzysztof Fijalkowski. Verso, 1996, pp. 1–33.

Rimbaud, Arthur. *Une Saison en Enfer/Les illuminations*. Translated by Enid Rhodes Peschel, Oxford UP, 1973.

Robinson, Cedric. *Black Marxism: The Making of the Black Radical Tradition*. U of North Carolina P, 2000.

Rodríguez, Emilio Jorge. "Bojeo a las revistas literarias caribeñas: Su función liberadora." *Literatura caribeña: Bojeo y cuaderno de bitacora*. Letras Cubanas, 1989, pp. 28–51.

Rodríguez Feo, José. "George Santayana, crítico de una cultura." *Orígenes*, no. 1, Spring 1944, pp. 35–38.

———. *Mi correspondencia con Lezama Lima*. 1989. Era, 1991.

Rodríguez Matos, Jaime. *Writing of the Formless: José Lezama Lima and the End of Time*. Fordham UP, 2017.

Rodríguez Navas, Ana. *Idle Talk, Deadly Talk: The Uses of Gossip in Caribbean Literature*. U of Virginia P, 2018.

Romero, Cira, and Marcia Castillo, editors. *Cuestiones privadas: Correspondencia a José Antonio Portuondo (1932–1986)*. Oriente, 2002.

Rosemont, Franklin, and Robin D. G. Kelley. *Black, Brown, & Beige: Surrealist Writings from Africa and the Diaspora*. U of Texas P, 2009.

Roumain, Jacques. "Guinea." Translated by Nicolás Guillén. *Gaceta del Caribe*, no. 3, May 1944, p. 13.

———. "Is Poetry Dead?" *New Masses*, Jan. 1941, pp. 22–23.

———. "La poésie comme arme." *Cahiers d'Haïti*, vol. 2, no. 4, Nov. 1944, p. 22.

———. "La poesía como arma." *Gaceta del Caribe*, no. 1, Mar. 1944, p. 15.

Said, Edward W. *Orientalism*. 1978. Vintage Books, 1979.

———. *The World, the Text, and the Critic*. Harvard UP, 1983.

Saldaña-Portillo, María Josefina. *The Revolutionary Imagination in the Americas and the Age of Development*. Duke UP, 2003.

Salgado, César A. "La futuridad del naufragio (Prólogo en dos estelas)." *La futuridad del naufragio,* Orígenes, *estelas y derivas*, edited by Juan Pablo Lupi and César A. Salgado, Almenara, 2019, pp. 9–48.

Salkey, Andrew. *Havana Journal*. Pelican, 1971.

Sartre, Jean Paul. "Orphée Noir." *Anthologie de la nouvelle poésie nègre et malgache de langue française*, edited by Léopold Senghor, Presses Universaires de France, 1948, pp. ix–xliv.

Schwarz, Roberto. "Misplaced Ideas: Literature and Society in Late-Nineteenth Century Brazil." *Misplaced Ideas: Essays on Brazilian Culture*. Translated by John Gledson, Verso, 1992.

Sealy, Karl. "Money to Burn." *Bim*, no. 5, Feb. 1945, pp. 38–40, 89–91.

Seligmann, Katerina Gonzalez. "Cabrera's Césaire: The Making of a Trans-Caribbean Zone." *MLN*, vol. 134, no. 5, 2019, pp. 1037–1058.

———. "Caliban, Why? The 1968 Cultural Congress of Havana, C.L.R. James, and the Role of the Caribbean Intellectual." *The Global South*, vol. 13, no. 1, 2019, pp. 59–80.

———. "Poetic Productions of Cultural Combat in *Tropiques*." *South Atlantic Quarterly*, vol.115, no. 3, 2016, pp. 495–512.

———. "Un-nationalisms of the Federated Archipelago." *Small Axe*, no. 61, 2020, pp. 69–77.

———. "The Void, the Distance, Elsewhere: Literary Infrastructure and Empire in the Caribbean." *Small Axe*, no. 62, 2020, pp. 1–16.

Seymour, A. J. *Edgar Mittelholzer: The Man and His Work*. National History and Arts Council of Guyana, 1968.

Seyrig, Henri. MS. NAF 19792. Letter from Aimé Césaire, 2 Apr. 1945. Bibliothèque nationale de France, Paris.

Smorkaloff, Pamela Maria. *Readers and Writers in Cuba: A Social History of Print Culture, 1830s–1990s*. Garland, 1997.

Steil, Benn. *The Battle of Bretton Woods: John Maynard Keynes, Harry Dexter White, and the Making of a New World Order*. Princeton UP, 2013.

Stieber, Chelsea. "The Haitian Literary Magazine in Francophone Postcolonial Literary and Cultural Production." *French Cultural Studies for the Twenty-First Century*, edited by Masha Belenky and Kathryn Kleppinger, U of Delaware P, 2017, pp. 21–38.

Stokes, Dick. "Dominica Trek." *Bim*, vol. 1, no. 2, 1943, pp. 25–27.

Torres-Saillant, Silvio. *Caribbean Poetics: Toward an Aesthetic of West Indian Literature*. Cambridge UP, 1997.

———. *An Intellectual History of the Caribbean*. Palgrave, 2006.

Trouillot, Michel-Rolph. *Silencing the Past: Power and the Production of History*. Beacon, 1995.

Véron, Kora. *Aimé Césaire, configurations*. Ed. Seuil, 2021.

———. "Césaire at the Crossroads in Haiti: Correspondence with Henri Seyrig." *Comparative Literature Studies*, vol. 50, no. 3, 2013, pp. 430–444.

———. Personal conversation with the author. New York City, 18 June 2018.

Véron, Kora, and Thomas Hale. *Les écrits d'Aimé Césaire: Bibliographie Commentée (1913–2008)*. Honoré Champion, 2013.

Villasana, Angel Raúl, and Alberto Amengual. *Viernes; índice*. Instituto Autonomo Biblioteca Nacional y de Servicios de Bibliotecas, 1978.

Vitier, Cintio. *Ese sol del mundo moral: para una historia de la eticidad cubana*. Siglo Veintiuno Editores, 1975.

Walcott, Derek. *25 Poems*. Guardian, 1948.

Walcott, Ursula. "The Theater Tickets." *Bim*, no. 3, Dec. 1943, pp. 37–40, 97–99.

Waters, Erika J. "'Music of Language': An Interview with George Lamming." *The Caribbean Writer*, vol. 13, 1999, pp. 190–210.

Whitfield, Esther. "Guantánamo, Cuba: Poetry and Prison on Divided Ground." *Comparative Literature*, vol. 72, no. 3, 2020, pp. 299–315.

Whitney, Robert. *State and Revolution in Cuba: Mass Mobilization and Political Change, 1920–1940*. U of North Carolina P, 2001.

Wilder, Gary. *Freedom Time: Negritude, Decolonization, and the Future of the World*. Duke UP, 2014.

Wilks, Jennifer M. *Race, Gender, and Comparative Black Modernism: Suzanne Lacascade, Marita Bonner, Suzanne Césaire, Dorothy West*. Louisiana State UP, 2008.

Williams, Eric. *From Columbus to Castro: The History of the Caribbean*. 1970. Vintage, 1984.

Williams, Erika Renée. "The Queer Gift of Black Folk: Double Consciousness in Du Bois's Detective Story 'The Case.'" *Studies in American Fiction* (forthcoming).

Williams, Jan. "Arise, My Love." *West Indian Stories*, edited by Andrew Salkey, Faber & Faber, 1968, pp. 148–155.

———. "The Shilling." *Bim*, no. 3, Dec. 1943, pp. 1–2.

———. "The White Dress." *Bim*, no. 5, Feb. 1945, pp. 2–4, 49, 51, 53.

Williams, Raymond. *Marxism and Literature*. Oxford UP, 1977.

Wimmer, Andreas, and Nina Glick Schiller. "Methodological Nationalism and Beyond: Nation-State Building, Migration, and the Social Sciences." *Global Networks*, vol. 2, no. 4, 2002, pp. 301–334.

Wood, Yolanda. "Revistas y trayectorias culturales en el Caribe." *Small Axe*, no. 50, 2016, pp. 85–91.

Wynter, Sylvia. "Afterword: Beyond Miranda's Meanings: Un / silencing the 'Demonic Grounds' of Caliban's 'Woman."' *Out of the Kumbla: Caribbean Women and Literature*, edited by Carole Boyce Davies and Elaine Savory, Africa World Press, 1994, pp. 355–366.

———. "Ethno or Socio Poetics." *Alcheringa: Ethno Poetics; A First International Symposium*, edited by Michel Benamou and Jerome Rothenberg, Boston University, 1976, pp. 78–94.

———. "Unsettling the Coloniality of Being / Power / Truth / Freedom: Towards the Human, after Man, Its Overrepresentation—an Argument." *CR: The New Centennial Review*, vol. 3, no. 3, 2003, pp. 257–337.

Yanique, Tiphanie. "The Bridge Stories: A Short Collection." *How to Escape from a Leper Colony*. Graywolf, 2010, pp. 15–30.

Zambrano, María. "La Metáfora del Corazón." *Orígenes*, no. 3, Oct. 1944, pp. 3–10.

Index

About the Author

KATERINA GONZALEZ SELIGMANN is a scholar of Caribbean literature, history, and social theory, and assistant professor of Latin American literature in the Department of Writing, Literature, and Publishing at Emerson College, Boston.

Available titles in the Critical Caribbean Studies series:

Giselle Anatol, *The Things That Fly in the Night: Female Vampires in Literature of the Circum-Caribbean and African Diaspora*

Alaí Reyes-Santos, *Our Caribbean Kin: Race and Nation in the Neoliberal Antilles*

Milagros Ricourt, *The Dominican Racial Imaginary: Surveying the Landscape of Race and Nation in Hispaniola*

Katherine A. Zien, *Sovereign Acts: Performing Race, Space, and Belonging in Panama and the Canal Zone*

Frances R. Botkin, *Thieving Three-Fingered Jack: Transatlantic Tales of a Jamaican Outlaw, 1780–2015*

Melissa A. Johnson, *Becoming Creole: Nature and Race in Belize*

Carlos Garrido Castellano, *Beyond Representation in Contemporary Caribbean Art: Space, Politics, and the Public Sphere*

Njelle W. Hamilton, *Phonographic Memories: Popular Music and the Contemporary Caribbean Novel*

Lia T. Bascomb, *In Plenty and in Time of Need: Popular Culture and the Remapping of Barbadian Identity*

Aliyah Khan, *Far from Mecca: Globalizing the Muslim Caribbean*

Rafael Ocasio, *Race and Nation in Puerto Rican Folklore: Franz Boas and John Alden Mason in Porto Rico*

Ana-Maurine Lara, *Streetwalking: LGBTQ Lives and Protest in the Dominican Republic*

Anke Birkenmaier, ed., *Caribbean Migrations: The Legacies of Colonialism*

Sherina Feliciano-Santos, *A Contested Caribbean Indigeneity: Language, Social Practice, and Identity within Puerto Rican Taíno Activism*

H. Adlai Murdoch, ed., *The Struggle of Non-Sovereign Caribbean Territories: Neoliberalism since the French Antillean Uprisings of 2009*

Robert Fatton Jr., *The Guise of Exceptionalism: Unmasking the National Narratives of Haiti and the United States*

Rafael Ocasio, *Folk Stories from the Hills of Puerto Rico / Cuentos folklóricos de las montañas de Puerto Rico*

Yveline Alexis, *Haiti Fights Back: The Life and Legacy of Charlemagne Péralte*

Katerina Gonzalez Seligmann, *Writing the Caribbean in Magazine Time*